DATE DUE

The Canon of Sir Thomas Wyatt's Poetry

The Canon

of

Sir Thomas Wyatt's Poetry

Richard Harrier

Harvard University Press

Cambridge, Massachusetts

1975

Publication of this book has been aided by a grant from the Hyder Edward Rollins Fund

Library of Congress Catalog Card Number 74-82812
IBSN 0-674-09460-3
Printed in the United States of America

To the Memory of Hyder E. Rollins

Preface

The purpose of this study is to determine within reasonable limits the canon of Sir Thomas Wyatt's poetry. Despite publication of three editions of collected "Wyatt poems" since 1949, little effort has been devoted to study of the manuscripts associated with Wyatt's name. Yet a careful account of the history and physical make-up of these documents can greatly reduce the number of poems among which final decisions concerning authenticity must be made on grounds of style and content.

The general conclusions of this study have already appeared in part in my review of the *Collected Poems of Sir Thomas Wyatt*, ed. Kenneth Muir and Patricia Thomson (Liverpool University Press, 1969), published in *Renaissance Quarterly*, XXIII (1970), 471-474. But the detailed evidence here presented has a significance that goes far beyond supporting those general conclusions. Future editors of Wyatt may benefit from the argument presented here that the Egerton MS 2711 (British Museum) is the keystone of the Wyatt canon. Further, the transcript and description of the Egerton MS, which report deletions, individual handwritings, modes of entry, punctuation, and probable errors, constitute the only sound and comprehensive study yet made. Its importance is underscored by the fact that the integrity of the Egerton MS was challenged by Raymond Southall in *The Courtly Maker* (Oxford, 1964), and his skepticism was carried over into the Muir and Thomson edition of 1969 through the device of adding a note on "Authorship" to each of the Egerton poems, as if each had to be defended without regard for its presence in a consistently presented body of poems among which are the only extant holograph poems by the poet himself.

Similar treatment is here given the problematic Devonshire MS 17492 (British Museum) and the so-called Blage MS (Trinity College Library, Dublin). It was not possible—nor indeed necessary—to make a line-for-line transcript of these documents, although they were scrutinized in both the originals and photos. Since 1961, when Muir first published *Sir Thomas Wyatt and His Circle: Unpublished Poems* (Liverpool University Press), the value of the Blage MS as a source of Wyatt's poems has been greatly inflated, until in the 1969 edition it took second place to the Egerton MS. As the bulk of the doubtful poems appear in these two manuscripts I consider my analysis of them equally important with my defense of the Egerton MS.

All of the minor manuscripts have also been studied. Among

these, the most interesting is the Parker MS 168 (Corpus Christi College, Cambridge), which contains one of the poet's most daring political allusions.

It is a pleasure to acknowledge the many debts that have been incurred over some twenty years of work. I wish to thank the President and Fellows of Harvard University for a grant that made possible my first research in England in 1952. For a similar grant I wish to thank the American Philosophical Society. I am grateful to the Trustees of the Folger Shakespeare Library in Washington, D.C., for financing a summer of study there. A grant from my own university, New York University, enabled me to go to Dublin. On many occasions I have been generously aided by the staffs of the British Museum Manuscripts Room and Reading Room, as well as of the Public Record Office. Twice I was kindly received in the library of Corpus Christi College, Cambridge, most recently by the librarian, R. I. Page.

Others to whom I am in debt for aid or inspiration are Louis B. Wright; John Stevens of Magdalene College, Cambridge; Walter Starkie, when he was at the Instituto Britanico en España; T. S. Wragg, Keeper of the Devonshire Collections at Chatsworth; Felix Hull, Archivist for the County of Kent; E. A. P. Hart, Librarian of the Inner Temple; and James A. Frere, Bluemantle Pursuivant of Arms. I was warmly received at the Maidstone Museums and Art Gallery by L. R. A. Grove and Tony Tynans. On a visit to Allington Castle I was courteously shown around by Joan M. Swingle, Superior of the Institute of Our Lady of Mount Carmel.

I am deeply appreciative of the generosity extended to me by His Grace the Duke of Norfolk, who in 1952 allowed me and H. A. Mason to microfilm the Harington MS at Arundel Castle. We were aided in that task by His Grace's former private secretary, W. Groves. Since 1952 I have been enlightened by the published work and private correspondence of H. A. Mason. Our meetings in Cambridge, London, and Arundel are a pleasant memory. In preparing this study, however, I was unable to use Mason's extensive review, *Editing Wyatt: An Examination of "Collected Poems of Sir Thomas Wyatt" together with suggestions for an improved edition* (Cambridge: Cambridge Quarterly, 1972). In reading Mason's book-length review of Kenneth Muir's work, I found that Mason and I still take essentially different views of the Egerton MS. While Mason has a number of brilliant suggestions for emending Egerton, he does not take it seriously as the cornerstone of the Wyatt canon and therefore the key to Wyatt's poetic identity. At the same time his evaluation of the Blage MS is far too high. Our two studies may serve as complementary guides for the next editor of Wyatt's poems.

Others to whom I owe special debts are Ruth Hughey of Ohio State University, William A. Wiatt of Indiana University, and Russell A. Fraser of the University of Michigan.

My oldest and deepest obligations are to Hyder Rollins and B. J. Whiting, who guided me in the inception of this work at Harvard University. Frequently I was aided and instructed by William H. Bond and the late William A. Jackson of the Houghton Library. In all the stages of this work my wife, Constance Smith Harrier, has been invaluable as a typist and editorial adviser.

Contents

Abbreviations

Foxwell   Agnes K. Foxwell, ed., *The Poems of Sir Thomas Wiat* (2 vols., London: University of London Press, 1913).

Hughey   Ruth Hughey, ed., *The Arundel Harington Manuscript of Tudor Poetry* (2 vols., Columbus: Ohio State University Press, 1960).

M1   Kenneth Muir, ed., *Collected Poems of Sir Thomas Wyatt* (London: Routledge and Kegan Paul, 1949).

M2   Kenneth Muir, ed., *Collected Poems of Sir Thomas Wyatt* (London: Routledge and Kegan Paul, 1963).

M3   Kenneth Muir and Patricia Thomson, eds., *Collected Poems of Sir Thomas Wyatt* (Liverpool: Liverpool University Press, 1969).

UP   Kenneth Muir, ed., *Sir Thomas Wyatt and His Circle: Unpublished Poems* (Liverpool: Liverpool University Press, 1961).

Nott   George F. Nott, ed., *The Works of Henry Howard Earl of Surrey and of Sir Thomas Wyatt the Elder* (2 vols., London, 1815-1816).

T   Hyder E. Rollins, ed., *Tottel's Miscellany*, 2nd ed. (2 vols., Cambridge: Harvard University Press, 1964).

V   Russell A. Fraser, ed., *The Court of Venus* (Durham, N.C.: Duke University Press, 1955).

Sigla

A Harington MS, Arundel Castle
B Blage MS, Trinity College, Dublin
C Parker MS 168, Corpus Christi College, Cambridge
D Devonshire MS 17492, British Museum
E Egerton MS 2711, British Museum
G Nicholas Grimald: emendations in *E*
H Harleian MS 78, British Museum
P Park-Hill MS (Add. MS 36529), British Museum
R Royal MS 17 A. xxii, British Museum
U University MS Ff.5.14, Cambridge University Library
Q *Certayne psalmes chosen out of the psalter of Dauid . . .*
    drawen into, englyshe meter by Sir Thomas Wyat Knyght
    (London, 1549)

Part One.

Textual Studies

The Egerton Manuscript

History

Since the Egerton MS 2711(*E*), now in the British Museum, is the cornerstone of the Wyatt canon, its history and nature must be described in some detail. Two notable studies of *E* have already been published. By far the more important is that of Ruth Hughey,[1] but the observations made by Raymond Southall are also relevant.[2] Hughey's study is primarily concerned with a companion volume to *E*, the Harington MS at Arundel Castle (*A*), but the true nature of *E* cannot be perceived except in that companion relationship.

Historically, *E* was one of a group of four manuscripts, which during the eighteenth and nineteenth centuries were together in the possession of the Harington family of Bath, descendants of the Tudor Haringtons of Stepney and Kelston. This group of manuscripts consisted of two prose and two poetry volumes. Although the prose volumes may be largely ignored, some of their characteristics illustrate the relationship among the four and thus account for certain aspects of *E* and *A*. The prose manuscripts have twin bindings similar to the twin bindings of *E* and *A*, the two poetry volumes. All four were rebound early in the nineteenth century. The prose volumes have flyleaves watermarked 1810, while *E* and *A* have flyleaves watermarked 1807. According to Christie's catalogue for a sale of 1888, both *E* and *A* were rebound by the firm of Charles Hering.[3] The prose volume called by Hughey Prose II, containing letters dating from about 1540 to 1575, includes handwriting from the Commonwealth days similar to that which now partly fills and disfigures *E*.

Portions of the old covers of *E* and *A* survive. These are pasted as insets on the flyleaves of their respective transcripts, also in the British Museum. The transcripts were done at the order of G. F. Nott about 1800 when he began to edit Surrey and Wyatt. It is known that the old covers were on *E* and *A* when they were used by Bishop Percy at the end of the eighteenth century, for a note in Percy's hand appears on the fragment of the *A* cover. Nott's transcript of *E* (Add. MS 28636) is not nearly so accurate as the one of *A* (Add. MS 28635), which is understandable, since *E* is much the harder to read.

The first folio in *E* is a modern leaf watermarked "Taverham 1807." Thus, f. 2 is the first of the original leaves, and the last original leaf is number 120. Beyond f. 120 are nine modern leaves, the last of which is backed with the cover paper. On the recto of what would be f. 126 is the note: "120 Folios. AG. January 1889/ Ex [?] S. S."

Between the present f. 2 and 3 are bound two stubs of original leaves. On the verso of the second stub survive the following rhyme-endings written in a scribal hand:

erne

eight
rough
able

old
und

I have not yet been able to identify this rhyme scheme within the Wyatt canon.

On f. 3r a scribe made the following false start then broke off:

Behold love thy poure how s

On f. 4r perhaps the same hand begins the full text of the poem and continues to copy additional poems as described below.

Although at least one leaf is lost between f. 7 and 8, there is no stub, and the binder did not indicate a known loss by binding in a modern leaf. However, a modern leaf is bound between f. 13 and 14. Folio 18 is a stub numbered 18, showing Wyatt's holograph signature "Tho." A modern leaf is bound between f. 21 and 22, but neither the stub of an original nor a modern leaf appears between f. 28 and 29. By contrast, both a stub and a modern leaf are bound between f. 45 and 46, and f. 46 is repaired with about half of a modern leaf. Between f. 48 and 49 is an old stub paginated recto and verso with the numbers 95 and 96. Single modern leaves are bound between f. 78 and 79 and between ff. 83 and 84. Folio 85 is repaired in its lower half with modern paper. Between f. 87 and 88 are both a modern leaf and an original stub bearing one visible number, 173. A single blank unnumbered old leaf occurs between numbered f. 99 and 100; three such leaves occur between f. 107 and 108; and another single old leaf comes between f. 111 and 112. Another modern leaf occurs between ff. 114 and 115.

By assuming one original leaf for each modern leaf bound in, totaling the number of stubs, and calculating obviously lost lines, one gets a total of 17 or 18 lost original leaves.[4] I assume that the binder had before him a volume that ended with the present f. 120.

All entries in *E* were made in single columns, with a lavish use of space suitable to a volume primarily devoted to fair copies. Wyatt was specially prodigal of space, sometimes placing only two ottave on one side of a leaf. In running copy the usual average for linage per side of a leaf is 26 lines. Thus, with an outside total of 18 lost leaves, there could be 468 missing lines. This estimate must be considerably reduced, however, in view of the fact that Wyatt wrote chiefly short lyrics, so that much of the space on the lost leaves would have been simply left blank for divisions between short lyric poems.

One need not look far for the poems now missing from *E*. In Tottel's *Miscellany* (*T*) there are 18 poems in the Wyatt section, none of which is extant in *E*: nos. 74, 76, 77, 78, 80, 81, 84, 105, 106, l07, 108, 109, 113, 114, 117, 119, 269, and 270, or a total of 368 lines of verse. Three of these poems (nos. 74, 77, 78) recently turned up in the Blage MS (*B*), but all of the others remain unique to Tottel's book. In view of the general authority of Tottel's attributions, there is no reason to challenge these poems. Thus, the simplest explanation for either Tottel's editor or Tottel himself printing these poems as Wyatt's is that they were then in *E* and also in the manuscript probably standing in sequence between *E* and *T*, namely *A*. In short, the Wyatt canon is almost complete with *E, A,* and *T*: and one would expect to find only a few more poems that were once also in *E* and probably rejected by Tottel's editor for special reasons. Unless the other MSS, such as the Devonshire MS (*D*) and (*B*), can show an independent authority, they should not be expected to add a large number of poems to the canon.

The early history of *E* can be determined from a study of its various handwritings. The earlier group of hands are here lettered A-H, the later and less essential group are numbered 1-8.

The Egerton MS is clearly not a working manuscript showing Wyatt's gradual development but an album of fair copies ready for final correction and polishing. The original entries are primarily in two hands, that of an amanuensis (hand A) and Wyatt's own (hand B). Two additional amanuenses (hands C and D) added a few poems, after which Wyatt himself continued until he died or gave up possession of the volume. Many of the poems entered by hand A have corrections in Wyatt's own hand. Those in his own hand also show revisions. One copy in particular, *What rage is this?* on f. 69v, is a remarkable specimen of a poem in the process of being written.

From what can be surmised about Wyatt's life, it is possible to tell something about the lateness of entries in *E* but nothing at all about their exact chronology of composition. Several poems in *E* can be placed within a likely time scheme:

> f. 7v *Who so list to hount*, about Wyatt's
> resignation of Anne Boleyn to "Caesar"
> (Henry VIII) around 1526-1527 or
> slightly later.
>
> f. 40r *Some tyme I fled*, probably referring
> to a trip from Dover to Calais in October
> 1532.
>
> f. 66v *If waker care*, announcing that Wyatt
> has taken a new mistress in place of Anne
> Boleyn, who had set England in a roar ,
> sometime between October 1532 and the
> end of 1537.
>
> f. 67r *So feble is the threde*, a verse letter to a
> mistress from a distant land, most likely from
> Spain after 1537. In fact, the poem is headed
> *In Spayne*, in italic script, which was probably
> added later by Wyatt.

Not included in this list is the poem *You that in love*, which alludes to unhappy experiences of the poet in "May." Although as Southall remarked, Wyatt was imprisoned in May 1534 and again in May 1536, the Chaucerian convention of lamenting love's unkindness in connection with the rites of May is too common to justify using this poem as evidence of chronology.[5]

The first continuous entries in *E* now begin on f, 4r, and it maybe assumed that *Who so list to hount* on f. 7v was written after 1526. Moreover, at least one leaf was lost between ff. 6 and 7. Therefore, nothing definite can be said about the dating of the poems before f. 7v, that is, of the very first entries in *E*. However, the bulk of the volume was entered after 1526, and Wyatt's first entry in his own hand on f. 50r comes after a poem he had written in 1532, copies on f. 40r. There is no evidence of entering poems in sections according to genre up to f. 69v. But Wyatt's psalms are isolated on ff. 86r-98v, and the so-called "Song of Iopas," an incomplete poem, comes last of all Wyatt's poems in *E* on ff. 100r-101r.

Since it is unlikely that a large gap of time existed between the first entries in *E* and the poem on f. 7v, they show that *E* was probably started about 1526 or slightly later. The most important conclusion from them, however, is a negative one, namely, that the poems in *E* are _not_ entered in order of composition. For only one poem is there some evidence of a date before 1526.

On f. 37v appears a copy of *A Robyn,* a lyric for which a musical setting is extant, the work of William Cornish, whose will was proved on 14 December 1523. Although *A Robyn* has a traditional opening, the traditional portion of the lyric is not likely to include the first twelve lines, all of which are part of the setting. Moreover, Wyatt did not write all the *E* poems beyond f. 7v later than 1526, since he was born around 1503. The possibility must therefore be accepted that some poems in *E* were written before 1526, and that no evidence of their first forms remains.

In fact, a general caution is relevant to all the manuscripts. Since most of the poems in *E* are in scribal copies, it is not known how many stages of composition they represent. All that is known is whether Wyatt approved or further revised the copies in *E* after 1526.

Up to Wyatt's death in 1542, *E* contained only those portions written in hands A-D. At Wyatt's death the manuscript probably went to his eldest son. Foxwell guessed that the volume went to Nicholas Grimald (1519-1562), since Grimald soon put his marks on *E*, but it would be hard to explain why the younger Sir Thomas Wyatt should give away permanently so valued a family document. Further, if *E* were in the possession of the younger Wyatt, there is a logical connection of *E* with the Harington family and the other Harington manuscripts. In 1554, the younger Wyatt was imprisoned in the Tower for leading the rebellion that subsequently brought about his execution.   Also in the Tower that year was the elder John Harington of Stepney (c. 1520-1582). It is probable that the younger Wyatt, being so close to his death, brought with him his father's personal volume, which also contained his father's version of the Penitential Psalms in his own hand.

Also in the Tower at that time was Sir John Cheke, from 27 July 1553 to 13 September 1554. One of Cheke's letters actually written in the Tower is preserved in the Harington Prose MS 2.[6]

The Egerton MS was no doubt in the possession of the younger Sir Thomas Wyatt in 1549 when the Penitential Psalms of the elder Wyatt appeared in print. This book is described on the title page as: "Imprinted / at London in Paules / Churchyarde, at the sygne / of thee Starre, By / Thomas Raynald, / and John Harryngton."

It is dated in the colophon: "M.D.XLIX. The last / day of December." It also has a dedication: "To the right honorable / and his singular good Lord, Willi- /am, Marqueshe of Northampton, / Earle of Essex, Barone of Kendal, / Lord Parre, a knight of the most no /

ble ordre of the Garter." This dedication is signed "John Harrington."

The "John Harryngton" of this book has been taken to be the John Harington, who compiled the Arundel MS and passed it on to his son, Sir John Harington (1561-1612), who translated *Orlando Furioso*. This seems unlikely, however. For one thing, John Harington of Stepney, father of the famous Sir John, was imprisoned in the Tower when the book appeared in 1549. Further, the existence of another John Harryngton, a London bookseller, is attested to by some evidence. This John Harryngton died in 1550, and one of his last books was the *Certayne Psalmes* of William Hunnis. His widow later published a volume of Thomas Sternhold's version of the psalms.[7] The more likely date, therefore, that John Harington of Stepney began his work with both *A* and *E* is the later one of 1554.

The 1549 *Penitential Psalms* did, however, leave their mark on *E*. In his dedication the bookseller John Harryngton remarked that he had proceeded "by thaduise of others (bet / ter learned then my self)." Among those learned gentlemen was very probably Nicholas Grimald, for John Bale recorded as among Grimald's works: "Restitutionem psalmorum Thome Viati libraris corruptorum cum prefatione ad Marchionem, li. i. A Restoration of the Psalms of Thomas Wyatt, corrupted by copyists, with a preface to the Marquis.. 1 vol."[8] The "preface to the Marquis" identifies Grimald's effort with the 1549 volume dedicated to the brother of Catherine Parr, Sir William Parr, marquis of Northampton (1513-1571).

The apparent explanation is a familiar occurrence of the sixteenth century. .The younger Wyatt was persuaded to put *E* at the disposal of an editor and a printer because corrupted versions of his father's psalms were in circulation. Grimald apparently was the middleman, since his editorial marks are notable in *E*, especially on the opening pages of *E*, on which he made a detailed study of Wyatt's prosody and orthography.[9] When he came to the psalms, however, he proceeded to re-edit them thoroughly, as the variants will show. One unmistakable sign of Grimald's presence as editor of the psalms is his insistence on a punctuated caesura. On f. 7v in *E*, Grimald rewrote Wyatt's poem *O restfull place* with each of the first eight lines divided at the caesura by a colon or a comma. Thus, it begins:

O restfull place : reneewer of my smart :

and ends:

Bysprent with teares, my bedde, I thee forsake. Although Grimald's peculiar spelling is not apparent in the 1549 volume, each line is neatly divided at the caesura by a comma, a practice only occasionally followed by Sir Thomas Wyatt in his holograph version. No doubt Grimald concluded from his study of the poems at the beginning of *E* that a thorough re-editing of the psalms was necessary. Ironically, therefore, the effort of the younger Wyatt to protect his father's work put into print an idiosyncratic version.

That *E* remained in the Harington family until the nineteenth century is evident. First of all, Sir John Harington (1561–1612) copied his version of the Penitential Psalms into *E*, and at the end of the eighteenth century the volume was still in the possession of the Haringtons of Bath. Moreover, it was probably a member of the Harington family who began copying Wyatt's first letter to his son on f. 71r. At least, the person had some knowledge of the Wyatt family and was obviously writing for others with personal knowledge of the Wyatts who might see the volume, for he headed the letter: "from him out of spayne to his son then xvii [?] yeres old". The "him" suggests that the copyist and his readers knew that *E* was Wyatt's personal book.

Although a number of other hands can be discerned in *E* and the order of their activities is relatively clear, no other person can be identified as working with *E* until the time of Bishop Percy, who left a note dated 1792 on f. 2r. It may be assumed that *E* remained under Harington family control and that all the hands in *E* represent either members of the family or their friends. In any case, nothing further of significance to Wyatt's work, with the exception of two poems, developed in *E* until it came to the attention of G. F. Nott, its first modern editor, in 1815–1816.

Description

E is a sound cornerstone of the Wyatt canon, being the only poetry manuscript in existence containing some of Wyatt's poems in his own hand, in both fair and working copies. There is no serious evidence to deny the assumption that all the poems in *E* likely to have been entered before Wyatt's death in 1542 are in fact his. The first task is to eliminate the material in *E* irrelevant to Wyatt's poetry.

There are twenty hands in *E* that must be initially considered as possibly relevant to Wyatt's work. About half of these are finally not crucial to the original formation of *E*. In order to distinguish them from the more important hands, they are numbered 1-8, while the important hands are lettered A-H.

The most modern hand (hand 1) is the note making of Bishop Percy, bishop of Dromore. The note that identifies his work occurs

on f. 2r: "In this Volume such Poems / are pointed out as have
been / discovered to be already / printed among "The / "Songs &
Sonnets of / "the Earl of Surrey / "& Others, 1557." / 1792."
Percy's indications of poems in *E* that are also printed in *T* begin on
f. 4r and continue throughout the volume. In another note on f.
43v, which has *My lute awake,* Percy wrote on the inner margin:
"Surrey [meaning *T*] / fo. 33 / + / ascribed to / Lord Rochfort / in
Nugae / Antiquae / vol. 3 / p. 256."

The next two hands to be eliminated are of the seventeenth century. Hand 2 is the most troublesome in the volume, since it has
covered many of the leaves with religious and mathematical discus-
sions and mathematical calculations, sometimes crossing out verses
to make its progress easier, sometimes turning the volume upside
down before beginning. Hand 2 has recorded the dates "August
1638" and "May 1639" on f. 6v. The extent of its operations
beyond leaves contining verses serves to identify early leaves and
give an idea of the relative position of poetry to other matter in the
volume. Hand 2 fills or partly fills ff. 2v-3v, 70v, 73v-74v (75r
is faded beyond deciphering), 75v-78v (79r is blank), 79v-83r
(83v is blank), 84rv, 99rv, 101v (102r is blank), 107v-109r (109v
is blank), 113r-115v, 116v-117r (117v is blank), 118r-119r
(119v is blank), and 120r (120v is blank). In general, hand 2, a
seventeenth century hand, has made use of almost every side of
every leaf at the beginning and end of the volume, besides impos-
ing itself on verses that its maker considered unedifying.

Hand 2 is briefly accompanied by hand 3, a fairer seventeenth-
century hand, on ff. 84v-85r. Hand 3 has copied two notes, signed
"Thomas ffairfax," the first being headed: "the Summons of Sir
Thomas ffairfax to P Rupert." Between these notes is a brief ack-
nowledgment, signed "Rupert." All three entries are probably
memoranda copies, since all of the texts and signatures are in one
hand.

Five additional hands occur after hand 3. Immediately following hand 3, on f. 85v, appears hand 4, an italic hand, which has
copied Surrey's *The great Macedon* as a proem to Wyatt's holograph
Penitential Psalms beginning on f. 86r. The poem is identified as
Surrey's by an "HS" monogram in the upper margin. On the inner
margin are the initials "IH," which probably indicate that the copyist was John Harington the elder. This hand is similar to that of
his son, Sir John, represented by the psalms copied in hand 6.

Hand 5, a Tudor hand, has copied *sententiae* in both English
and Latin on ff. 102v-103r. Immediately after f. 103v, which is

blank, hand 6, that of Sir John Harington, has copied his own version of the Penitential Psalms on ff. 104r-107r. Hand 7, an italic
hand probably of the seventeenth century, has copied some French
verses on ff. 110r-112r. Hand 8, a late Tudor hand, has copied a
recipe at the top of f. 117r.

Every leaf after f. 70v that does not contain verses or prose
traditionally attributed to Wyatt is now accounted for. All of these
folios are primarily dominated by hands 1-8, are blank, or are
modern blank unnumbered leaves. There are innumerable scribbles
by other hands that are not worth mentioning.

As for the location of the Wyatt material, his poetry occurs on
ff.4r-70r.   Following f. 70v, occupied by hand 2, appear Wyatt's
two letters to his son on ff. 71r-73r.   Wyatt's Penitential Psalms
are on ff. 86r—98v, and his "Song of Iopas" is on ff. 100r-101r.
This completes the analysis of all sections of the volume according
to their materials.

The texts of the Wyatt material are in eight hands, identified
by letters. Folios 4r-49v are in a strikingly neat secretary hand,
hand A. Folio 50r has two ottave in Wyatt's own hand, hand B.
Hand A resumes copying on ff. 50v-54r. Folio 54v has two more
ottave in Wyatt's hand B. Folios 55r through to the upper half of
f. 62r are continued by hand A.

A second secretary hand, hand C, begins copying on the lower
half of f. 62r and continues through f. 63v.[10] A third secretary
hand, hand D, appears on ff. 64r-65v. Wyatt himself (hand B) resumes on f. 66r, and hand C returns to continue on f. 66v. Wyatt
continues on ff. 67r-69v, and f. 70r has two isolated lines of poulter's measure at the top of the leaf in Wyatt's familiar book hand.
Wyatt's book hand (hand B) next appears on ff. 86r-98v, with his
Penitential Psalms. His so-called "Song of Iopas," actually titled
Iopas Song and never completed, covers ff. 100r-101v.

Thus, the texts of all of the poems usually attributed to Wyatt
from *E*—with two minor exceptions to be discussed—are in four
hands, one of which is Wyatt's own book hand. Furthermore,
Wyatt's hand interweaves with the other three from recto to verso, and the only large separations are between poems in Wyatt's
hand in distinct genres, namely, the Penitential Psalms and a
longer poem in poulter's measure. In view of the fact that not
one of the poems is specifically attributed in *E* to anyone other
than Wyatt, and not one of them is attributed elsewhere to anyone else on a better authority than *E*, the volume forms a safe
basis for the Wyatt canon. Indeed, these poems are the only

really secure group of Wyatt poems, and all judgments of style should be based on them and no others.

Four additional hands in *E* affect two additional poems and the two letters of Wyatt to his son. On the lower half of f. 7v, Nicholas Grimald has copied in his own hand (hand E) a version of the first stanza of *O restfull place.* A slightly different version of this poem, beginning *The Restfull place,* occurs in *D* on f. 18r, and unlike many other poems in *D*, this one is specifically sub- scribed with "ffynys *quod* Wyatt ᴕ." It thus seems to be the text of a poem probably once appearing in *E* between ff. 7 and 8, where a leaf or more has been lost.[11]

On f. 24v of *E*, beneath the poem *Madame withouten many Wordes,* an italic hand (hand F), has inserted a poem beginning *Of few wourdes sir you seme to be* and headed *Aunswer.* It clearly is a woman's reply to Wyatt's poem inserted sometime later, perhaps by a woman. This *Aunswer* also occurs in *B*, and there is no reason to consider it a poem by Wyatt. Although the dominant copyist of *E*, hand A, began entering poems in econom- ical fashion, after the first five entries he habitually began a poem at the top of a leaf or side of a leaf, leaving much space for later insertions. It is, therefore, remarkable, that the *Aunswer* is the *only* miscellaneous poem inserted between ff. 4r-69v. One may infer that the absence of poems other than the *Aunswer* between ff. 4r-69v is implicit confirmation that the Tudor possessors of the volume knew it to be the album of Wyatt's poems entirely and thus added their own poems only in the unfilled concluding portions of the volume.

On f. 70r, beneath the two lines of poulter's measure in Wyatt's own hand, another italic hand, hand G, has copied the *ottava Vulcane bygat me Mynerua me taught.* This poem was printed in *T* among Wyatt's poems. Evidence for this ascription appears on f. 49v, where Wyatt revised a scribal copy of what became *The furyous gonne.* The second version of the revised first line clearly shows the word *bombard* in the large italic hand that copied the *Vulcane* poem on f. 70r. The change from secretary to italic hand must have been suggested in both cases by the nature of the ma- terial. The term *"bombard"* was a foreign technical term, and the *Vulcane* poem is based on a Latin riddle, to which the answer is "a gun." Since Wyatt's normal hand appears above the word *"bombard,"* the conclusion follows that Wyatt in fact wrote two hands, secretary and italic, the latter usually called forth by Latin or by technical language. Hence, hand G on f. 70r must be designated as another of Wyatt's hands.

A much smaller, more refined italic hand, hand H, begins the first of Wyatt's letters to his son on f. 71r, heading it *"from him out of spayne to his son then xvii [?] yeres old."* After copying eighteen lines and a portion of the nineteenth, hand H stops. The copying is resumed in a still smaller italic hand quite similar in style. Whether or not this smaller hand is a new one is difficult to say. All that is known about hand H is that it was clearly later than Wyatt's time and was probably not that of the younger Wyatt, because of the heading to the first letter. It was, however, by someone who could designate Wyatt simply as "him" and who knew the age of the younger Wyatt. It must have been someone close to the Wyatt family, who knew that E was Wyatt's personal book.

The seventeenth-century hand 2 respected the letters as moral documents and also respected the *Vulcane* poem. Hand 2, however, crossed out Wyatt's two lines of poulter's measure at the top of f. 70r and filled in the rest of the leaf above and below the *Vulcane* poem. Similarly, hand 2 filled f. 70v, and continued at the top of f. 73v after the copy of Wyatt's second letter.

Thus, the texts of all Wyatt's poems in *E*, with the exception of the single stanza copied by Nicholas Grimald, are in five hands, two of which are Wyatt's own. None of the three secretary hands ascribed any poem to anyone. The poems are simply entered. Hands A and C do not even append the usual term "finis" beneath a poem. Hand D uses a "finis" on ff. 64v and 65r.

Signs of authorship do occur and, with one exception, are not at all obscure. Beneath the poems in his own hand Wyatt usually added an interlaced monogram signature "TV". This signature also occurs on f. 64v beneath the last line of the poem on the lower half of the leaf in hand D. The poem above it merely has "finis." as does that on f. 65r. The copy of Psalm 37 also in hand D on f. 65v has neither a "finis" nor anything else, probably because it is an unfinished poem. This combination suggests that Wyatt gave his initial approval to a text by adding his monogram signature. A number of poems in *E* also show his corrections, a practice that explains why he later added in his own hand an informal *"Tho"* or *"Tho."* in the margin of many a copy. As Southall observed, the form is so familiar that it must have been done by a member of Wyatt's own family. In fact, it is Wyatt's own signature, and not a sign of authorship but of approval for work done by the scribe.[12]

One set of entries in *E* probably began as a designation of authorship. This sequence includes simply the word "Wyat," which occurs in a small italic hand on the inner margin of about a dozen poems. It first occurs on f. 7v beside the poem *Who so list to hount,* beneath which Nicholas Grimald made his copy of *O restfull place.* Like some other poems in *E, Who so list to hount* was heavily corrected by Grimald according to his ideas of spelling and pointing. These "Wyat" entries were not continued far as a system, and at a crucial point the sign does not occur at all. On f. 86r, where Wyatt's psalms begin, there is no such entry to mark off Wyatt's work from the proem by Surrey on f. 85v. What probably happened is revealed by the contents of f. 7v. On that folio the writer of the "Wyatt" entries found the strange hand of Grimald and a text apparently not by Wyatt. Thus, his first "Wyat" was added to distinguish a well-known Wyatt work from what was presented to be another's work. Further checking of the volume soon convinced the writer that the designations were pointless, and they were dropped.

Although the writer of the "Wyat" entries cannot be identified by name, he or she can be pinned down to the one intrusive text among the Wyatt material up to f. 70r. A comparison of ff. 7v, 20v, and 24v shows that the writer of the "Wyat" entries was hand F. Hand F copied the text of the lady's *Aunswer,* but not the title itself, on f. 24v, which matches the "Wyat" entries and also the word *Petrarke* in the head margin of f. 20v. Hand F was probably that of a woman who wrote in the late sixteenth or early seventeenth century.

The person who added the heading *Aunswer* to the text of hand F on f. 24v also added to the title the phrase "2 ent?". This exemplifies an inconsistent system of classification in *E,* comprising an arabic numeral plus the word "enter" abbreviated. The general system was as follows:

"1 ent?." for shorter lyrics or songs
"2 ent?." for fourteen-line sonnets
"3 ent?." for longer lyrics
"4 ent?." for psalms
"5 ent?." for satires
"6 ent?." for the prose letters.

The last of these numerals shows that the system was imposed on *E* late in the sixteenth century or even later. There is no extant manuscript or book that conforms to this system, other than *E* itself.

The term "Sonet" also occurs sporadically at the head of some

poems in *E*, and Agnes Foxwell took the word to be part of the numbered system. Such is not the case, however. Whoever added the
term "Sonet" was using it according to the older meaning of "sonnet"
as "little sone." In the numbered system the number 2 stands for
true (fourteen-line) sonnets, while the term "sonet" is added indis-
criminately and in a different hand.

One more set of classifications appears in *E,* made by Wyatt himself. This system is shown to be the poet's because the pen and inking
are integral with the text of the holograph poems. It consists of roman numerals, occurring as follows:

"Vij"	f. 29v
"Viij"	f. 32r
"IX"	f. 37r
"X"	f. 40r
"iij"	f. 40v, cut off at the top of the leaf
"V"	f. 50r
"iiij"	f. 54v

That Wyatt should have added these numerals to poems in ottava
rima suggests his special interest in the form. Just why they were
added, however, is a question that cannot be answered.

In conclusion, *E* is a fully understandable document and beyond
any question Wyatt's own. Furthermore, Wyatt's work within *E* is
clearly identifiable from later accretions, and the poems so designated may serve as the cornerstone of the Wyatt canon.

Significant Details

In the holograph Penitential Psalms, Wyatt's hand is most
obvious in the headings he added, because of the similarity of
ink between heading and text. In order to distinguish the Wyatt
headings from others, comparison should be made with the Penitential Psalms of Sir John Harington on ff. 104r-107r. This
shows that in most cases the heading *Psal:* plus a number was
added by Harington. Harington made such additions for Psalms
6 and 32 (cf. ff. 87v, 89v, 104r), Psalm 51 (cf. ff. 93r, 105r),
and Psalm 102 (cf. ff. 95r, 106r). A similar matching occurs for
Psalm 130 (ff. 97r, 106r), but the deleted "129" on f. 97r does
not reappear, which suggests that the error was first made when
Harington read Wyatt's psalms, perhaps in preparation for his
own work. There is a stylistic similarity for Psalm 38, but on f.
104v the heading is briefer, appearing as "Ps. 38."

For Wyatt's handwriting, one must focus on f. 98r, where

Harington found no need to add anything. Here there is a close match between the heading and the text in color of ink and sharpness of point as well as in general style of writing. But the heading is the Latin incipit in Wyatt's italic hand, followed by a roman number. This is clearly by Wyatt, since the writing and ink match the text of his familiar book hand.

The same incipit appears on f. 95r in a similar but slightly larger script, and it was probably added to Psalm 102 after that text had been copied, because the ink matches that of Psalm 143 more than Psalm 102. The Latin incipit of Psalm 130, f. 97r, also closely tallies with its text and is therefore by Wyatt. But the incipit on f. 93r for Psalm 51, in black ink, contrasts with the hand of both Wyatt and Sir John Harington. Apparently Sir John found it there when he added his numbered heading. It may have been by his father.

The incipit for Psalm 38 was written by Wyatt but added later, since it matches the ink of Wyatt's revisions in the text. Also, this incipit was fitted in around the TV monogram to the preceding poem rather than being given a line of its own. The style of the incipit for Psalm 32, f. 89r, is more open, but as it is similar to the others and matches the ink of the text, it is Wyatt's.

Although the incipit for Psalm 6 is cut off, a few letters are still visible at the top of the leaf: *"Dne ne in ʄ"*

To this Harington added a full heading in black ink.

These examples prove that Wyatt used italic as well as book or secretary hand. They support the argument that the italic of f. 70r, which also matches words and headings on preceding folios of *E,* is a specimen of Wyatt's hand. Those preceding headings are: *In Spayne* on f. 67r and *In Spayn* on f. 69r. The inking of the word *bombará* in the revision of the first line on f. 40v (Poem 61) does not match as well as the others, but the style is the same.

There is one difference between the italic on f. 70r (Poem 109) and the italic used for the incipits of the Penitential Psalms. In the former a closed *e* is used, and in the latter an open *e.* One probable reason for this difference could be a time lapse of several years. According to H. A. Mason *(Humanism and Poetry,* pp. 204-206), the Penitential Psalms were most likely written about 1536, during the Anne Boleyn tragedy. The headings that match Poem 109 indicate a time several years later, when Wyatt was in Spain, or even after his return. A note of reminiscence appears in the headings, phrased simply "In Spain."

Two other headings in Wyatt's italic hand are the Latin incipit for Psalm 37 on f. 65v and the title "Iopas Song." on f. 100r.

The punctuation of *E* is very difficult to analyze. In each instance, however, I have tried to determine whether the punctuation marks were made by the scribe, by Wyatt, or by some other hand. The simplicity of Wyatt's usual system is striking, in view of the large bulk of his holograph verse and of the scribal texts corrected by him. Wyatt generally used only the virgule and the full stop for punctuation, occasionally putting both in the same place, which indicated a change of mind. Even the use of the comma is not plentiful.

Evidence of a concern with meter, even to the counting of syllables, is rare, but it does occur. In this regard one must remember that *E* contains mostly fair copies and that many earlier corrections and refinements were no doubt made. The Penitential Psalms and Poems 61 and 68, in particular, show evidence of the range from light pointing to intensive revision. The last two poems are unique in having double or triple punctuation. They are also written in ottava rima, a form that may have had a special interest for Wyatt in leading to metrical experiment.

The Arundel Harington Manuscript

History

In 1933, Ruth Hughey rediscovered in Arundel Castle the lost manuscript that G. F. Nott had designated Harington MS no. II. In 1935 she published an extraordinary study of it, and in 1960 she produced a definitive edition.[1]

The Arundel Harington MS (*A*) retains 145 of its original 228 leaves. Its paper is ruled with 38 lines to the page, which indicates that if it was once filled with verse, about 5300 lines have been lost, while about 10,000 survive. The compilers of *A* were John Harington of Stepney and his more famous son, Sir John Harington of Kelston, translator of *Orlando Furioso*. Within its covers are represented most of the important and many minor-poets from the generations of Wyatt and Surrey to those of Sidney and Greville.

Two periods are significant in the provenance of *A*. The better known started in 1769, when *A* was still in the possession of the Harington family of Bath, Iineal descendants of the Tudor Haringtons of Stepney and Kelston. In that year Henry Harington (1755-1791), second son of Dr. Harington, physician of Bath, edited the first volume of *Nugae antiquae*. The young man undertook this task when he was merely fourteen years of age. The result was tragic for *A*, since many of the original leaves were sent to the printer and lost or destroyed in the process. Hughey concluded from a study of the surviving manuscript texts of poems published in *Nugae antiquae* that some of them were faithfully printed, while others differ so greatly that other manuscript sources besides *A* were obviously used by the editor and printer. This occurrence led G. F. Nott to note that *Nugae antiquae* as edited by Henry Harington in 1769, 1775, and 1779 has the authority of a manuscript. Hughey's analysis supported this conclusion, at least about the general substance of the texts, as opposed to orthography and exact phrasing. It is therefore possible to place among the poems probably written by Wyatt those included in *Nugae antiquae*.

The second period began somewhat later, when through the courtesy of Dr. Harington, *A* was loaned to persons planning editions of *T* and earlier Tudor poetry. In 1792 Bishop Percy of Dromore made use of *A*, as he also did of *E*, leaving his manuscript annotations in both volumes and on their flyleaves. He was soon followed by Nott, who consulted *A* for his printed but unpub-

lished edition of Tottel's *Songs and Sonnets,* as well as for his
monumental edition of Surrey and Wyatt, published in 1815–1816.
Nott's handwriting has also been traced in *A* by Hughey. Owing
to her recent discovery of Nott's correspondence with Dr. Harington, Hughey was able to determine that the one responsible for
the early nineteenth-century bindings of *A* and *E* was Nott himself, who employed the firm of Hering to do the work. Thus, all
four of the Tudor Harington volumes, *E, A,* and Prose I and II,
have similar early nineteenth-century bindings. Early in 1842, after the death of Dr. Nott, his library was sold. The bookseller
Thomas Rodd, who may have been acting as an agent for the
Duke of Norfolk, bought the volume. In any case, *A* was in the
library of Arundel Castle by 1862, when Canon Tierney wrote a
note on its flyleaf.

The early history of *A* is obscure, but some probable lines may
be laid down, at least in relation to *E* and Wyatt's poetry. John
Harington the elder was no doubt personally acquainted with
Wyatt, George Blage, and the other middle-class courtiers of Henry
VIII, since he was a member of the royal household from about
1538 on. Harington was about seventeen years younger than the
elder Wyatt, eight years younger than Blage, and approximately the
generation of the Earl of Surrey. It is probable that Surrey knew
Harington at first simply as a favorite musician of the king. But in
view of Harington's later service with the Seymour family, he must
have been associated from the early forties in Surrey's mind with
an enemy faction. Since Harington was a skilled musician, he probably began composing words for popular tunes and other verses
from about 1540 at the latest. Like many others, therefore, he must
have become aware of Wyatt's skill in verse and have begun collect-
ing his poems. The copies of Wyatt's poems in *A* were probably
made between 1542 and 1554, many of them directly from *E*. Some
of them were also made from the circulating copies that also came
to be collected in *D.*

Logical dates for Harington's personal use of *E* were suggested by
Hughey, who pointed out that when the Earl of Surrey was executed in 1547, his possessions were seized by the Seymours. Among
those could have been Wyatt's personal manuscript, *E,* which could
have passed from the younger Wyatt to Surrey during their days of
close companionship. More likely, however, is an earlier or later date:
either 1542–1546, when Harington could have made personal contact with the younger Wyatt, or 1554, when he was a fellow prisoner
of the younger Wyatt in the Tower.

Harington was imprisoned twice in the Tower, about February 1549 to early 1550, and again about 8 February 1554 to late in that year. On the first occasion he was imprisoned as a follower of Sir Thomas Seymour, then Lord High Admiral. It might be thought that such a situation would not encourage the writing of love poems, but in fact Harington seems at the time to have courted Isabel Markham, daughter of the Lieutenant of the Tower, Sir John Markham. A more serious fruit of this imprisonment was a translation of Cicero's *De amicitia,* published 1550. The second occasion of imprisonment was more serious, for Harington had been implicated in the rebellion of the younger Wyatt and the plot to put Lady Jane Grey on the throne. It seems likely that the younger Wyatt brought his father's book, *E,* with him when he entered the Tower, for it held not only love poems but also the elder Wyatt's satires on court life, stoical reflections, and versions of the Penitential Psalms in his own hand. Although it is possible that Harington had begun earlier to collect Wyatt's poems, on this occasion he probably made an extensive record of the poems from *E* into *A,* including the Penitential Psalms.

That John Harington of Stepney was not the John Harryngton, London bookseller, who was instrumental in the publication of Wyatt's Penitential Psalms, is shown by both the imprisonment of Sir John Harington in the Tower when the book actually appeared and from evidence of the separate existence of the bookseller John Harryngton. The connection of John Harington with *E* and its influence on the contents of *A* more probably took place in 1554, when both the elder Harington and the younger Wyatt were in the Tower. The younger Wyatt probably left *E* in the possession of John Harington simply because he was soon to be executed for his leadership of the rebellion.

In June 1557, Tottel published his renowned *Songs and Sonnets,* comprising 40 poems of Surrey, 97 of Wyatt (later reduced to 96), 40 of Grimald, and 94 by Uncertain Authors. Although the identity of Tottel's editor is not known, Hughey pointed out that the person was probably not Grimald, since his peculiar orthography was inconsistently followed in *T.* Furthermore, in the second edition of July 1557, Grimald's section was reduced to ten poems, and his name was replaced by his initials. John Harington himself remains a logical candidate for Tottel's editorship, although it is not possible to pinpoint his full contribution to the volume. More important than the question of editorship, however, is the relation of *A* to *T* and to *E.*

Hughey's analysis of many readings in *E, A,* and *T,*[2] led to a fair, if not unchallengeable, conclusion that *A* was in a medial position between *E* and the *T*. It is evident that the editor of *T* had in hand both *A* and other manuscript sources. Both in wording and attribution of authorship, *T* is based heavily on *A*, although in a few instances of attribution, *T* ignores the grouping in *A*.

One fact about the relations of *E*, *A*, and *T* emerges from a study of Hughey's chart of the relative positions of poems in each volume. Of all the manuscripts extant, only *E* and *A* show sectional groupings of poems in exactly the same order, which sometimes agree between the two manuscripts but also include groups congruent in *E*, *A*, and *T*. This would happen naturally when a copyist used one text as the source for the second. The importance of such symmetries is most notable for *A*, which emerges as the only extant manuscript likely to stand in direct descent between *E* and *T*. The symmetries may be represented as follows:

	E	*A*	*T*
Yf amours faith	f. 12v	f. 65r	no. 98
Farewell love	f. 13r	f. 65v	no. 99
My hert I gave	f. 13v	f. 65v	no. 100
Som fowles	f. 19v	f. 66r	no. 47
Bicause I have	f. 20r	f. 66rv	no. 48
I fynde no peace	f. 20v	not present	no. 49
Though I myself	f. 21r	f. 66v	not present
My galy charged	f. 21v	f. 66v	no. 50
Auysing the bright	f. 22r	f. 67r	no. 51
Ever myn happe	f. 22v	f. 67r	no. 94
Love and fortune	f. 23r	f. 67rv	no. 95
How oft have I	f. 23v	f. 67v	no. 96
Like to these	f. 24r	f. 67v	no. 97

The slight reversal of sections in *T* could be accounted for by the process of printing, with the continuity of copy in this instance being disturbed only slightly by the editor or compositor. Not counting the Penitential Psalms, which are shared by *E* and *A*, additional symmetries between them are:

	E	*A*
Was I never yet	f. 11r	f. 63rv
Eche man me telleth	f. 11v	f. 63v
Patience though I have not	f. 28r	f. 75v
Paciens for my devise	f. 29v	f. 75v
Processe of tyme	f. 55r	f. 97r
After great stormes	f. 55v	f. 97rv

Additional symmetries between *A* and *T* are:

	A		*T*
Suche vayne thought	f. 67 (2)v		no. 41
Vnstable dreame	f. 67 (2)v		no. 42
You that in love	f. 67 (2)v, 68r		no. 43
If waker care	f. 68r		no. 44

Other small parallels among the three volumes are:

	E	*A*	*T*
Some tyme I fled	f. 40r	f. 68v	no. 71
He is not ded	f. 40r	not present	no. 72
The furyous gonne	f. 40r	f. 68v	no. 73

The missing poem in *A* may have been close to the others, since a blank leaf is bound into *A* after f. 68, indicating a loss of material. The next folio in *A* is numbered 75.

These symmetries, together with the analysis of readings presented by Hughey, lead to the conclusion that *A* is the only surviving manuscript directly descended from *E* and likely to have served as the basis for the edited copy from which the *T* was printed.

Description

Considering the number of known Wyatt poems in *A*, the grouping is remarkably solid. A total of 49 poems are in *A*, numbered 96–144 in Hughey's edition, of which 45 are confirmed by *E*. Two of the exceptions, Hughey nos. 96 and 97, are placed among Wyatt's poems in *T*, which shows Tottel's dependence on *A* for attribution. The third exception, no. 98, *Was never ffile yet half so well yfyled*, is the variant version of Hughey no. 108, *There was never fyle half so well fyled*. Of these two, no. 98 represents the version that circulated independently of *E* and also got into *D*, while no. 108 is the *E* version. The fourth exception comes at the end of the series, no. 143, *In Greece somtyme theare dwelt a man of worthie fame*, which Tottel placed among his "Uncertain Authors." In this instance the placement of Tottel should stand, for he must have had other authority for denying the grouping that he otherwise followed consistently. One of the reasons for supposing that *A* preceded *T* is simply that *T* departs from *A* occasionally in wording and attribution. One would expect that if *A* had been copied from *T*, the copyist would have followed *T* more closely. After Tottel had publicly proclaimed no. 143 as not being by Wyatt, one would expect the copyist of *A* either to group it elsewhere or to make some deliberate sign of knowledge about the poem's authorship. Tottel's editor no doubt was the later worker and had another authority. No. 143 must therefore be placed among the poems of uncertain authorship.

The Penitential Psalms of Wyatt are grouped in *A* as nos. 154-169, and between nos. 145 and 154 are a number of miscellaneous poems. One of these, however, no. 145, may be the very end of the Wyatt group in *A.* After no. 144, *Myne olde dere En'mye* (also in *E*) is a lacuna of two leaves, and the next poem is no. 145, *But Lorde how straunge is this / that to the iust befall.* Because of the lacuna, it is uncertain whether the Wyatt section in *A* continued up to the present no. 145, although it may have. As the poem stands, no. 145 is the conclusion of a poem begun on one of the earlier missing leaves. Hughey was ambiguous about this poem. At one place she remarked, "I concur in the opinion that No. 145 was very probably written by Wyatt." But elsewhere she wrote more accurately that, although the Haringtons may have regarded the poem as Wyatt's by its position, "the style and content of the fragment suggest a closer relation with Surrey's biblical paraphrases than with Wyatt's poetry.[3] She also pointed out that the verses of no. 145 compare well with Wyatt's other biblical paraphrases, but that those seem different because they are in terza rima. There is no other information on this poem, because it occurs nowhere else as yet discovered. In this instance, therefore, one must be guided by the probable grouping of an authoratative manuscript. In brief, the Haringtons probably placed it at the end of a Wyatt group that ran beyond the present no. 144 through two missing leaves, ending on f. 105r. The poem was no doubt ignored by Tottel because it was unsuitable in content. As a religious reflection, it would do well coming last in *A*, and the three leaves intervening between it and the Penitential Psalms may well have originally been left blank for more Wyatt poems. It must therefore be included among poems probably written by Wyatt.

On Tottel's authority, two more poems must be added to the Wyatt canon. They are isolated on a single verso of a leaf later in *A*, f. 216v. They are *The flamyng Sighes that boile within my brest,* a double Shakespearian sonnet (*T* 101), and *Stond who so list vpon the Slipper toppe* (*T* 118). How these two poems became separated cannot be explained. There is no reason to add to the Wyatt canon any other poems in *A*, although a few have been proposed. The two poems on f. 216v do not constitute a strong enough group to justify adding to them contiguous poems. To do so would require some outside authority, which is lacking.

Nugae antiquae

Nugae antiquae (1769), edited by Henry Harington, comes mainly from *A*. A few other poems printed in *Nugae* are probably from *A* but no longer extant in it because of the loss of leaves, as noted by Hughey. Among these are a group of 11 poems, beginning with *I fynde no peace* and concluding with *Caesar when that the traitour,* both of which are confirmed by *E*. Three others in the series are also in *E*, and two are confirmed by *T* as well as by the Park-Hill MS, B.M. Add. MS 36529[P]. All of these poems together, as Hughey showed, would have fitted nicely on the missing ff. 61-62 and 69-74, as two subsections within the extant Wyatt group. Furthermore, her demonstration of the generally close nature of *P* to *A*, since *P* is another of the Harington family manuscripts, leads to the conclusion that groups of poems still extant in *P* could once have been in *A*. Such an example is the group of four additional poems printed in *Nugae*, which are no longer extant in *A* but still extant in *P*. They are *Vengeaunce must fall (P* f. 35r), *Spring of all woe (P* f. 35r), *Playne ye, myne eyes (P* f. 33r), and *I see my playnt (P* f. 33r). These four poems must be added to those probably written by Sir Thomas Wyatt, taking the *P* texts as primary.

In one instance *Nugae antiquae* contradicts both *T* and *E*. In the 1775 volume, *My lewt, awake* is identified in the heading as written by Lord Rochford, according to a manuscript dated 1564. There may have been such a manuscript, but its date alone would discredit it beside the testimony of Wyatt's own volume and the public testimony of Tottel, which surely would have provoked wider comment if it had been false.

The Devonshire Manuscript

History

The early history of the Devonshire MS (*D*) as outlined by Raymond Southall is sound in the essentials, with the one caveat that his construction "was arrived at simply by collating the disposition of the hands in the manuscript with the known histories of Mary Shelton (A), Mary Fitzroy (B), and Margaret Douglas (C)."[1] I am not convinced that these three handwritings occur in *D* just where Southall found them. The general truth of his account nevertheless remains unchallenged, simply because these three ladies are the only ones who can reasonably be connected directly with the volume. To them must be added their lovers and courtly servants: Thomas Clere, Henry Fitzroy, and Lord Thomas Howard.

D still has its original London binding, examples of which are on record for the years 1525–1559. The front cover is stamped with the initials "M.F." and the back with "S.E." The modern foliation, 1-96, is the only visible one. Portions of the original flyleaves survive, mounted on ff. 1 and 94. As Southall remarked, "all the jottings on the [front] flyleaf are enigmatic," but two marks are worthy of recognition. The only clear name on the front portion is "mary shelton." The word "marayg" on the same flyleaf is written in a hand "remarkably similar to that of Margaret Douglas later in her life."[2]

Several internal markings support these clues as to the possession or use of the volume. On f. 7r, beneath the last line of a poem, is:

> ondesyrd sarwes
>> reqwer no hyar
>>> mary   mary shelton.

The full name following the isolated first name indicates that the writer later realized another Mary (Mary Fitzroy) was also identified with the book. And on f. 22v, beneath two fragments of verse —neither of which is related to her doggeral, however—Mary Shelton wrote:

> awel I hawe at other lost
> not as my nowen I do protest
> bot wan I haue got that I hawe mest
> I shal regoys among the rest
>> mary shelton.

There also appears on f. 68r, above more rime doggeral of Mary Shelton's:

>   Madame margeret
>   et madame de Richemont
>   Je vodroy bien quil fult.

These lines are in a neat secretary hand, in vivid contrast to Mary Shelton's scrawl.

The "margeret" of this last inscription was undoubtedly Lady Margaret Douglas (1515–1578), child of Henry VIII's sister Margaret, who was first married to James IV of Scotland and later to Archibald Douglas, sixth earl of Angus. As a niece of the king, Lady Margaret was for a time close to succession to the throne, since both Elizabeth and Mary had been declared illegitimate. Perhaps with the approval of Anne Boleyn, Lady Margaret made a secret betrothal with Lord Thomas Howard, the poet Surrey's half uncle. This act was treasonable, since it involved a successor to the throne and was without the king's knowledge or desire. In 1536, in the midst of the accusations against Anne, the secret marriage was discovered and Lord Thomas was imprisoned in the Tower, where he died in October 1537. Despite the political implications of the marriage, the troth between the lovers seems to have genuinely been a matter of the heart, as sections of *D* reveal.

Lady Margaret had followed her husband to the Tower in 1536, but because of illness she was soon removed to the Abbey of Syon. She was released a few days before her husband died. Although the birth of Prince Edward removed her from immediate succession to the throne, Lady Margaret was again in trouble in the autumn of 1541 for a courtship with Sir Charles Howard, third brother of the queen. Again she was imprisoned in Syon House.

In July 1544, Lady Margaret was finally married with royal approval to Matthew Stewart, earl of Lennox, in a ceremony performed at St. Jame's Palace. Her son by this marriage was Lord Darnley, later to become father of James I of England. Verses by Lord Darnley, perhaps addressed to Mary Queen of Scots, are copied with unusual neatness in *D* on f. 57r. They conclude: "your humble seruant Hary Stuart."

The connection of Lady Margaret, Lord Thomas, and Mary Shelton with *D* was first outlined in detail in 1871 by Edward A. Bond of the British Museum.[3] Bond detected the name "Margaret How[ard]" on the front flyleaf, about an inch above that of Mary Shelton, where it is still faintly visible. Specific sections in *D* described by Bond as the fruit of the secret betrothal of Lady Margaret and Lord Thomas are ff. 26r-30r, 40r-44r, 44v-47v, and 89v-92r. He was also the first to observe that the copy of Surrey's poem *o happy dames* on f. 55r is in the hand of Mary Shelton.

Bond also corrected one of G. F. Nott's readings, which removed the cornerstone of Nott's view of the manuscript. Bond remarked that Nott "fell into a mistake when he read a half-effaced subscription to the sonnet beginning 'My fearful hope' as 'Finis qd Wyatt', and that to the response to it as 'Finis qd Surreye,'" and printed them as Surrey's. The subscriptions are 'Finis qd Nobodye,' and 'Finis qd Sumbodye'." Bond added that the two poems are more likely to be Wyatt's than Surrey's, because there are more poems by Wyatt in *D*. However, Bond could find no trace of Wyatt's hand in the volume. The importance of this finding was that it removed the best evidence for Nott's supposition that *D* was an album recording the poetic exchanges of Wyatt and Surrey. Although it is possible that Surrey read Wyatt's poems in *D*, since it was primarily a Howard family book, neither Wyatt nor Surrey was probably connected directly with it.

In *D* the lovers Lord Thomas and Lady Margaret adapted the verse of earlier English poets to their situation of mutual loyalty and distress, as shown by Ethel Seaton, who discovered that the verses on ff. 89r-92r are actually excerpts from Hoccleve's *Letter of Cupid*, Sir Richard Roos's *La belle dame sans merci*, *Anelida & Arcite*, and Chaucer's *Troilus and Cressida*, Bk. II. Another stanza was taken from *The Remedy of Love*. All of these verses occur in Thynne's 1532 edition of Chaucer.[4] It is likely, therefore, that they were copied from the 1532 Chaucer rather than from a variety of manuscripts. The hand that copied these excerpts from Hoccleve and others is the same as that of ff. 26r-30r, folios that Bond described as having "verses by Lord Thomas Howard, apparently in his own handwriting, on ruled lines." Since I do not have a lengthy specimen of Lord Thomas' script, I cannot verify Bond's statement. There are eight poems on ff. 26r-30r, and all except one of them were addressed by Lord Thomas to Lady Margaret. The sixth in the series is Lady Margaret's reply to her faithful lover and husband. Scattered throughout the other poems are allusions to "my wife" and the disparity of their estates, as well as to the threats and snares faced by the prisoner in the Tower. Beneath the poem by Lord Thomas on f. 26v is what looks like a genuine signature or name used in direct address, "margrt." This single word is probably the only word actually written by either of the two. The rest is in a neat scribal hand.

As Seaton showed, the last poem in this sequence is a remarkable example of borrowing from the past to suit a personal situation. The verses on ff. 29v-30r are "carved out of the fine lament to Fortune by Troilus" (Bk. IV, 11. 288-308, 323-329). Where Cressida's name occurs in Chaucer's poem, two blanks are left by the copyist for the name of Lady Margaret.

A distinctly different hand copied the verses on ff. 44v-47v, two of which are subscribed "T. H." This fact casts doubt on the supposition that Lord Thomas himself copied the earlier section, since he was more likely to sign his own verses with "T. H." than simply the "fynis" that occurs in the earlier section. In the absence of a lengthy specimen of his copybook script, it is unsafe to conclude that all the material in *D* up to f. 47v was entered no later than 1537, a conclusion that could be hazarded if it were certain that the latter group was indeed in the hand of Lord Thomas.

The verses of ff. 89v-92r are more general in character than those of the section on ff. 26r-30r. They are partly in praise of women, partly in defense of women against slanderers, with several contrasting protests against *"la belle dame sans merci."* The handwriting connects them with Lord Thomas and Lady Margaret. They could, of course, be from an earlier stage in their courtship, but in view of the position of the verses in *D*, it is more likely that the copyist was either Lady Margaret herself or one of her friends at a later time.

The "madame de Richemont" of the inscription on f. 68r is the sister of the poet Surrey, Mary Howard. Mary was married to Henry Fitzroy, duke of Richmond and illegitimate son of Henry VIII. Surrey and Fitzroy were companions from 1532 until the latter's sudden death in 1536. The initials "M. F." on the front cover of *D* probably refer to Mary and Fitzroy, who were either the original owners of the volume or soon took possession of it, stamping their initials on the cover. As Southall suggested, the hand that both he and I designate as hand B may be that of Mary Fitzroy.

Mary Shelton is best known as the sweetheart of Surrey's friend Thomas Clere, for whom Surrey wrote an epitaph. Thomas Clere should be distinguished from Sir John Clere, Surrey's squire. Mary was the daughter of Sir John Shelton of Shelton, Norfolk. Her mother was a daughter of Henry Parker, Lord Morley, whose other daughter, Jane or Joan, married Lord Rochford, brother of Anne Boleyn. After the death of Clere, Mary Shelton became Mrs. Hevingham. She remained very close to Surrey until his execution and was examined by the authorities in their attempt to get evidence against the poet.[5]

Because it is difficult to make a certain connection between signed inscriptions and a copy of a poem in attempted or successful copyist's script, I have not followed Southall in dividing the bulk of *D* among the hands of Mary Shelton, Mary Fitzroy, and Margaret Douglas. This could safely be done only if one had at hand a holograph letter also signed by the writer, and as I have not seen such documents for these women, I cannot place them in *D*, except for the hand of Mary Shelton. For that reason I have kept largely to the anonymous designations of hand A, B, C, and so forth, as they occur in *D*.

For the most part I agree with Southall's identification of Mary Shelton's hand.[6]   There are some important exceptions, however. The neat hand of ff. 26r-29v is not the scrawl of Mary Shelton. Nor is it her hand on ff. 89v-92r, again a neat hand and no doubt the same as that on ff. 26r-29v. In other words, Southall lumped a distinct hand, which does range throughout the volume, with that of Mary Shelton. This difference of opinion does not affect Southall's conjectured history of the volume, for it remains clear that Mary Shelton was an early possessor of the volume, and that she remained in contact with those who later had it.

One further conjecture about her is possible. Southall lists two additional hands, designated D and E, as starting the volume with her. I would reduce his D and E to one hand, plus her scrawl. However, the beginning hand of the volume on f. 2r is possibly what Mary Shelton would have produced had she tried to do a copyist's work. It is by no means a professional hand and makes frequent errors. Perhaps what has been taken as an addition to the poem on f. 3r is simply Mary Shelton lapsing from script into her scrawl before recovering on the next attempt.

Another activity of Mary Shelton is evident in *D*. After the bulk of the volume had been filled in, she went through it marking certain poems for copy, memorization, or musical performance. Her usual mark was "and thys," which occurs on ff. 4r, 6v (beside the poem to which she added the comment about undesired services), 9v, 12r, 13v, 14v, 24r, 70v, 71v, 72v, 73r, 73v, 78r, and 80v. Two additional markings appear: on f. 17v, "and thys chefly," beside *And wylt thow leve me thus;* and on f. 81r, "lerne but to syng yt," above the first line of *now all of chaunge / must be my songe.* Thus, she seems to have made good use of *D* as an album of courtly games, verbal and musical.[7]

In view of both the letters stamped on the binding of *D* and the internal markings, Southall's sketch of the volume's early history

is reasonable. It was probably purchased in London by Henry Fitzroy about 1533 and was first used by him and his connections,
among whom were Mary Howard and her friend Mary Shelton.
That the volume remained primarily a Howard family album is
shown by its use for the love verses exchanged by Margaret Douglas and Surrey's half uncle, Lord Thomas Howard. Lady Margaret
Douglas must have taken the volume with her when she married
Matthew Stewart, earl of Lennox, in 1544. At her death it was
probably left to Charles Stuart, younger brother of Lord Darnley.
That would account for how the book got to Chatsworth House
and for the initials "S. E." on the back. For Charles Stuart married
Elizabeth Cavendish, daughter of George Talbot and Bess of Hard-
wick, earl and countess of Shrewsbury. Thus, the initials on the
back cover were added to signify Stuart and Elizabeth.[8]

Since both Wyatt and Surrey made the voyage from Dover to
Calais in October 1532, it is likely that their relationship started on
that date and that it continued in some fashion until the fall of
Anne Boleyn in 1536. This conjecture coincides with the purchase
of D as a Howard family volume. It is certain that D is not Surrey's
personal record of Wyatt's work, although in it are copies of
Wyatt's poems collected by Surrey's sister Mary and her companions. These copies begin with some degree of reliability in the work
of hand B.

Although Anne Boleyn confided in the ladies who used D, she
never made use of it herself. Southall followed Foxwell in the error
of supposing that certain fragments of writing on f. 67v include a
signature by Anne Boleyn. These jottings, above the scrawl of Mary
Shelton, are:

> am el mem
>   anem e
>   as I haue dese
>   I ama yowrs an

The top three lines of this inscription are indeed a riddle, but
Southall did not solve it by transposing them thus:

> a lemmen
>   amene
> ah I saue dese
>   I ama yowrs an

Even if one allows the transposition and reads "lemmen" as the
Middle English word for "sweetheart," the result makes little sense.
More important, this handwriting is not Anne Boleyn's.[9] As the
position of the "an" in the last line shows, it is not even a signature

but the start of the new word "and." The hand that wrote these words and fragments is the same as that occurring on ff. 89v-92r and 26r-30r.[10]

Description

G. F. Nott, who essentially defined the Wyatt canon in his edition of 1815-1816, had an incorrect view of D's general nature, but his less systematic and more sensitive approach allowed him to exclude some of the poems in D that probably are not Wyatt's but crept into the canon later. Although Nott saw clearly that D was a Howard family volume, he believed "that Surrey and Wyatt were in the habit of frequently communicating their verses to each other."[11] With this in mind, he printed one pair of poems as if written by Wyatt and Surrey in verse correspondence and doubtless assumed that many others in D were a record of the two poets matching their skill. Without stating it explicitly, Nott assumed that D was Surrey's manual of Wyatt's work, from which Surrey learned and then gradually departed. That cannot have been the case, however, since D contains not a trace of either Surrey's or Wyatt's hand.[12] Although little more of certainty can be stated about D until all the hands are identified, the volume was never the personal book of either Wyatt or Surrey but of their admirers, friends, and relations.

Nott also began the useful editorial practice of scrutinizing the poems in D according to the continuity of handwriting and the nature of each group. However, his observations of handwriting continuity were unfortunately inaccurate, as shown by comparing his list of contents with D itself. At the head of his list, Nott remarked: "Those Pieces which have a Star prefixed, are either in the hand-writing of the original Copyist, or have Wyatt's signature [sic] subscribed. The others are in the handwriting of different other persons." As the stars show, Nott mostly saw the same hand running throughout D, whereas a number of changes in handwriting and in procedure of entry actually occur. Furthermore, the phrase "Wyatt's signature" covers a large variety of signs, none of which is actually Wyatt's signature.

Foxwell also advanced a faulty view of D's relation to E, based on two known facts about the manuscripts. First, a number of "ballets" or songs either by Wyatt or by someone else appear in D but not in E. Second, in most instances D does not have the revised readings of the poems in E, but rather has a different reading or the "earlier" of two. On the basis of these facts, Foxwell theorized that

Wyatt began as a writer of "ballets," mainly in lines shorter than pentameter, and that the record of these early experiments is D.[13] She conjectured that Wyatt had much greater difficulty writing pentameter than he did writing tetrameter or trimeter, which led him to study Trissino's handbook and Pynson's Chaucer so as to perfect his own verse. As he improved, he selected from D the poems he most prided himself on and had them copied into E. Many of these poems were difficult exercises in translation from the Italian into a pentameter line. Naturally, Foxwell argued, Wyatt would have cherished most the poems that were harder to write and illustrated his line of development.

To support her view, Foxwell created two fictions. One was that the large group of poems in D beginning on f. 69r are signed with Wyatt's monogram signature "TV." On the contrary, they are signed merely "fs" or "fs." Another fiction was that late in life Wyatt chose Mary Howard, the duchess of Richmond, as the "Phyllis" who replaced the lost Anne Boleyn in his affections. Foxwell also conjectured that the lines about *A face that shuld content me* were addressed to Mary Howard.[14] But even aside from Sir Edmund Chambers' identification of Phyllis with Elizabeth Darrell, there is no evidence for assuming that Mary Howard might be Phyllis.

In one instance Foxwell perceived the actual nature of D, when in discussing the rondeau *Thou hast no faith* and its metrical peculiarities, she remarked, "This rondeau probably circulated in MS. before it was copied into D MS. and was altered during its circulation."[15] The question arises as to why Wyatt should have allowed a corrupted version to be copied into his own manuscript while laboring at the problems exemplified by the corruption. The truth is that D was not Wyatt's book and that many copies in it are not directly from E but from circulating copies, as Foxwell conjectured. Therefore, wherever the same poem does not occur in E, there is no knowing whether it is a true copy of a Wyatt poem, an earlier version of a Wyatt poem, a corrupted copy, or simply a poem by someone else.

The latest edition of Wyatt's poetry, by Kenneth Muir and Patricia Thomson, continued to ignore the problems presented by D. That edition allowed only six pages for the relationships among all of the manuscripts, and while most of those pages were devoted to D, they offered only an argument by analogy (*M3*, pp. xx–xxv). Thus, Muir showed that wherever the same poem occurs in D and in E, the D text usually does not include Wyatt's revisions. Hence, some *D* versions are in a sense "earlier." On this there is no dispute, except that the precise meaning of "earlier" is unclear.

Muir then made a false leap: "It is a reasonable hypothesis that the poems peculiar to D were also written early and it is strange that Wyatt did not include them in his own MS. Some pages have been torn from E, but not enough to have contained all the D poems assumed to be Wyatt's. One can only suppose that he had another MS. from which the poems in D, A, P, H, T, and B were ultimately derived" (*M3*, p. xxiv). This statement contains its own refutation, since it would be strange indeed for Wyatt not to include so many of the *D* poems in his own book if they were his. It also obscures the fact that *D* is not in the same relation to *E* as are *A* and *T*, for among the latter group is overwhelming evidence of direct contact and continuity. Since *E* is made up of fair copies, there must have been at least one manuscript on which it is based, and perhaps several. But this is only negative evidence and the task remains of evaluating the features of those copies that are peculiar to *D*, namely, manner of entry, ascription (if any) grouping, and stylistic integrity.

By including *That tyme that myrthe dyd stere my shypp* among the "Wyatt poems" (*M3, CLXXIII*), Muir was creating an ambiguity, for that poem has been used to argue that *D* was possibly Wyatt's book, in which Anne Boleyn inscribed her devotion to the poet. In his biographical study of Wyatt, Muir observed concerning two poems: "Wyatt conveys the totality of an experience. This does not necessarily mean that the two poems are autobiographical, though one could hazard a guess that the lady of the first poem is the one who wrote in the poet's book:

> I am yours, you may be wel suer,
> And shall be whyle that Lyffe dothe duer."[16]

These lines are quoted, however, not from *D* but from *B*, and it may be that Muir was here claiming that *B* was "Wyatt's book." Elsewhere in his study, however, he indicated that he was alluding to the story about a mistress who declared her submission to Wyatt in *D*: "On a later page of the Devonshire manuscript, someone has written: 'I ama yowres An' [*sic*]. But there is no evidence that the Devonshire manuscript ever belonged to Wyatt, and his handwriting does not appear in it. If this inscription is related to the above poem it would seem probable that the poem was not, after all, Wyatt's. If, however, the poem is Wyatt's, as I believe, the inscription may be unrelated to the poem, or it may have been written after the poem by someone who knew that it had been addressed to Anne Boleyn."[17]

In brief, Muir argued that *D* was never Wyatt's book but that this poem was probably written by Wyatt to commemorate an occasion when Anne wrote the words "I am yours, Anne" in his book. Muir assumed, however, that the inscription later in *D* was not essential to his argument. Perhaps he was suggesting that the poem was once in *E*, which was Wyatt's book, and that such an inscription was made by Anne in that volume. Neither the inscription nor the poem, however, can be removed from their context in *D*. The explanation is more simple.

The inscription on f. 67v of *D* is correctly transcribed *I ama yowrs an*. As Muir noted, it is not by Anne Boleyn. Rather, it is part of the line "I am yours and will be sure," or something similar. Neither poem nor inscription concerns Wyatt but both are the record of the love affair of Lord Thomas Howard and Lady Margaret Douglas. The handwriting of the inscription is the same as that on ff. 89v-92r and 26r-29v. Among the verses borrowed from *La belle dame sans merci* on f. 90v is the line:

> So am I yowrs and wylbe ueryly.

Thus, the inscription is a fragment of either this line or a more concise version of the earlier pair:

> I am yowres, yow may well be sure,
> And shall be whyle my lyff dothe dure. (*D* f. 17v)

The letters "an" are simply the uncompleted word "and." Since the same hand wrote not only the fragment on f. 67v and the quotation on f. 90v but also the whole section ff. 26r-29v, and since the section 26r-29v is undoubtedly the fruit of the secret marriage of Lord Thomas and Lady Margaret, it is reasonable to conclude that the earlier lines on f. 17v refer to the same affair. Thus, the inscription no longer ties the poem and the book to Anne Boleyn and Wyatt.

Muir indicated that *D* and *B* are mutually supporting, but did not make clear how. In totaling up the number of Wyatt poems, for example, he stated: "It is highly probable that he wrote at least 28 of the poems in the Blage MS (apart from those also included in *E*); that he wrote at least 23 of the Devonshire poems—apart from those included in *B* and *E*."[18] However, in order to make a case for twenty-eight poems in *B* that do not occur in *E*, one would have to support them either from *D* or *A*. The other possible argument would be a reversal of direction: that *B* is its own authority and supports *D* and *A*. About either of these possibilities, however,

Muir was uncertain. As he wrote: "There is no definite proof that Wyatt wrote this or any of the remaining poems in the Blage MS; but there is, after all, no certainty that he wrote many of the poems in the Devonshire MS; and as Blage was a close friend of Wyatt's and the compiler of D is unknown, the former was probably in a better position to collect Wyatt's poems than the latter. It is true that only two of the poems are definitely ascribed to him, but only one of the known Wyatt poems in the manuscript bears his initials; and the absence of these cannot be taken as an indication that he was not the author of other poems."[19] This argument was neatly refuted by Southall: "Muir.. . . is at this point arguing that the absence of certainty as to Wyatt's authorship of many poems in the Devonshire MS. is a point in favour of supposing him to have written many of the unascribed poems in the Blage MS!"[20] This paradox, unfortunately for both D and B, is the only argument one can make for many of the poems.

Southall offered the most skeptical view of both D and E. In fact, his view of E would wipe out the entire Wyatt canon, for not even any judgments of style could be made, since there would be no bona fide poems of Wyatt on which to make them. But his severe view of D is more right than wrong. Of the group numbered 133-167 (except 162) in Muir's second edition (M2) and "written in a single hand," Southall remarked: "The fact that some 'known' Wyatt poems are found amongst a number of poems of unknown authorship in a manuscript in which poems by several authors are collected tells us no more than that Wyatt was one of these authors. That all of the poems in one particular section of one manuscript have been entered by one scribe does not suggest that they are all the work of one author. There are no reasonable grounds for assuming that any of the unascribed poems in the Devonshire MS. are by Wyatt in the absence of other evidence."[21] These two caveats serve as negative guides; that is, they indicate what not to assume about groupings in D as a whole or about particular sections.

Southall's criticism of the assumptions underlying Muir's choice of poems for M2 applies also to M3, since most of the Devonshire poems are still included solely on the authority of D. Muir has shifted the burden, however, from D to B wherever B offers a text of the same poem. A comparative table of the largest group of Devonshire poems as printed in M2 and M3 follows:

M2 133 from D = M3 CCVI
M2 134 from D = M3 CLVIII from B
M2 135-M2 149 from D = M3 CCVII-CCXXI

M2 150–*M2* 151 from *D* = *M3* CXIII and CXXVI from *B*
M2 152–*M2* 155 from *D* = *M3* CCXXII-CCXXV
M2 156 from *D* = *M3* CXLVIII from *B*
M2 157 from *D* = *M3* CLXXIV from *B*
M2 158 from *D* = *M3* CCXXVI
M2 159 from *D* = *M3* CXXVIII from *B*
M2 160–*M2* 166 from *D* = *M3* CCXXVII-CCXXXIII
M2 167 from *D* = *M3* CXL from *B*

Thus, in the case of seven poems Muir took as his authority in *M3* not *D* (as in *M2*) but *B*. This followed from his placement of *B* as the second source after *E* in *M3*. But this strategy further weakens the case for all of these poems, because uncertainty of authorship in one manuscript does not support certainty of authorship in another, unless additional and firmer evidence is forthcoming. Since in fact *B* is a slenderer reed than is *D*, the structure of *M3* is more confused—if not weaker—than that of *M2*.

When reduced to making a decision about authorship entirely on grounds of style, one must rely on poems specifically ascribed to Wyatt in some manuscript. Since the only extant manuscript that Wyatt ever saw or wrote in is *E*, Wyatt's identity as a poet must be based entirely on the poems in *E*. Those in *D*, even ones specifically ascribed to him, may include any number of verbal inaccuracies, as shown by checking them with *E*. The same objection applies to *B*. The only other manuscript that shows signs of having been copied directly from *E* is *A*, which frequently incorporates Wyatt's own corrections and contains many poems in almost the same order in which they occur in *E*.

I agree with Southall that it cannot be assumed that groups of unascribed Wyatt poems exist throughout *D* merely on the basis of one or more continuous handwritings. *D* is clearly a miscellany, not only of early Tudor poems but also of earlier poems by Chaucer, Hoccleve, and others. In general, the unascribed poems from *D* should be accepted into the canon only when the style of a poem has a strong resemblance to Wyatt's style represented in *E*.

In instances of doubt about style, however, the groupings in *D* become significant. The style of a poem is frequently inconclusive, especially since many of the poems in *E* are not distinguished. For that reason the different kinds of groupings in *D* must be taken into account.

The general error made in past handling of *D* has been an imprecise and inconsistent evaluation of its different sections and groups. They are markedly different, with some being far more impressive than others. In the past, mere continuity of handwriting in a group, together with the presence in it of known Wyatt poems, has been taken as the rule for a Wyatt group. This practice is unsound. In fact, three kinds of groups are exemplified in D, which have varying degrees of reliability as guides to authorship. A group is basically a number of poems entered by one hand in a characteristic way.

The first group includes poems specifically ascribed to Wyatt as well as to other people. It is therefore not likely to include among its unascribed poems any by Wyatt. The second group of poems is made up only of some ascribed to Wyatt and others not ascribed to anyone. It has more possibility of containing additional poems by Wyatt, depending on how many and where the Wyatt ascriptions were made. For example, a copyist might wish to indicate a Wyatt group by specifically ascribing the first poem in a series to him. The third group is made up entirely of unascribed poems. In this case one must judge the content. For example, a group of thirty-seven continuous poems of which twenty-nine are confirmed Wyatt poems suggests that the other eight might also include Wyatt poems. On the contrary, a group of twenty-nine poems among which occur only two Wyatt poems that are confirmed by good authority must be viewed as more doubtful. Both such groups actually occur in D.

In the past, unfortunately, an editor did not demand that a Wyatt group even begin with a confirmed Wyatt poem; it could occur anywhere in the series. Ideally, a Wyatt group should begin and end with known Wyatt poems, but at the least it must begin with one. It is unlikely that both the first and last poems in a series would have been lost from E or from one of the other manuscripts that made their way into T.

When a series of poems occurs in both D and E, anything that can be noted about the possible copy used for D in relation to that of E also tells something about the group. Thus, a D series containing a pair of poems that occurs in E on exactly the same folio, recto and verso, and in exactly the same order, is a much better group than one not showing such characteristics. In discussing different versions of Wyatt poems in various manuscripts, J. C. Maxwell used "superior version" to indicate approval of the text in one manuscript as opposed to another. But it ought to refer simply to the version's relation to the text in E, which is the basis of all "superiority." Aside from correcting for mere scribal nonsense, one must base one's judgment on what Wyatt himself saw and approved. This rule should be extended to the search for similar phrases in Wyatt's poems and prose when a poem does not occur in *E*.[22]

Finally, some poems are ascribed to Wyatt in *D* with "ffinis qd Wyatt" or "finis qd W," others merely with "W" or "T. W." or the like. Usually Wyatt signed his own poems in *E* first with a "TV" monogram beneath the last line in the center of the leaf, then added a "Tho." in the margin after he had looked over the copy. Neither of Wyatt's characteristic ways of signing is duplicated in *D*.

It is sometimes suggested that Wyatt's brother-in-law, Anthony Lee, was the source of Wyatt's poems in *D*, simply because one poem is subscribed "ffynys qd anthony lee." But this single objective ascription is not adequate evidence for Lee's personal connection with *D*. It would be safer to assume that Edmund Knyvet was instrumental in the volume because two poems are subscribed "EK" (f. 63v) and "E knyvet" (f. 59v). Edmund Knyvet could well have provided authorial copy for the scribe who wrote Knyvet's poems into *D*, for he was an intimate of the Howard family until his quarrel with Surrey. These two examples point out that the way in which poems are ascribed by a copyist may be additional evidence of their reliability.

Section 1

The first section of *D* showing an inner consistency of scribal hand and habit begins on f. 2r and continues through f. 6r. This section is mainly in one hand but shows the aid of two others, and there is one link with the next section.

Hand A began the volume on f. 2r and continued through f. 3r, leaving f. 3v blank, then continued on f. 4r through f. 6r, also leaving f. 5v blank. Hand A is notable for several habits: uncertainty of movement, frequency of errors, and leaving poems as fragments. Thus, its work of seven and a half lines on f. 3r had to be continued by another hand (hand C). In similar fashion, the work of hand A on f. 4r broke off after twelve lines and was continued by still another hand (hand D) before resuming on f. 4v. The six poems or fragments copied into *D* by hand A have no "finis" or any mark of authorship. On f. 2r appear two scribbles in still another hand, which are probably flourishes but could be taken as letters. As letters they resemble not "TW" but "TH", and since Surrey's half uncle Lord Thomas Howard is prominent later in *D*, he is doubtless the one intended, if indeed anyone is.

The note in *M3* for the first poem printed from *D* (CLXXVIII) is entirely fanciful: "*Authorship:* Signed 'Th.W' in D." The scrawls or doodles on f. 2r in *D* contain no dots of abbreviation, are unlike any other signature in the volume, and if they do indicate an ascription, are as much like "TH" as "TW."

Of the six poems copied by hand A, Muir printed two from *D* (*M3* CLXXVIII and CLXXX) and two from their parallel texts in *B* (*M3* CXIV and CLXX). Yet the list of contents of *D* (*M3*, pp. xiv-xv) refers to the *B* text rather than the *D* text wherever one is available. This procedure does not allow for an accurate list of *D* but does follow Muir's policy of shifting authority from *D* to *B*. Nor does the list indicate which of the poems are fragments. If these four poems are treated as a group, there are two possible reasons for including them among Wyatt's poems, both of which are decidedly weak.

First is the possibility that two fragments of Wyatt poems are included among them. On f. 2v, hand A has copied a version of lines 13-30 of *Alas the greiff,* which is known to be Wyatt's because it occurs in *E* on f. 5v. It is clear, however, that hand A did not see *E*, since lines 1-12 are missing from *D*, and the large ornamental "O" of line 13 in *D* is meant to represent the beginning of a poem. Hand A, therefore, found a fragmentary and inaccurate copy of *Alas the greiff* and copied the lines into *D*.

Similarly, the twelve lines on f. 3r (in two hands, A and C) are a fragment of *My hert I gave the not to do it payn*, which occurs again in *D* on f. 75v. Both copies in *D* are defective. The twelve lines of this sonnet on f. 3r (occurring in *E* on f. 13v) omit lines 10 and 11, while the copy on f. 75v of *D* omits line 11. The sequence of error is obvious. Hand A first copied seven and a half lines of the sonnet on f. 3r. Much later, after the volume had been mostly filled, hand C tried to complete the poem from the copy on f. 75v of *D* and compounded the error by omitting another line besides that already omitted on f. 75v. Neither of these copies came from *E*, since both have numerous variants.

There are six poems by hand A in *D*, two of which are fragments of Wyatt's poems. The fragments are clearly not from *E*, and hand A probably had no idea what the accurate texts were. Of the other four poems, two are unique to *D*, and two occur elsewhere. *At last withdrawe yowre cruelltie* also occurs in *B* f. 67r, and *To wette yowr Iye* occurs in *B* f. 170r. These facts, however, indicate nothing whatever about Wyatt's authorship; they merely suggest the kinship of *D* and *B*, of which there is much further evidence.

In sum, the work of hand A in *D* has no bibliographical soundness whatsoever. Thus, these poems could be placed in the Wyatt

canon only on the basis of style, which is impossible, as they are
thoroughly undistinguished. At best, they are what Muir described
as "by imitators."

The first of the dubia from *D* are:

  f. 2r *Take hede be tyme leste ye be spyede*
  f. 4rv *At last withdrawe yowre cruelltie*
  f. 5r *To wette yowr Iye withouten teare*
  f. 6r *I lowe lovyd and so doithe she*

Section 2

The second section in *D*, a remarkable one, is entirely in hand B,
a legible and consistent secretary hand but not of professional re-
finement. The entries of hand B follow, with ascriptions, possible
location in *E*, and occurrence in Muir's edition.[23]

  f. 3v *My pen take payn a lytyll space fynys* [*M3* CLXXIX,
      followed by three entries in hand A]
  f. 6v,7r *Suffrying in sorow in hope to attayn*
      ffynys ᴙ[deletion] *ondesyerd serwes reqwer no hyar mary*
      mary shelton [*M3* CLXV]
  f. 7v *My ferefull hope from me ys fledd fynys qd nobodye* [?]
  f. 8r *Yower ferefull hope cannot prevayle fynys qd*
      somebodye [?]
  ff. 8v,9r *Bownd am I now and shall be styll fynys*
  ff. 9v,10r *Ffarewell all my wellfare fynys*   [*M3* CLXXI]
  f. 10v *May not thys hate from the estarte ffynys qd anthony lee*
  f. 11r *Yff I had sufferd thys to yow vnware ffynys qd*
      *Wyatt*ᴙ[l. 25ff of   [l. 25ff of *Hevyn and erth and all that*
      here me plain in *E* ff. 47v,48r; missing folio?]
  f. 11v *The hart and servys to yow profferd fynys* [*M3* CLXXXII]
  f. 12r *At most myscheffe ffynys qd* Wyatt ᴙ[In *E* f. 34rv]
  ff. 12v,13r *What menythe thys when I lye alone fynys qd*
      Wyatt ᴙ[*M3* CLXXXIII]
  f. 13v *Pacyence tho I have not fynys qd Wyatt* ᴙ [In *E* f. 28r]
  f. 14r *Ys yt possyble fynys qd Wyatt* ᴙ[*M3* CLXXXIV]
  ff. 14v,15r *My lute Awake performe the last labor*
      fynys qd Wyatt ᴙ[In *E* ff. 43v, 44r]
  ff. 15v,16r *Alas poore man what hap have I ffynys* [*M3* CLXXXV]
  f. 16v *Marvell nomore Altho ffynys qd Tas Wyatt* ᴙ
      [In *E* f. 35rv]
  f. 17r *And wylt thow leve me thus fynys qd W.*ᴙ
      [*M3* CLXXXVI]

f. 17v *That tyme that myrthe dyd stere my shypp* *ffynys*
    [*M3* CLXXIII]

f. 18r *The restfull place Revyver of my smarte* *ffynys*
    qd Wyatt ⮜[*M3* CLXXXVII]

f. 18v *All women have vertues noble and excelent* *fynys qd*
    Rychard Hattfeld ⮜

f. 19r *What no perde ye may be sure* *fynys qd Wyatt* ⮜
    [In *E* f. 31v]

f. 19v *To my* [blank, then in a later italic hand, not B] *Was*
    neuer yet fyle half so well fylyd *ffynys* ⮜[In *E* f. 14v]

f. 20r *As power and wytt wyll me Assyst* *fynys*
    [*M3* CLXXXVIII]

f. 20v *Sum tyme I syghe sumtyme I syng* *fynys*
    [*M3* CLXXXIX]

f. 21r *Pacyence of all my smàrt* [A line is drawn across the
    second column after l. 30 of this poem; *M3* CXC]

    `*Who wold haue euer thowght* [continuation of the foregoing
    entry] *fynys* ⮜[*M3* CXCI]

f. 21v *In faythe methynkes yt ys no Ryght* [*M2* 119]

f. 22r *And sure methynkes yt ys best way* *fynys qd A. I.* ⮜

This group displays a remarkable consistency, not only of hand
but of habit. Every entry except one has either a "finis" with ascription or simply "finis." The entry on f. 21v without either nota-
tion is very likely incomplete, since the leaf contains two stanzas,
with space left blank for a third, an arrangement that would exactly match the three stanzas parallel to it on f. 22r.

Nine poems of this group are specifically assigned to Wyatt,
and a tenth to "W." Of these ten, six are confirmed as Wyatt's by
their occurrence in *E*. A seventh, *The restfull place*, probably was
in *E*, since one of its stanzas occurs in the hand of Nicholas Grimald
on f. 7v, at which point at least one folio is missing. It is therefore
probable that hand B knew what he was doing when he specifically assigned a poem to Wyatt in *D*.

Another poem, *Was neuer yet fyle half so well fylyd*, has only
"ffynys⮜" beneath it. Much the same poem occurs in *E* on f. 14v,
but the first line is a variant, *There was never ffile half so well
filed*. Both versions occur in *A*, the *E* version appearing among the
certain group of Wyatt poems in *A*, and the *D* version appearing
among a possible but isolated group of Wyatt poems. On f. 59v of
A are a number of verses signed "ffinis Jo hn Har ington ." Beneath them, and on succeeding folios, in a neat scribal hand appear
the following poems:

f. 59v *With Petrarke to compare theare may no wight ffinis*
f. 60r *It was the day on whiche the Sonne depryved of his
  Light ffinis*
  I ne can close in short and conning vearse ffinis
f. 60v *The piller pearisht is whearto I Lent ffinis*
    [*M3* CCXXXVI]
  A Ladye gave me a gyfte she had not ffinis [*M3* CCXXXVII;
  Was never ffile yet half so well yfyled ffinis
    ff. 61-62 are missing in *A*, then starts the solid Wyatt
    section]
f. 63r *The Longe love that in my thought doth harber ffinis.*

There follows a group of Wyatt poems, then on f. 65v begins
There was never fyle half so well fyled, concluded on f. 66r with
"ffinis." Thus, *A* shows the existence of two versions of a Wyatt
poem, one that was recognized as authoritative (*A* ff. 65v, 66r)
and one that was not (f. 60v). Clearly, the writer of hand B in *D*
saw only the variant version, which so far as he knew was of unknown origin. This explains why he did not specifically ascribe it
to Wyatt, as he did nine others.

Only two poems in this group are specifically assigned to Wyatt
but not confirmed by *E*, and a third is assigned to "W" but not
confirmed by *E*. These too may be safely given to Wyatt because
there are no strong objections on the basis of style. In fact, *Ys yt
possyble* is a superior poem, and *What menythe thys* reads like a
preliminary exercise for *What rage is this?* The poem assigned to
"W," is not witty but it is a gay song. *And wylt thow leve me thus?*
may therefore be included on the authority of hand B.

In the group copied by hand B there are four types of classification. Some are assigned to Wyatt or "W"; others to people named,
like Wyatt's brother-in-law Anthony Lee or "Rychard Hattfeld."
A third pair have probably been given pseudonymous names, like
"nobodye" and "somebodye"; while the fourth class is left unmarked. One of the unmarked poems was apparently directed to
Mary Shelton, the sweetheart of Surrey's friend Thomas Clere, in
token of which she wrote on f. 7r beneath the poem her sentiment
as a "daungerous" lady to an aspiring servant.

The logical conclusion is that when hand B knew the author of
a poem and dared to record it, he did so. The unassigned or pseudonymous poems are likely to be intimately concerned with persons close to the writer of hand B, or in fact with hand B himself.
Those named, Wyatt and the others, seem like outsiders, who are
included because their poems illustrate the same love-game being

played by Mary Shelton and her friends. Therefore, one must have the most compelling reasons on grounds of style, or other outside information, to place in the Wyatt canon one of those poems left unassigned by hand B.

Other occurrences of the unassigned poems are not helpful. As in the case of *Was neuer yet fyle*, hand B assigned a poem to Wyatt on good authority when available and avoided doing so when in doubt. Three other parallel occurrences among the manuscripts suggest the same procedure, as I shall now illustrate.

Two of the unassigned poems occur in *B. Suffryng in sorow*, the poem that Mary Shelton took to be directed at herself, occurs on *B* f. 159r. This fact undermines the authority of *B* as a Wyatt collection, for *B* has no authority on its own to give as support to other manuscripts. The other poem is *That tyme that myrthe dyd stere my shypp*, on *B* f. 175r.

A third poem occurs in two versions in *A Boke of Balettes*, published probably in the 1550s, and in *The Court of Venus*, published between 1561 and 1564.[24] These printed version are not evidence of authorship, only of popularity.

Aside from the poem addressed to Mary Shelton, which must be excluded from the Wyatt canon, ten entries remain unassigned to anyone. None of these poems should be included in the Wyatt canon, although some have been on the basis that they represent Wyatt's style or an incident in his life. One of the group, *Bownd am I now*, has never been included. Another of the poems, *Ffarewell all my welfare*, is written from a woman's point of view and has none of Wyatt's manner as exemplified in *E*. In fact, the poem reads like a fifteenth century song or an imitation of it by a woman. It does not belong in the Wyatt canon.

A third poem was brought into the Wyatt canon on the basis of an erroneous biographical argument and, on investigation, provides still further evidence that the unassigned poems concern persons in the Howard family who did not dare to have their names recorded. *That tymethat myrthe dyd stere my shypp* expresses the resolve of a servant to remain loyal to his lady, whom he has dared to love above his degree. He remarks that on one occasion of good fortune:

> Then in my boke wrote my maystresse
> I am yowres yow may well be sure
> And shall be whyle my lyff dothe dure.

To confirm or support this experience, on f. 67v, among other fragments, someone has written: "I ama yowrs an". This was taken by Foxwell, and tacitly accepted by Muir, as the work of Anne

Boleyn writing in Wyatt's book a declaration of her love. This
is not the case, however, for the words on f. 67v are not in Anne
Boleyn's hand, nor are they a declaration with a signature. On
f. 90r of *D*, the same hand as that on f. 67v has copied out lines
229-236 of Sir Richard Roos's *La belle dame sans merci*, which include the line: "So am I yowrs and wylbe ueryly". Clearly, the
fragment on f. 67v is simply the uncompleted line: "I ama yowrs
and wylbe ueryly" or the like. If one adds the fact that *D* was
never Wyatt's book and that a better candidate for the role of the
lover appears in *D,* the whole case for the poem as Wyatt's col-
lapses. The servant who loved above his degree and remained faithful to death was in fact Surrey's half uncle, Lord Thomas Howard.
Thus, this lyric may safely be placed among the lyrical exchanges
of Lady Margaret Douglas and Lord Thomas Howard.

Three additional poems offer no evidence at all of Wyatt's style
or of biographical significance. *As power and wytt wyll me Assyst*
is an archaic carol suitable for round dancing. These opening words
are in fact the burden of a traditional carol, rhyming with the refrain line "Evyn as ye lyst". As a poem, it is a pastiche of clichés
and proverbial expressions, which could be by anyone, and there
is no reason to think that Wyatt wrote dancing carols, since he
carefully revised the form by dropping the burden in *E*. His poem
A Robyn should not be confused with the carol form, since *A
Robyn* is a dramatic dialogue very different in tone. On considera-
tions of style, therefore, *As power and wytt* must be removed
from the canon. An even less distinguished poem must follow it,
Sum tyme I syghe sumtyme I syng.

The third poem of this subgroup, *The hart and servys* (*M3*
CLXXXII), changed its character between Muir's two editions. In
his first edition (*M1*, p. 99) it was a thoroughly abject, singsong
address of a servant to his lady, vowing total subjection and service "secrettly," but with an unusual line:

Ffor all my servys and my fyer
Reward your servante lyberally.

Since at least one critic had noted the importance of "fire" as a
thematic word in Wyatt's vocabulary, the appearance of "fyer"
here seemed of significance in ascribing the poem to Wyatt. However, Muir later corrected the error, and *D* actually reads: "Ffor all
my servys and my hyer" (*M2*, p. 99). This fact raises suspicion
about Wyatt's authorship of the poem, as does the occurrence of
the adverb "gentily" as a trisyllable in rhyme position, which occurs nowhere else in Wyatt's known work: "But take yt to yow

jentylly" (*M3*, p. 193). Similar perversity of a singsong kind may be the solution to this line: "At your commawndement humbly." Should we read "humbly" as the trisyllable "humbily"? If so, we must exclude this poem from the canon.

The seventh unassigned entry is also not likely to be by Wyatt. *In faythe methynkes yt ys no Ryght*, f. 21v, consists of two rhyme royal stanzas, which probably were once followed by a third. The parallel poem on f. 22r is also in rhyme royal, and it reads so much like a companion poem that I suspect the "A. J." named on f. 22r to be its author. Like Wyatt, that author expressed an independent view of women:

> And sure I thynke yt ys best way
> to love for love alyke agayn
> & not to make ernest off play
> as I to love & she to ffayn
> ffor syns fansy so muche dothe rayn
> the suryst way nedes take I must.

In this stanza's first line, the "And" strikes the ear as a continuation, making it either a companion poem or actually part of another. The poem concludes:

> By trustyng I was dysceavyd
> ffor when I thought my self most sure
> another had me Begylyd
> & shortly made her to hys lure
> but now that she ys past Recure
> & thus fro me hathe tane her flyght
> Best let her go & take hytt lyght.
>
> Should I take thowght when she ys glad
> Or shuld I wake when she dothe slepe
> yet may I say that ons I had
> & nother sobbe nor syght nor wepe
> nor for her love on knee to crepe
> ffor surely thys ryght well I wott
> happyest ys he that hathe her nott.
>
> ffynys qd A.J.s.

This poem skillfully uses the falcon imagery, but except for the last line, it is more diffuse than Wyatt usually is. Because *In faythe methynkes* has the same independent attitude toward women and the same rhythmic movement, it must be excluded from Wyatt's poems as probably the work of "A. J." Muir suggested this same conclusion when, in discussing the inscription on f. 69r of *D*, he remarked that the "an" of the inscription cannot be the "A. J." of the earlier section. He added: "A.J.'s poem is written in reply to Wyatt's poem 'In faythe methynkes yt ys no Ryght' (No. 119), unless indeed we ignore the gap in the MS and assume that A.J. wrote the 'Wyatt' stanzas too."[25] One should not "ignore the gap," however, since it indicates the existence of a parallel third stanza in the first of the two poems.

With seven of the ten entries rejected, there would have to be an unusually strong argument that any of the other three poems is in Wyatt's style before accepting it as his work, which appears not to be the case. *Alas poore man* (*M3* CLXXXV) has some wit, but so does the poem by "A. J." *My pen take payn* (*M3* CLXXIX) was thought by Nott to be a parody of Wyatt's *My lute awake*. If so, there is all the more reason to expect that the writer of hand B should have known it and assigned it to Wyatt, as he did Wyatt's other poems. If it is a parody of Wyatt's poem, it need not, of course, have been written by Wyatt himself.

The remaining entry is really two poems copied together. Hand B entered 48 lines in a double column on f. 21r. Either the writer of hand B or someone else later recognized that two poems had been run together and that only lines 1-30 belong to the "patience" theme of the opening line *Pacyence of all my smart*. The speaker of the "patience" poem is resigned, while that of lines 31-48 is resentful and determined to learn from his error. Nott recognized this fact and did not include lines 31-48 in his edition. Muir, who first followed Foxwell in printing all 48 lines as one poem by Wyatt, later printed lines 31-48 as a separate poem (*M3* CXCI).

Two poems by Wyatt having the "patience" theme occur in *E*, and they have the same metrical form as *Pacyence of all my smart*, ababcc in iambic trimeter. Identity of meter, however, is not in itself proof of authorship. If it were, all rhyme royal poems and all sonnets written in the early Tudor period could be claimed for Wyatt. Two additional facts about "patience" poems outweigh the matter of metrical identity. The first is that one of Wyatt's "patience" poems in *E* does in fact occur in this same group copied by hand B. *Pacyence tho I have not*, on *D*, f. 13v, is significantly subscribed "fynys qd Wyatt." Again one wonders why hand B should specifically include one "patience" poem by Wyatt, while adding another of his leaving it unassigned. It is more likely that the unassigned poem is someone else's imitation of Wyatt. The second fact is that one more stanza in the same form and on the same

"patience" theme occurs later in *D*, on f. 82v, and there is no basis
for assuming all the poems in that later section to be Wyatt's without specific support from another authority. Thus, every poem on
the "patience" theme cannot be assumed to be Wyatt's. In fact,
only the two in *E* are his.

The second part of the *Pacyence of all my smart* entry was at
first sight—and perhaps permanently—indistinguishable as a separate poem to the writer of hand B. It reads like a companion poem
or second part, in which the speaker resolves to break out of the
obsequious servant state of mind. Both halves are likely to have
been by the same writer. Unless *Pacyence of all my smart* can be
confidently placed in the canon, there is no reason for including
its companion.

In sum, eleven poems in ten entries unassigned by hand B in *D*
are not safe poems for the Wyatt canon. One of them may be by
Thomas Clere and is addressed to Mary Shelton. The others probably concerned members of the Howard family, including Lord
Thomas Howard and his secret bride, Lady Margaret Douglas. At
the same time, hand B provides the texts of four Wyatt poems
available from no other source.

Section 3

Hand E, an ornate hand at the top of f. 22v, marks a new section in *D*, continuing through f. 25r, with f. 25v blank. Hand E
copied only three poems in *D*. It began with a four-line fragment
of *The knot which fyrst my hart dyd strayn* at the top of f. 22v,
beneath which it added "fynys quod Jhon." The complete poem
was recopied on f. 23rv, beneath which occurs only "ffynys." A
third copy of the poem occurs later in *D*, on f. 33rv, beneath
which is neither a "finis" nor any ascription. This combination of
occurrences leaves the poem definitely in the doubtful class.

Even if one assumes that Wyatt was continuing the opening of
another poet, a John Heywood, for example, it is clear that at least
two different copyists in *D* could not definitely ascribe it to anyone other than the original "Jhon." As a "songe" (line 36) it is not
distinguishable from many others. It must certainly be put into the
doubtful category.

Hand E also made a copy of *A Robyn* on f. 24rv, with the
slightly variant beginning "He Robyn Joly Robyn tell me." Beneath the last line on f. 24v is "ffynys qd 5813." These numerals
were probably a cipher for "Wiat," although I cannot confirm this
from diplomatic correspondence in the Harleian MS 282 and else-

where. In any case, I am quite sure that Southall was wrong in reading "5813" as the word "Saiz."[26] It is impossible to tell whether hand E knew the significance of the cipher or not.

The only other work of hand E is a thirteen-line fragment of *It was my choyse yt was no chaunce* on ff. 24v-25r, breaking off without an ascription or sign of any kind. It is generally true that hand E can offer no positive evidence of Wyatt's authorship without confirmation from another source.

Section 4

From ff. 30v to 39v is a remarkably fine continuity of handwriting, the work of hand F:

f. 30v *It was my Choyse yt was no chaunce* [also on ff. 24v, 25r *M3* CXCII]

A blank unnumbered folio follows in the manuscript. Then:

f. 31r *Suche Vayn thowght as wonted to myslede me*   T W [In *E* f. 38r]

f. 31v [blank]

f. 32r *So Vnwarely Was never no man Cawght*   W [*M3* CXCIII]

f. 33v [blank]

f. 33rv *The knott whych ffyrst my hart dyd strayn* [*M3* CLXXII]   [The single line 35 of this copy was omitted by hand F. It was supplied thus: "yowr gret dysdayn ᵹ."]

f. 34r [blank]

f. 34v *Yff fansy wuld favor* [In *E* f. 30rv]

f. 35r [blank]

f. 35v *The Wandryng gadlyng in the Somer tyde*   W [In *E* f. 32r]

f. 36r [blank]

f. 36v *The lyvely sperkes that yssue frome those Iies* [In *E* f. 32v]

f. 37r [blank]

f. 37v *Tho I Can not yowr Crueltie constrayne* ᵹ [In *E* f. 38v]

f. 38r [blank]

f. 38v *Somtyme I fled the fyre that me brent*   T Wiat [In *E* f. 40r]

f. 39r [blank]

f. 39v *What Deth ys worse then thys* [In *E* f. 42r]

Thus, hand F copied into *D* a total of ten poems, seven of which are confirmed by their occurrence in *E*. Of those seven in *E*, hand F specifically ascribed three to "TW" or "W" or "T Wiat." *So Vnwarely* may be confidently ascribed to Wyatt on the basis of his "W." Additional poems entered by hand F probably existed between the first two extant poems, where a blank folio indicates loss of material.

Two poems are neither confirmed by *E* nor ascribed to anyone by hand F: *It was my Choyse* and *The knott whych ffyrst*. Since four of the poems confirmed by *E* do not have any ascription, one might assume that hand F was recording a Wyatt group without comment. However, there is too much against that argument. To safely assume a Wyatt group, there should be a series, introduced by a poem either definitely ascribed or confirmed by other evidence. Yet the first poem in this series is neither ascribed nor confirmed by *E*. Also, if hand F were recording a solid Wyatt group, he would hardly take the trouble to ascribe some of them or to scatter four ascriptions among ten poems.

Moreover, the poem *The knott whych ffyrst* occurs three times in *D*. Hand E copied a fragment of it on f. 22v, beneath which was written "fynys quod Jhon." Then hand E copied the full poem on f. 23rv, beneath which he wrote only "ffynys." A collation of the version by hand F on f. 33rv with that by hand E on f. 23rv suggests that hand F was following either that of hand E or a common source. There are no significant variants to negate this conclusion, and one to confirm it. The only verbal variant is in line 30, where hand E has: "of burning syghes and fervent love;" while hand F wrote: "with burnynge syghes & fervent love." At the same time, hand F followed hand E or their source in a peculiar division of the word "always" in line 4, both hands writing it "All was." Also, hand E made a correction in line 41, repeated by hand F. Thus, hand E wrote: "Sens well ye know this paynfull syghte [deleted] fytt." And hand F copied: "Syns well ye knowe this paynfull fytt." Thus, the source of hand F's copy of *The knott whych ffyrst* is either its earlier occurrence in *D* or their common source. Hand F did not ascribe it to anyone in particular because he had no better authority than had hand E. Because of the incomplete ascription of the poem's opening lines to "Jhon," this poem must be placed in the doubtful class.

The remaining poem neither ascribed to anyone by hand F nor confirmed by *E* is *It was my Choyse* on f. 30v. The position of this poem in *D* further clarifies the relations of hands E and F. Like *The knott whych ffyrst*, *It was my Choyse* was copied earlier by hand E, and significantly, it was the last poem entered by hand E on ff. 24v and 25r, while it was the first poem entered by hand F on f. 30v.

The reason for the repetition in this case was simply that hand E completed only lines 1-13 of the poem before breaking off without ascription. Hand F recorded the complete poem. A collation shows no important variants in the thirteen lines except for line 8, which is straightened out in the second version. Thus, on f. 25r hand E wrote: "Accepted yt Ide Wys Refuse [?]" later attempting to correct the line by writing "with" over "Ide" and adding an "o" before "Wys." Hand F records the correct line: "Acceptyd be with owte Refuse." Since hand F added twenty-two lines not entered by hand E, there must have been a source other than the uncompleted copy now in D. This fact suggests that both poems common to the two hands came from a common source. Hand F was conscious of the work of hand E, picking up where hand E had left off and adding additional poems.

The poems copied by hand F in D and also occurring in E are from a particular cluster that took a similar position in E. This can be shown by listing the folios in E on which the same poems occur. Their order in E is: ff. 38r, 30rv, 32r, 32v, 38v, 40r, and 42r. Thus, one of the pairs in D occurs on the same folio, recto and verso, in E, and another folio of E (f. 38) has two more of the poems in D, but this time occurring separately in the sequence of D.

Although it might seem that the copies were made directly from E into D, this was not the case. There are too many significant variants in the whole group. *Suche vayn thought* has a correction by Wyatt himself that does not occur in D. *If fansy would favor* loses a whole stanza in D. *The wandering gadlyng*, however, has no significant variants in D; nor does *The lyvely sperkes*, both on E f. 32. There are a number of spelling variants in these two poems. *Tho I cannot* omits from D an important revision of the last line made by Wyatt in E. The same is true of the poem *Some tyme I fled*, where the second line revised by Wyatt does not appear with the revision in D. *What Deth is worse* has an important correction in line 3 of the E version not made in D. Altogether there is no positive evidence that the D copies were made directly from E and a great deal of negative evidence. What probably happened was that some of the same copies used to make up this section of E (ff. 30-42) also provided copy for those that made up ff. 30-39 of D.

The general relations of hands E and F can therefore be summarized. Hand F picked up the work of E where it was left incomplete. In the case of two poems they probably had the same copy. What is not known is whether the copy of those two poems was from the same source as that for the other eight poems, which was very good copy, close to that of E. It is unliely, however, that all

of the copy was distinctly marked as Wyatt's work, since hand F
scattered only four ascriptions to Wyatt among ten poems, or
among eight if the copy for the eight also in *E* was of distinct origin. The other significant fact is that as hand F was undoubtedly
conscious of hand E's work, he probably let hand E's ascription of
The knot whych fyrst to "Jhon" stand uncorrected because
he had no better knowledge than hand E. The poem must
remain suspect.

There is no clear evidence against *It was my choyse*, however,
and it is probable that when eight out of ten poems are surely or
very likely Wyatt's, there may be a ninth. In this case, too, the
style of the poem is compelling. In view of the skill with which the
stanzas of the poem are interlinked, it is more reasonable to include *It was my choyse* than to exclude it.

Between ff. 40r and 47v appears the section of *D* produced by
the love affair of Lord Thomas Howard and Lady Margaret Douglas. Only one of the poems in this section has ever been included
in the Wyatt canon. That poem is *How shold I*, on f. 43r, after
which the copyist added only "ffynes." This poem has been included in the Wyatt canon mainly because it occurs later in *D*, on
f. 77rv.

At this point in the editing of *D*, Muir made a surprising change
between his second and third editions. *Thy promese was to loue
me best*, from f. 40r, appeared among the doubtful poems of *M2*,
but Muir noted in *M3* (p. 419): "This was printed as a doubtful
poem in M. But it is at least as likely to be W's as many of the D
poems printed as his by Nott and F." Although this statement is
true in general, because the "many" could apply to many different
poems from many different sources, the unfortunate implication
for *D* is that no section is any better than any other, despite the
available knowledge. A comparison of ff. 39v and 40r clearly
shows that on f. 40r a childlike scrawl has replaced the ornate
book hand of the previous section. The contents entered by these
two hands show distinct differences, including the fact that one
hand entered seven poems confirmed by *E* (hand F), while the
childlike hand entered none confirmed by *E*. It is more reasonable,
then, to look for Wyatt poems among the other texts entered by
hand F and to keep the texts of the childlike hand (a woman's?)
among the doubtful poems.

The next poem in *M3*, CXCV must also be covered by the same
note, since it follows on f. 40v and was No. 215 in *M2* among the
Doubtful Poems.

Section 5

After the entry signed "T. H." at the top of f. 47v, another hand, hand G, has copied eighteen lines of the poem *Hartte aprest with dessperott thoughtes*, which occupies the rest of f. 47v and the top of 48r. This poem was rightly placed in the doubtful category in *M2*. It also occurs in *A* on f. 217r. It is possible that a Wyatt section occurs on f. 216v of *A*, but there is no reason to think that f. 217 is a continuation of it. This poem must therefore remain in the doubtful class.

Section 6

After f. 48v, which is blank, there is a continuity of scribal handwriting in *D* (hand H) extending from ff. 49r through 54v. The first lines of these entries and their subscriptions follow:

ff. 49r-50v *So feble is the therd that dothe the burden staye* ffins [In *E* ff. 67r-68v]

f. 51r *ffull well yt maye be sene finis* [*M3* CXCVII]

ff. 51v-52r *Synes loue ys suche that as ye wott ffinis* [*M3* CXCVIII]

f. 52v *Lo how I seke & sew to haue ffinis* [*M3* CXCIX]

f. 53r *My loue ys lyke vnto theternall fyre ffinis* [*M3* CC]
    Synes so ye please to here me playn ffinis [*M3* CCI]

f. 53v *Yf in the worlde there be more woo ffinis* [In *E* ff. 62v-63r]

f. 54r *Now must I lerne to lyue at rest ffinis* [*M3* CCII]

f. 54v *fforget not yet the tryde entent* [*M3* CCIII]

There is only one inconsistency of entry in this group of poems: the last one lacks the "ffinis" of the others. It may be that the copy is not complete, although the variation in the refrain of the last line recorded would suggest a complete poem.

Only two of this group are confirmed by copies in *E*, the first and the seventh. The *D* copies of these poems differ in accuracy. The first poem, *So feble is the therd*, despite the inversion of the letters in the word "thred," is a copy of the poem as corrected by Wyatt in *E*. That such copies were available is shown by the appearance of the poem in its corrected form in *A* ff. 97v-98v, where it is also marked "ffinis," and in *T*. The *E* text is in Wyatt's own hand, with many corrections and signed "TV." The other poem, *Yf in the worlde*, shows several variants that indicate a different line of descent for the copy in *D*.

All the other seven of the nine poems are unique to *D*. There is little on which to base their authorship except style. If, however, one or more of them was included within the canon, there would be little point in excluding the others, since the copyist was almost entirely consistent in habit, and the whole group starts off with a known Wyatt poem. If the last one were also confirmed by *E*, there could be little basis for arguing that this is not a Wyatt group. The last poem, however, even lacks the "ffinis" that the others have. Making fine distinctions among the seven is nevertheless risky. They are of consistently high quality, and to include any one of them simply assumes the probability of a Wyatt group of poems, all left unassigned by the copyist, who began the series with a known Wyatt poem. One should therefore either exclude all seven or take them into the canon. Considering the consistency of style and the consistency of the scribe's habit of entry, I believe that they must be included in the canon as probably by Wyatt.

Section 7

Between ff. 55r and 68v in *D* is a chaos of entries in a medley of hands. The sequence begins with a copy of Surrey's *O happy dames* on f. 55r, probably by Mary Shelton's hand. No grouping of any kind is notable.

Eight poems or fragments in this section have a bearing on the Wyatt canon. As they are all in the same hand, hand H, they have been assumed to be a group. However, since they are interrupted consistently, there is no basis for this assumption. Following are the folios on which they occur, together with other entries in other hands:

f. 58v *O myserable sorow withowten cure finis* [*M3* CCIV]
f. 59v *Wyly no dought ye be a wry* E knyvet *finis*
    To dere is bowght the doblenes finis [In *A* f. 18v ascribed to "E Knevet"]
f. 60v *Myn vnhappy Chaunce to whome shall I playn*[27]
f. 61v *Go burnynge siths vnto the frosen hert finis* [In *E* f. 16v]
f. 62v *In places wher that I company* [fragment of 5 lines]
    I speke by that And mene by this [one line]
f. 63v *If that I cowld in versis close* E K

These scattered entries include two signed by or assigned to Edmund Knyvet. A third is known to be Knyvet's from the ascription in *A*. Among these entries is one of Wyatt's poems also in *E*, but a single such entry coming fifth in a divided series constitutes no basis for assuming a scribal intention of grouping. The only ground for including the first of the series within the Wyatt canon would be the poem's style. Since it is in fact a wretched piece, there is no reason to include it.

The only other poem between ff. 55r and 68v that has entred the Wyatt canon occurs on f. 64rv in hand H. It is *Blame not my lute*, which may be taken as a variation on Wyatt's poem *My lute awake*. There is, however, some evidence of authorship in *D* on 64r. Someone, probably not the copyist of the poem, wrote "W" in the margin of f. 64r after line 21 of the poem. It is unlikely that the copyist should do so in that position, since he had another side of the leaf to fill. There is no "finis" or ascription beneath the last line of the poem. However, in view of the style of the poem and the authority of the "W," it must be included in the Wyatt canon.

Section 8

The largest continuous section almost entirely in one hand and style of entry in *D* runs from ff. 69r to 85r. It is separated from the preceding material by a blank unnumbered leaf and from what follows by a change of handwriting. This section is the work of hand I, the most economical of copyists in *D*, frequently using double column entries and filling in the second column in very small writing. Hand I sometimes finished an entry with the double sign "fs͛, but more frequently simply with "fs."[28] From f. 73v, the "͛" disappears entirely. The handwriting remains consistent, however, up to f. 81v, after which all the entries are in a single column and larger letters, but still in hand I. Then on f. 82v is a break of continuity, where *Patience for I haue Wrong* is in an italic hand and concludes not with "fs" but with "finis," also in italic. The first line of *Wyll ye se What Wonderous love hathe Wrought* on f. 84r, although in extra large letters, is probably also by hand I. It is not possible to say whether the single poem in italic is by hand I or was later inserted by another hand. However, the italic poem occurs in the section after f. 75r, which is a markedly different group of poems.

Since none of the poems in this section of *D* is assigned to anyone, they must be examined for internal grouping. Such an examination reveals two distinct halves. The first thirty-seven items copied by hand I begin and end with poems also occurring in *E*; *To cause accorde or to agree*, *D* F. 75v and *E* f. 53r; and *Eche man telles me I change most my devise*, *D* f. 75v and *E* f. 11v. This group of thirty-seven poems includes no less than twenty-nine poems also occurring in *E*. Scattered among them are eight poems,

seven of which are unique to *D.* The eighth odd poem also occurs
in *B.* At no point do any two of the unconfirmed poems occur
in sequence. All eight are preceded and followed by a poem also occurring in *E.* Therefore, all thirty-seven may be safely accepted as a
Wyatt group, since there are no objections on grounds of style.

What follows these thirty-seven poems is totally antithetical in
character. With *Payne of all payne the most grevous paine* on ff.
75v-76r begins a sharp discontinuity. This poem was not included
in the canon by Nott, who recognized its archaic nature. When
Foxwell brought it into the canon, she nevertheless remarked:
"The poem is signed in the usual fashion with Wiat's monogram
signature, but I strongly suspect that it has been erroneously included as Wiat's." Muir agreed that Foxwell was wrong in reading
the "fs" of hand I as Wyatt's monogram signature, which is decidedly different. There is no logical reason, therefore, for continuing to include *Payne of all payne* in the canon.

This fact indicates a break in the continuity of entries. From
Payne of all payne on f. 75v to *I am as I am* on f. 85r are twenty-
nine entries. Among this group is only one poem also occurring in
E, I finde no peace, D f. 82rv and *E* f. 20v. Twenty of this group
are unique to *D,* and an additional six poems also occur in *B.* One
more poem, *Mye love toke skorne,* receives support from *T* as a
Wyatt poem, if it is assumed that Tottel had better authority than
this group in *D. Mye love toke skorne* is a sonnet, and Tottel's editor may have selected it out of this group because of his interest in
sonnets. Two additional sonnets appear in this group, which are
decidedly inferior, *Dyvers doth Vse* on f. 77v and *I abide and
abide* on f. 81v, the last being so loose in form and rhythm that
only its fourteen-line total suggests that it might be a sonnet.

So far the totals alone show that this is not a group of Wyatt
poems, contrasted with what precedes it, twenty-nine poems with
only one confirmed by *E* and another by *T.* Further negative evidence comes from a copy on f. 77rv of *howe shulde I,* which also
occurs earlier in *D* on f. 43r, where it is marked merely "ffynes."
Since that section of *D* is devoted mainly to the love poems which
passed between Lord Thomas Howard and Lady Margaret Douglas,
neither section supports the other as a Wyatt section of *D.* Rather,
the combination throws suspicion on the poem. Further, the poem
now all of chaunge on f. 81rv of *D* also occurs in *A* on f. 17v in a
section considered by Hughey to contain miscellaneous authors.
Patience for I haue Wrong may also be a later insertion. Finally,
several others of this group were excluded by Nott as of suspicious

nature: *The losse is small* (f. 77v), *Grudge on who liste* (f. 78v), *ffortune doth frowne* (f. 78v), *Greting to you both* (f. 79rv), *lengre to muse* (f. 80r), *wyth seruing still* (f. 81r), and *whan that I call vnto my mynde* (ff. 82v-83r). Muir was therefore speaking only for himself and Foxwell when he noted concerning the odd quatrain *Ffortune doth frowne* (*M2*, p. 138): "This quatrain is copied in the same hand as the surrounding poems, which are all assumed to be Wyatt's." Since Foxwell's assumptions were denied by Muir himself, he in fact included them primarily on the continuity of handwriting. The pattern of grouping, however, that goes with the handwriting must exclude them entirely, unless some other authority can show that an occasional Wyatt poem has crept into the group by chance. *M2* 141-167 must therefore join the other doubtful poems of *D*. In *M3* these are numbered: CCXIII-CCXXXIII and CXIII, CXXVI, CXLVIII, CLXXIV, CXXVIII, CXL.

One additonal and clinching fact concerns the concluding poem in this group, *I am as I am* on f. 85r, which has been admired for its stoical directness, an occasional characteristic of Wyatt's poetry. This stylistic connection is suspect, however, for the admired opening phrase is traditional. In fact, a shorter version of this same poem occurs as a fifteenth century carol.[29] The *D* version is an expansion of the carol, which could be by anyone. Moreover, the first poem in this questionable group, on f. 75v, is another carol, *Payne of all payne*. The defining limits of this group as well as its internal makeup compel the conclusion that it is not a group of Wyatt poems. Only individual poems within it may be attributed to Wyatt on other authority.

Section 9

Only two Wyatt entries remain in the rest of *D*. Another hand, more ornate than hand I, made a copies of Wyatt's *My nowne John poyntz* on ff. 85v-87r, concluding it "fs," and of the first thirteen lines of Wyatt's *My mothers maides* on f. 87v, breaking it off after the first word "And" of the fourteenth line. These two entries cannot support all of the preceding twenty-nine entries as a Wyatt group.

The Blage Manuscript

History

The manuscript once in the possession of Sir George Blage (1512-1551), an intimate of Wyatt, and now in the library of Trinity College, Dublin, was recently edited by Kenneth Muir as a major addition to the Wyatt canon.[1] However, the authority of *B* as a Wyatt manuscript is undermined by the facts about *D*. Previously a number of poems in *B* were assumed to be Wyatt's because of their presence in *D*. However, as their position in *D* now places them in the doubtful category, they can no longer be used to bolster the authority of *B*. Like the other manuscripts, *B* must stand on its own history and physical make-up, as well as on its relation to the more authoritative documents, *E*, *A*, and *T*. In the end, the value of *B* is slight. Curiously, Muir himself suggested this fact by titling his edition *Sir Thomas Wyatt and His Circle: Unpublished Poems*, and within his text the lines of probable authorship remain for the most part vague.

B is contained in MS. D. 2. 7 in the library of Trinity College, Dublin. However, only ff. 57-186 of this manuscript constitute *B*. The whole of MS. D. 2. 7 is made up of "three volumes bound in black cloth in a black slip case. This latest rebinding dates from 1920."[2] *B* is contained in volumes two and three of the set. Until 1742 the two *B* volumes were a separate manuscript, a condition to which they have now been restored.

Following f. 162 in *B* is a blank unnumbered leaf, with a note on the verso that the binder "has displaced the pages: the third folio should come first." This probably means that f. 59, which contains a "tabula" listing poems under the letter "A," should come before f. 58, which is now the first leaf after the flyleaf (numbered 57). The note does not indicate, however, where the present f. 58 should come, unless it was originally left blank between the present f. 59r, with its "A" listings, and f. 60r, with listings for the letter "D." The fact of displacement is not vital to an analysis of *B*, however, since *B* is unique among Tudor poetry manuscripts in being organized primarily under alphabetical headings. It is still in an alphabetical arrangement, no doubt almost exactly as originally arranged. The surviving portions of the original catalogue for letters "A" and "D" indicate that the arrangement was not followed strictly for letters after the first letter of the first line, but simply that all poems beginning with an "A" were included in any order in a section headed "A." Another unusual binding feature is that, to preserve f. 178, which could not be bound in, the binder mounted it by its left edge to the verso of f. 177. However, the water mark of an open hand, all five fingers visible, shows that f. 178 is on the same paper as the rest of *B*. The handwriting of f. 178 is also consistent with a major portion of *B*.

The flyleaves and evidence of dating *B* show that, although volumes two and three of MS. D. 2. 7 may be called the "Blage manuscript," there is reason to doubt that Sir George Blage was the original compiler and owner of the manuscript. The dated inscription of f. 61r, which Muir misread as "in the xxviith yere of . . ." actually reads ten years later, thus: "that [ ] I george blagge gentleman hatthe payd vnto johne deyne [   ] off Rochestere the xxvith day of nouember in the xxxviith yere of [   ] for mysterys whytte sumtyme one of the abbey & monastery of dart [ford?] ."[3] Since the date of this inscription is undoubtedly calculated by the regnal year of Henry VIII, it follows that Blage entered it between 22 April 1545 and 21 April 1546, three years after Wyatt died, rather than the year 22 April 1535 and 21 April 1536, before Wyatt had gone to Spain, as implied by Muir.

Perhaps Muir's calculation was what led him to suggest that "loose sheets of different dates (c.1532-1551) were arranged in alphabetical order."[4] Although it is possible that some of the copies in *B* were made about 1532, there is no evidence that they were made under the direction of Blage. Further, it is unlikely that Blage should have made a financial note on a loose sheet somewhere, since it might have gotten lost. Finally, Blage's inscription on f. 61r is in a legal hand, which appears in only one other place in *B*, at the bottom of the flyleaf, now f. 57r, where Blage wrote in the same hand: "In the name of god amen." Thus, one must conclude that *B* was a bound volume in the year 1545-1546, when Sir George Blage made a financial note in it and a pious dedication of the volume on the flyleaf. Since Blage's legal hand was not suitable for poetry and sententiae, another way of following his work in *B* is through the signed copies of verses in his italic hand. For example, the center of the flyleaf is occupied by the inscription: "G / Ameriti sermio." These words are in Blage's italic hand.

The top of the flyleaf was pre-empted, however, by the hand of the copyist, who made most of the entries for letters "A" to "I." This can be seen by comparing the first "I" entry on f. 105r with the fragmentary note at the top left of the flyleaf: "In ye yer of [   ]." For the peculiar down-turned "r" of the word "yer," see the word "wer" on f. 109r. Although the date of this inscription is lost, it was definitely earlier than 1545, because the alphabetical organization of the manuscript clearly preceded the additions made in the italic hand of Blage.

There is sufficient evidence that the alphabetical arrangement was original and primary to the organization of *B* as a whole. This can be demonstrated by reference to the distinct handwritings in *B*. The designations used for these handwritings, however, do not necessarily mean that they belonged to different people, since one person can write differently at different times with a change of habit. The designations refer simply to a set of distinct habits of letter formation and manner of entry on the leaf. Since *B* was planned to receive the entry of a poem at the top of each recto under a letter heading, only those handwritings are noted that occupy the primary position in relation to the letter heading on each recto of a leaf. No verso of a leaf has a letter heading, as versos were used simply to complete a poem started on the recto. All other materials in verso position are later additions.

There are three primary organizing handwritings in *B*. Hand A is a small, precise Tudor secretary hand, which took first possession of the following folios:

f. 57r (flyleaf)
f. 59r ("tabula A")
f. 60r ("tabula D")
ff. 63r-71r (nine poems under letter "A")
ff. 72r-74r (letter "A" only)
f. 75r (one poem under letter "A")
ff. 76r-77r (two poems under letter "B")
ff. 78r-79r (letter "B" only)
ff. 80r-81r (two poems under letter "C")
f. 82r (letter "C" only)
ff. 83r-89r (seven poems under letter "D")
ff. 90r-92r (letter "D" only)
ff. 93r-95r (letter "E" only)
(Letters "F" and "G" are no longer extant.)
ff. 96r-100r (five poems under letter "H")
ff. 101r-104r (letter "H" only)
ff. 105r-108r (four poems under letter "I")
f. 109r (letter "I" and four lines of a poem)
ff. 110r-111r (letter "I" only)
f. 121r (two poems under letter "L," with letter "L" itself
     by hand C).

Many opportunities were left between ff. 59r and 111r for other copyists to continue under the organization set up by hand A, which is what occurred. One significant recurrence of hand A takes place after another copyist had filled in under hand A's organizing work to f. 121r. In order to show the linking hand A with hand B, the listings under letter "A" of the "tabula" on f. 59r follow:

alone musyng	fo j
absence alas	flo
absence abcentyng	flo
alas fortune	flo
A my Harte	flo
alas Dere Harte	flo
at last w^t drawe yor Crueltie	flo
at moste myschyffe	flo v
Alas Dere Harte	flo ix
Alas all Sorofull	flo x
Away all care and payne	flo xj
Alack alack what shall I doo	flo xij
Alas that same Swete face	flo xiij
Alas my Dere	flo xiiij
all ye that know	flo xv
accusid though I be	flo xvj
Agaynst the Rooke	flo xvi
A. face that shuld	flo [
A.s from theys hyll*es*	fl [

The left brackets indicate where the edge of the leaf is torn away. None of the folio numbers listed is extant elsewhere in *B*. Note the peculiarity of the last two entries, where the letter "A" is separated from what follows it by a period. The separation indicates that hand B filled in two entries in the "tabula" after hand A had begun the line with an "A," forgetting that since something would later follow it, there should be no period. Beneath these last two entries started by hand A and completed by hand B are eight additional letters "A" down the leaf. In this series the first two and the fifth and sixth letters are also followed by an unnecessary period. Thus, it appears that hand B started where hand A had left off, although in continuing the "tabula," it did not carry on the work of hand A very far.

In addition to the link between hands A and B in the "tabula," a third hand, C, filled in some folios prepared by hand A with his letter at the top. The continuations of both hands B and C constitute the entire remaining organization of the manuscript. The designations of hands B and C follow:

f. 59r (hand B: the last two entries under letter "A" after the letter itself entered by hand A)

ff. 72r-73r (hand B: two poems under the letter "A," the letter itself entered by hand A)

f. 74r (hand C: one poem, the first appearance of hand C)

f. 82r (hand B: one poem under letter "C," the letter itself entered by hand A)

ff. 90r-91r (hand B: two poems under letter "D," the letter itself entered by hand A)

ff. 110r-111r (hand C: two poems under letter "I," the letter itself entered by hand A)

ff. 112r-114r (hand C: three poems under letter "I")

(Letter "J" is comprised in "I"; letter "K" is not extant)

ff. 117r-119v (hand B: four poems under letter "L")

f. 120r (hand C: one poem under letter "L")

ff. 125r-130v (hand C: eight poems under letter "M")

f. 136r (hand B: one poem under letter "O")

ff. 137-140r (hand C: four poems under letter "O")

ff. 145r-147r (hand B: three poems under letter "P")

ff. 154r-161r (hand C: eight poems under letter "S")

ff. 167rf171r (hand C: five poems under letter "T")

ff. 172r-174r (hand B: three poems under letter "T")

ff. 178r-179r (hand C: two poems by Surrey under no letter headings. Folio 178 was the one mounted onto f. 177v by its left edge.)

ff. 181r-183r (hand C: three poems under letter "W")

ff. 184r-185r (hand B: two poems under letter "W")

f. 186r has prose in a later hand

Not only does the work of the three copyists, hands A-C, in essence both fill and organize the whole of *B*, but none of these hands is that of Blage, who wrote in two different hands, one legal and one italic.

Although most of the leaves in *B* have now been accounted for, some gaps remain. These gaps are significant, for they help to prove that the original organization of *B* was alphabetical and that this arrangement did not meet all the requirements of later writers in *B*, including Blage. Thus, ff. 93r-95r were each headed with the letter "E" by hand A. At present, f. 93r remains blank except for the letter "E"; f. 94r has a poem in a hand later than A's, beginning with the word "O." Folio 95r has verses written right over the letter "E," beginning with the word "what." Since the verses on f.

95r fill about half the leaf, it is not likely that anyone imposed the letter "E" on top of the verses already on the leaf for possible future verses to suit that letter, for there would have been no room for such future verses. Thus, the section "E" was reserved for future entries that never appeared. The space remained unused or misused. Folios 101r-104r were reserved by hand A with the letter "H" at the top of the leaves. Later Blage, in need of space, copied his long poem *A voyce I haue*, which was out of order, on ff. 101r-103r, signing it "G. B." on 103r. Blage further violated the system on f. 104r, where the letter "H" appears by hand A above his copy of *your lokes so often cast*. There would have been no sense in adding the "H" after the pages had been filled with verses not relevant to the letter. Further, ff. 131r-135r were reserved with the letter "N" placed near the top of each leaf. Each of these folios has later verse or prose not appropriate to the letter "N" and, in the case of ff. 133r-135r, written right over the letter. The large italic "N" was probably entered by hand B, since it closely resembles the "N" in *Noli* written by hand B in the phrase *Noli me tangere* on f. 185r. Which copyist entered it, however, is not a crucial point. The letter system clearly preceded the material on the folios, which must have been left blank because suitable verses were not yet available. Similarly, ff. 141r-144r (except f. 143r) were each marked with the letter "O." These leaves are covered with later prose. Folio 153r has the letter "R" at the top and is otherwise blank. (The poem noted by Muir, *Only the elect*, is on the verso of this leaf.) Folio 165r has a "T" at the top crossed out and covered with the prose that continues from ff. 164r-166r. Folio 168r was originally headed "W." The writer of hand C, who was a careful worker, needed another leaf for a poem beginning with "Tho," which forced him to blot out the "W" and place a "T" beside it. This fact indicates either a miscalculation by hand C or, more probably, the prior entry of the "W" by hand A. Folio 180r has a neat "T" at the top of the leaf and a poem beginning with the word "When" by one of the later writers in the manuscript.

Altogether, then, one must conclude that *B* was assembled as a systematic alphabetical volume. It makes little difference whether the leaves were simply kept together or actually bound by the copyists, since many of them were pre-empted for the alphabetical system by the imposition of letters. Some of the leaves were left blank at the beginning of the volume for a "tabula," of which only portions of letters "A" and "D" survive. Other leaves later in the volume were left either completely blank or blank beneath the letter. Later unsuitable verse and prose reveals this fact.

The entries of Blage in *B* begin on the flyleaf (f. 57r), in both his legal hand and his italic hand. On the next leaf, now numbered f. 58r, Blage copied a poem, *whan shall the cruell stormes be past*, signing it with the small letters "gb" employed in the financial note on f. 61r. The text of this poem, however, is in his italic hand. In view of the fact that the binder had "displaced" the first and third folios of *B*, one cannot be sure of the original order at this point. However, the copyist of hand A had left two folios blank in close proximity to ff. 59r and 60r, which now contain the two portions of the "tabula." Blage showed no interest in reserving them for the completion of the "tabula." One he used for a financial note, and the other for a poem beginning with the line just quoted. The implication is that Blage did not order the preparation of the volume as it was assembled. He gained possession of it after someone else had arranged and bound it. Further, there is no reason to believe that the date of Blage's possession was much earlier than 1545, the date of the financial note onff. 61r, and three years after Wyatt had died. Although Blage did not consistently violate the alphabetical arrangement, he did so when necessary. It would have made little sense for him to order the volume in such a fashion and then use it in a way calculated to destroy that system.

Two other entries by Blage are *dysdayne not madam on him too louke* (f. 92r) and *A voyce i haue and yk a will to wayle* (ff. 101r-103r). The second poem is signed with the large initials "G. B.", the first example of whcih appears on the middle of the flyleaf (f. 57r). Its content shows that undoubtedly it dates from Blage's religious trouble with Bishop Gardiner in 1546, which adds to the evidence that Blage began to use the volume in the eyar 1545-1546.[5] Blage then entered the poem *your lokes so often cast* (f. 104rv) under the letter "H."

In the "L" section of *B* are two poems correctly placed. The first is *Lyue thowe gladly iff so thowe may*, which is marked beneath the last line "TW" on f. 123r. The other poem is *Let the hethen whyche trust not in the Lord* (f. 124rv), signed "B. G:" on the verso. Muir described this poem as "apparently an elegy on Jane Seymour."[6] It would hardly suit the young Jane, however, to write of her: "Lyke sara he [the Lord] sent me a blessid byrthe" (f. 124rv). The answer to this allusion comes later in *B*, on f. 177r: "A remembrance of the dethe of the vertuis Lady Quiene / Kateryn dowager Lat Wyffe to the Lord thomas seymour / vncle to the kynge hys m^ate :" again signed "B. G:" Thus, both the poem and the "remembrance" concern Catherine Parr rather than Jane Seymour. In 1548, the last year of her life, Dowager Queen Catherine Parr gave birth to a girl at Sudeley Castle, making the allusion to the late-bearing Sarah appropriate. As Muir noted, the lady of the poem is also compared to Hester, Abigail, and Lidia. Similar allusions were used by Nicholas Grimald in no. 144 of *T*, beginning:

To. l. K. S.

To you, madame, I wish, bothe now, and eke from yere to yere,

Stregth ẘ Debore, ẘ Iudith faith, ẘ Maudle zeal, Anns chere

With blessed Mary modest moode: like Sibill, life full long.

Rollins noted (*T*, II, 233) the suggestion that the "K. S." of this poem was Catherine Parr, widow of Henry VIII, later married to the Protector Seymour. It therefore seems almost certain that Blage, like Grimald, was complimenting Catherine Parr. Thus, all of the evidence for the datable activity of Blage in *B* places his use of the manuscript between 1545-1548 or later.

Additional copies by Blage in *B* are *In somer seson as soune as the sonne* (f. 115r) and *It now the tyme is that the dulfull daye* (f. 116r). Both these entries come correctly under "I." Under "P" is *pas fourthe my wountyd cries* (f. 148r). Under "Q" is *Quondam was I in my Ladys gras* (f. 150r). Under "R" is *Ryd of bondage free from kaer seuen years space and mor* (f. 152r), signed "G. B." on the verso. Under "S" Blage entered *Syns Loue is founde wyth parfytnes*, ascribing it with the letter "A" beneath the last line. Under "T" he placed *that tyme that myrthe dyd styr my shyppe* (f. 175rv). The Surrey verses *degrese of Lyghtnes Lefte be hynde* (f. 176v) are also in Blage's hand. These verses are immediately followed by the "remembrance" of Catherine Parr, signed "B. G:"

Description

The work of hand A, which made the incomplete "tabula" and thirty-three separate entries in *B*, including a solid block of initial poems, proves conclusively the original nature of the whole book. Of these thirty-three poems, which occur nowhere else in manuscript or print, Muir reproduced twenty-two in his edition of unpublished poems. They can be placed in the Wyatt canon only on the basis of style or because they constitute a Wyatt group. Muir employed both arguments noting: "in the same hand are seven of Wyatt's known poems. On the evidence of style alone, several of the other poems in this group can confidently be ascribed to Wyatt; and, although some of them are uninspired, their weaknesses of rhythm

and of repetitive vocabulary are characteristic of Wyatt's less successful poems."[7] The grouping of these poems, however, all beginning with letters "A-I," almost entirely eliminates the first basis for
inclusion. Of Muir's seven "known" Wyatt poems among those of
hand A, one is a ghost, *Goo burnyng sighes* (*M2*, 20), for the poem
is nowhere in the manuscript. Of the other "known" poems, my
analysis of *D* has shown that four (*M2* 104, 150, 151, 167) appear
in *D* among groups of the most doubtful character.[8] Three of
these four are positioned in *D* between ff. 75v-85r, where mere
continuity of handwriting has been presumed to be a sign of
Wyatt's authorship. Quite simply, this is a case of taking a double
uncertainty as evidence of certainty.

An additional poem from this group in *D* is printed by Muir as
an unrecognized poem in an expanded version. It is *Dryven by Desire I Dyd this Dede* (*M3* XIV), a poem of seven lines in *D* on f.
81v and of thirty-one lines in *B*. Referring to the *B* stanzas as a
"new" version, however, is a patent error. The *B* "poem," whose
first line of the second stanza is "Sens that my Language without
eloquence," is clearly two poems run together: one being the first
stanza, which occurs in *D* as a separate poem; the other being the
remaining twenty-four lines, which have no known genealogy.[9]
This fact is borne out by the rhyme scheme, for the first stanza is a
seven-line one of rhyme royal (*ababbcc*), and the following three
stanzas, each of eight lines, rhyme *ababbcbc*. Thus, this "new"
combination refers once again to the very questionable section of
D and to unknown sources.

Another example occurs in the "tabula" of *B*, of which Muir
noted that seven poems listed under "A" were lost from the manuscript. Among them is *absence abcentyng*.[10] This poem also occurs
in *D* on ff. 81v-82r in the group of poems identified only by continuity of handwriting. It is unclear whether *B* is supporting *D* or
D supporting *B*, and there is no reason for assuming that section of
D to be a section of Wyatt poems. In all of these instances, therefore, both manuscripts are assailable.

Another poem by hand A is *Durese of paynes & greuus smarte*,
on f. 83r in *B*. This poem is known only from a printed version in
The Court of Venus.[11] Two poems of unknown origin were listed
by Muir as Wyatt's, on f. 121. These are also in hand A, although
isolated from the opening group.

The only positive evidence that these thirty-three entries constitute a Wyatt group comes from two poems and a fragment of a
third. They are *Accusyd thoo I be*, which occurs elsewhere only in

T (74), among Wyatt's poems; *At moste myschyef*, which also occurs in both *E* (f. 34r) and *D* (f. 12r); and *If chaunce assygnyd*, a
four-line fragment in *B*, occurring complete in *E* (f. 44v) and *D*
(f. 70v). The four-line fragment yields no variants among all three
manuscripts. The variants for the complete poem show that in a
few instances *B* departs, through miscopying, from both *D* and *E*;
in one other instance *B* agrees with *D* but not with *E* (l. 37).

The conclusion is inescapable that the thirty-three entries of
hand A in *B* were not intended as a Wyatt group. Three certain
poems out of thirty-three in fact prove the opposite, that the copyist was arranging poems by various authors under alphabetical
headings. One is therefore forced to examine these poems entirely
on the basis of style and of external evidence through allusion.

The main difficulty in Muir's argument for adding the twenty-
two poems to the Wyatt canon on the basis of style is that a cliché
is taken as evidence of identity.[12] Listed as evidence of authorship
are "chaunge," "disdayne," "payne," "remedy," which were
among Wyatt's favorite words. But such favorites were too common to be a signature of authorship. The other evidence, similar
stanza forms or the linking of stanzas, is equally weak. In fact, the
parallels cited were so common as to be useless for Muir's argument. He also argued that Wyatt was the only one interested in
translating sonnets from the Italian, and that "No. V which has
lost a line somewhere reads like a translation of an Italian sonnet."[13] But another such translater was Surrey, with whom Blage
was also friendly and whose canon of poems seems strangely limited by the expansion of Wyatt's. Although the lines do not have
Surrey's grace, the text of the poem is probably not accurate. Giv-
en the doubtful origins of the whole group of poems, one should
hesitate to add a poem to Wyatt's canon simply because it is recorded with an irregularity of rhythm.

This problem is exemplified by the sonnet *Be belstred wordes I
am borne in hand*, for which Muir cited as parallels the common
phrases "borne in hand" and "wasted wynde." Two other sonnets
he considered similar, one of which, *I abide and abide and better
abide* from *D* f. 81v, is once again among the questionable poems
of that manuscript. Both sonnets are certainly not by Wyatt. Their
roughness is that of someone who could write verse neither grace-
fully nor with subtle variation. *There was never ffile half so well
filed*, a genuine Wyatt poem, which Muir suggested as being a similar effort, is in fact very different, having a significant syntactical
structure not shown in either of the other two sonnets, and its

rhythm is congruent with the syntax of the whole poem. The other sonnet that Muir cited as similar to Wyatt's begins: "Dryuyn to Desyre, a drad also to Dare, Bitwene two stoles my tayle goith to the ground;" and ends with the paradox: "Though Dowbell in Dedes, a inward perfit man." Both of these expressions, ignored by Muir, are exemplary of the misconceived Wyatt. He was colloquial, but never mixed fabliau phrases with a Petrarchan situation in a sonnet. Further, his mind was above the crude juxtaposition offered by the poet in the last line. Even the uninspired poems of *E* are not in the class of these two sonnets.

Of the twenty-two poems printed by Muir as characteristic of Wyatt's work, only the last deserves serious consideration. This poem has a traditional opening: "I muste go walke the woodes so wyld," as shown by another version cited by R. H. Robbins.14 The *B* version is seventy-five lines long, and in a narrative situation the elaboration is well employed to define the banished man's predicament. The pastoral elements are presented in a way that suggests a courtier viewing a greenwood landscape after more civilized surrounding, rather like Yeats looking back to Innisfree. All of this raises the possibility of Wyatt's adding another experiment to his *A Robyn* dialogue. Furthermore, the implied dialogue quality of the poem imparts a lively sense of the woman's awareness, while the man remains preoccupied with his own ego. This poem, then, is probably another Wyatt experiment.

Further evidence of Wyatt's authorship, beyond the cliché "banysshed from my blys," is the line "The wynter nyghtes that ar so cold" (l. 66), which is used by Wyatt in a similar lying-abed situation in *My lute awake* (ll. 21-25). Perhaps most important of all, the poet makes a sudden but indirect reference in the last stanza to the enemies of their love:

> A wofull man such desperat lyfe
> > Becummyth best of all,
> > But wo myght them befall
> That ar the causers of this stryfe,
> > And all for your Loue, my dere.

The understated wish and peculiar emphasis given to "them" are very like Wyatt.

One difficulty in this instance is an incomplete line in the manuscript:

> The wynter nyghtes that ar so cold
> > I ly amyd the [   ]
> > Vnwrapt in pryckyng thornes

> Remembryng my sorrowes old
> And all for your loue, my dere.

Muir made no attempt to remedy this loss, but one should be able to complete the line from Wyatt's work if it is truly his work. The only word that seems to fit the context is "storms," an imperfect rhyme with "thornes." The fact is, however, that Wyatt never used the word "storm" or "storms" in rhyming position, and he used the term "thorns" only once, in the line "Venemus thornes that ar so sharp and kene." The only possible conclusion is that the unusual pastoral nature of the poem made Wyatt consider a unique pair of rhymes, which he never decided upon. I am therefore inclined to place the poem among Wyatt's entirely on the basis of style.[15]

Of another set of poems (*UP* XXIII-XLIV) Muir remarked that they are "in a different hand (or hands), and this group also contains a number of Wyatt's known poems." But in no sense can these poems be called a group. They are arranged alphabetically, and unless all *B* poems are assumed to be Wyatt's, the alphabetical arrangement precludes the possibility that they are subgrouped as Wyatt's. The analysis of hand A showed beyond any doubt that his entries do not constitute a solid Wyatt group. There is as little ground for thinking that what follows his work, in alternating hands B and C, is a Wyatt group.

A closer examination of all the entries by the different hands B and C will give some idea of how rich their sources were in Wyatt copy and what sort the copy was. The two hands alternate from ff. 72r-185r, with hand C being far more dominant than hand B. In all, hand B must be credited with seventeen poems, and hand C with thirty-five (two of which are by Surrey), which leaves thirty-three entered by hand C as possibly by Wyatt or others.

There is no problem in distinguishing hands A, B, and C. Not only are they distinct in the ways they form letters, but their habits of finishing off their work are different. Hand A is the smallest and most regular of the hands, and it never makes any concluding sign of "finis" or mark of authorship. Hand B is not a professional hand, showing continual variations in slant and curve of line. Hand B is also in the habit of finishing off his work with similar signs, thus: ·∫·∫

Hand C has two characteristics, which may be seen by comparing ff. 74r, 110r-114r, and 178r-179r. Hand C usually begins the opening lines of a poem very neatly, but by the time he gets to the end of a poem, he is expanding his script and becoming irregular in letter formation. Another habit of hand C, an almost infallible sign of his work, is that he is the only Tudor hand in *B* who consistently concludes his work with "ffinis" or "finis," mostly the former. Thus, out of thirty-five entries by hand C, twenty-eight are concluded with a "ffinis" or "finis."

Most of the irregular entries by hand C can be accounted for in some way. Two poems of Surrey were marked with "HS" and "H" to set them off from the others. Three poems have no mark beneath the last line because the bottom of the leaf is lost (ff. 128, 140, and 155). Only three poems do not have the "ffinis," which suggests that they may be incomplete (ff. 156r, 158r, and 167r). However, only three lapses out of thirty-three entries still leaves sufficient evidence of a copyist's consistency. One may be quite sure, then, about distinguishing the entries of hands A, B, and C in the manuscript.

The entries of hand B are as follows:

f. 72r *a face that shuld* [*T* in the Wyatt group]

f. 73r *as from theys hylles* W [*E* f. 66r]

f. 82r *Cursyd be he* [*UP* p. 90]

f. 90r *dydo am I* [*UP* XXIII; *M3* CXXXI]

f. 91r *danger thy selff* [*UP* p. 90]

f. 117r *Loo what hytt ys to loue* [*E* f. 60r]

f. 117v *Leve thys to slander loue* [*E* f. 60v]

f. 118r *who most doth slander loue* [*E* f. 61v. These three poems on ff. 117r-118r are entered as an unbroken series, concluding on f. 118v.]

f. 119r *Lenger to troo ye* [*UP* XVIII; *M3* CXLVII]

f. 136r *O lord what chance* [*UP* p. 91]

f. 145r *Perdy I sayd hytt nott* [*D* f. 70v; the Wyatt group in *T* (91)]

f. 146r *patiens of all my blame* [*E* f. 26r, where the first line is "Patience though I have not]

f. 147r *patiens for my devyse* [*E* f. 28v]

f. 172r *To my myshap* [*D* f. 42r, in the hand of Mary Shelton; *T* (225), among "Uncertain Authors"]

f. 173r *the knott that furst ffynis* [*D* ff. 22v, 23rv, and 33rv]

f. 174r *ther was never fyle* [*E* f. 14v]

f. 184r *venus in sport* [*UP* XLIV; *M3* CLXXVII]

f. 185r *who so lyst to hunt* [*E* f. 7v]

A comparison of the entries of hand B with those of hand A shows a notable contrast. Hand A entered thirty-three-poems under letters "A," "B," "C," "D," "H," "I," and "L," of which only three are ascertainable as Wyatt's on other authority. Hand B entered seventeen poems under letters "A," "C," "D," "L," "O," "P," "T," and "W," of which eight are confirmed by *E* and a ninth by *T*. Even allowing hand B the advantage of having an additional letter heading to draw from, the proportion of Wyatt entries by hand B suggests both that he was interested in Wyatt poems and that he had access to sources close to Wyatt's own manuscript.

One odd irregularity in the habit of hand B may now be clarified. On f. 73r appear both his usual "finis" sign and, beneath that, a large "W." Examination of the original manuscript indicates that the "W" was added later in a browner ink. One may therefore conclude that hand B at no time specifically assigned any poem to Wyatt, even when that poem was certainly his. One may not conclude, however, that hand B entered only Wyatt poems, for among his entries is *To my myshap*, from f. 42r of *D*, where it is copied in the hand of Mary Shelton and marked merely "ffynys." This poem Tottel included among his "Uncertain Authors" (*T* 225). Muir included it among the "Doubtful Poems" in *M2*, where it belongs; he unwisely made it a member of his regular texts in *M3* (CLXXI).

One other irregularity of hand B is the fully written word "ffynis" at the end of "the knott that furst," which occurs in *D* three times, as a fragment on f. 22v, in full on 23rv, and again on 33rv. This single occurrence of the full word 'ffynis' in *B* suggests an unconscious following of his copy text. It is fairly certain, then, that there was no ascription of the poem to Wyatt in the *B* copy-text. The variants among the two full versions in *D* and the version in *B* indicate that *B* stems from an independent manuscript tradition, which farther confirms the fact that the poem was not attributed to Wyatt by copyists, and that the poem is probably not by Wyatt, based on its context in *D*.

Perdy I sayd hytt nott, however, is confirmed by the fact that *T* (91) placed it among Wyatt's poems. This poem occurs among the very solid group of Wyatt poems in *D* on f. 70v.

The case of the two "patience" poems, which also occur in *D*, *A*, and *E*, is difficult to assess. The problem is to decide whether the copy for *B* was closer to *D* or to the pair *E* and *A*. The variants show that although *B* sometimes takes an independent line, it more often agrees with *E* and *A* than with *D*, which suggests the superiority of hand B's readings over those of *D*.

Two poems by hand B were included by Muir among Wyatt's

unpublished poems. These are *dydo am I* (*UP* XXIII) and *venus in sport* (*UP* XLIV). The first exhibits nothing positive of Wyatt's style. Another aspect is the doubtful metrical placing of both proper names in the first line. In his other poems Wyatt placed both "Dido" and "Cartage" in a position to receive strong accents, thus:

> When Dido festid first the wandryng Toian knyght;

and:

> Off Cartage he that worthie warier.

It is odd, then, that the first line of this poem may be scanned either:

> Dydo am I the fownder furst of cartage;

or:

> Dydo am I the fownder furst of cartage.

Wyatt could have easily written "I Dydo am." Further, in this *ottava* the first line is the only one with an extra unaccented syllable at the end. Wyatt was fond of the extra syllable, but he used it consciously in combinations. This *ottava*, probably a translation, as Muir suggested, must remain in the uncertain category.

The second *ottava* may also be a translation, but that alone does not make it a poem by Wyatt. It begins:

> Venus In sport to plese therwith her dere
> dyd on the helm off myghty mars the red.

Here the phrase "dyd on" is used to mean "put on." A search of Wyatt's language shows that he never used this exact phrase. On one occasion, however, he employed the word "do" to mean "put," thus: "Arrise for shame / do away your sluggardie," which is line 3 of *You that in love find lucke*. This phrase is repeated twoice in the poem of *B*:

> priapus can ['gan] smyle & sayd, 'doway fordred,,
> doway, maddame, theys wepyns gret & grym.'

Wyatt was also fond of using both "therewith" and "therwithall" in adverbial phrases, such as: "Therewith to please your sight," which is line 20 of *Syns ye delite to knowe*.

Another rhetorical feature of the poem in *B* is the last line: "I, I for you am wepyn fytt and trym," which has a similar line in Wyatt's satires: "I cannot I, no no, it will not be," line 76 of *Myne owne John Poynz*. In so short a poem, because it is difficult to find a wholly characteristic tone, these more unconscious and mechanical features of style are a better guide. I would therefore include the poem among those probably by Wyatt.

Of the three other poems entered by hand B, one is an obscure allegory about Fortune and Cupid, which may be ignored (*O lord what chance*). A second is the advice of an older man to a younger, *danger thi selff loe for nothyng*. Apparently the young man has just been imprisoned for youthful lawlessness. The older man advises him:

> lyve vnder law and cache at goold
> who makes a nenmy bowght & sold.

As there is no irony in his advice about politic behavior to "styng" one's enemies, it does not sound like Wyatt. The third poem, however, in terza rima, with a total of forty-two lines or perhaps forty-three (one lost), has much the tone of Wyatt's verse letter to John Poinz, and should be included among poems possibly by Wyatt. The first line of the poem is "Cursyd be he that furst began.16

- f. 74r *Alas the grefe ffinis* [*E* f. 5v]
- f. 110r *Yf I myght hau ffinis* [*UP* XXIV; *M3* CXLII]
- f. 111r *I wyll all thow I may not ffinis* [*H* and *M2* 218– "Doubtful"; *M3* CXLIII]
- f. 112r *I knowe not where ffinis* [*UP* XXV; *M3* CXLIV]
- f. 113r *I have benne A lover ffinis* [*UP* XXVI; *M3* CXLV]
- f. 114r *In mornyng wyse ffinis* [*UP* XXVII; *M3* CXLVI]
- f. 120r *Love hath Agayne ffinis* [*M2* 156; *D* f. 80v; *M3* CXLVIII]
- f. 125r *My lut Awake ffinis* [*E* f. 43v]
- f. 126r *Mornyng my hart ffinis* [*UP* XXIX; *M3* CL]
- f. 127r *Madame I you requyer ffinis* [*UP* XXX; *M3* CLI]
  The Aunswere
  Your ffolyshe fayned hast [*UP* XXXI; *M3* CLII, where it is incorrectly listed in the Index as "Your foolish feigned heart"]
- f. 128r *Mestres what nedes many wordis* [*E* f. 24v]
  the Aunswer
  Of ffewe wordes sir ye syme to be [*E* f. 24v]
- f. 129r *Myght I as well finis* [*UP* XLIX; *M3* CLIII]
- f. 130r *My swet Alas ffinis* [*UP* L; *M3* CLIV]
- f. 137r *O what vndeseruyd creweltye ffinis* [*UP* XXXII; *M3* CLV]
- f. 138r *Ons in your grace ffinis* [*UP* XXXIII; *M3* CLVI]
- f. 139r *O crewell hart ffinis* [*UP* XXXIV; *M3* CLVII]
- f. 140r *O faythfful hart* [*UP* p. 91]
- f. 154r *Some men wold thynke ffinis* [*T* 82; not in *M*]
- f. 155r *Sche y̌ shuld most* [*UP* XXXV; *M3* CLXII]
- f. 156r *Sens ye delight to knowe* [*E* f. 47r]

f. 157r *Spytt off ther spytt ffinis* [*UP* XXXVI; *M3* CLXIII] 17
f. 158r *Syethe yt ys so* [*UP* XXXVII; *M3* CLXIV]
f. 159r *Suffryng in sorrowe ffinis* [*D* f. 6v]
f. 160r *Sythe I my selffe ffinis* [*UP* XXXVIII; *M3* CLXVI]
f. 161r *Sustayne abstayne ffinis* [*UP* p. xiii, Bannatyne MS.]
f. 167r *Thous slepest ffast* [*UP* XXXIX; *M3* CLXVII]
f. 168r *Tho some do grodge ffinis* [*UP* XL; *M3* CLXVIII]
f. 169r *Tho of the sort ffinis* [*UP* XLI; *M3* CLXIX]
f. 170r *To wette your yee ffinis* [*D* f. 5r]
f. 171r *Thoughe this thy port ffinis* [*E* f. 53v]
f. 178r *Suche wayward ways H S* [Surrey]
f. 179r *yf Ryght be rakt H* [John Harington. See Hughey, II,
    20-22.]
f. 181r *Wythe seruyng styll ffinis* [*D* f. 81r]
f. 182r *What wolde ye mor ffinis* [*UP* XLII; *M3* CLXXV]
f. 183r *Who lyst his welth finis* [*UP* XLIII; *M3* CLXXVI]

The letter "H" apparently distinguishes between Surrey ("HS")
and John Harington. The other poems in *B* marked with an "H"
are therefore probably by John Harington rather than Surrey.

Of thirty-seven entries by hand C, only six are confirmed as
Wyatt's by their presence in *E*. If the two of Surrey are subtracted,
it leaves a proportion of six confirmed Wyatt poems out of thirty-
five. Muir placed one additional poem in his doubtful poems in *M2*
(218), *I wyll all thow I may not*, which in *H* has the opening line,
"I will and yet I may not." This text has become CXLIII in *M3*.
The poem *Some men wold thynke* is included among Wyatt's
poems in *T*. But all four of the poems that occur also in *D* do so in
sections and manners that place them in the uncertain category.
There is a notable affinity in this group of four between *B* and *D*,
since two of the poems by hand C occur in *D* on the same folio
(f. 5), recto and verso, and a third occurs on f. 6v. The fourth occurs in the questionable section of *D* on f. 81r.

Further, a comparison of hand C's copies to those in *E* reveals
his carelessness and divergences of many kinds. Only one poem of
the six, *Thoughe this thy port*, may be said to be a more careful
copy in *B* than in *E*. Clearly there is no reason to believe that hand
C was the work of anyone with much interest in or contact with
Wyatt's work. Thus, there would have to be strong stylistic evidence to admit any of his copies into the canon. Yet Muir preserved twenty-one poems of hand C. Some of these are among the
most awkward and crudely patched poems of the early Tudor period (*UP* XXIV-XXVI). Most of the others are mosaics of clichés

(*UP* XXIX-XXXVI, XL-XLII, XLIX-L). Even the best of these
(*UP* XXXIII) is not like Wyatt's style. The last stanza is an abject
acceptance of death for love unrequited, most unlike Wyatt. Two
are written from a woman's point of view (*UP* XXXVII, XXXVIII),
a practice that cannot be assumed to have been Wyatt's.

The poem *In mornyng wyse syns daylye I increase* is a lament
for the men who were executed as Anne Boleyn's lovers (*M3*
CXLVI): "Rochefford, Norrys, Weston, Brewton, and Mark [Smea-
ton] ." As a poem, it is ordinary and drab, as J. C. Maxwell remarked. If this poem is by Wyatt, one would have to say that he
bungled one of the great moments in literary history. In phrasing
and especially in rhythm, the poem is very unlike Wyatt's longer
line. Two points of phrasing make it suspect. There is an easy assumption of life as a courtier, which Wyatt did not allow himself:

>   And we that now in court dothe led our lyffe.
>   Most part in mynd doth the lament and mone.

Such a sense of identity is incompatible with Wyatt's satires and
with another poem from *B* that is claimed for Wyatt within the
same context of Anne's tragedy. Also, the familiar address to
Smeaton as "Mark" suggests a closer relation between Wyatt and
Smeaton than can be documented. Muir cited Royal MS. 20B,
XXI, but it provides no evidence to connect Wyatt intimately with
Smeaton.   It merely connects Wyatt with George Boleyn, Lord
Rochford. Thus, Wyatt's reflections on the fate of Anne's accused
lovers cannot be found here.

Another poem, however, has a biographical context and an inscription above the first line suggesting that it is Wyatt's work.
Who lyst his welthe and eas Retayne is a Stoic reflection on the
dangers of court life, with a quotation from Seneca's *Hippolytus*
(*M3* CLXXVI). The third and fourth stanzas read:

>   These blodye dayes haue brokyn my hart,
>   My lust, my youth dyd then departe
>   And blynd desyre of astate;
>   Who hastis to clyme sekes to reuerte;
>   Of truthe, *circa Regna tonat.*
>
>   The bell towre showed me suche syght
>   That in my hed stekys day and nyght,
>   Ther dyd I lerne out of a grate
>   For all vauore, glory or myght
>   That yet *circa Regna tonat.*

The contrast between these stanzas and the lines quoted above from *In mornyng wyse* helps to establish the authenticity of *Who lyst his welthe and eas Retayne* and the alien nature of the former poem.

The *ottava Thou slepest ffast* reads like another translation from the Italian. Norman Ault dubbed this poem anonymous, and it must remain so.

In sum, neither copyist A nor C was particularly interested in Wyatt's poetry, and had no sources close to Wyatt's own manuscript, in contrast to hand B. To go on to the entries by George Blage, these are not always under the proper alphabetical heads, for he fitted his copies in where space had been left. They are:

> f. 58r *whan shall the cruell stormes be past* gb [*UP* p. 90; *M3*, p. 390]
>
> f. 92r *dysdayne not madam on hym too louke*   [*UP* XLVI; *M3* CXXXII]
>
> f. 101r-103r *A voyce i haue and yk a will to wayle* G.B.   [*UP* p. 90; *Life and Letters*, Appendix C]
>
> f. 104r *your Lokes so often cast* [*T* 78; *M3* CXXXVII]
>
> f. 115r *In sommer seson as soune as the sonne* [*UP* p. 90; *M3*, p. 402]
>
> f. 116r *It nowe the tyme is that the dulfull daye* [Not noted in *UP*; *M3*, p. 403]
>
> f. 123r *Lyue thowe gladly yff so thowe may* TW [*UP* XLVII; *M3* CXLIX]
>
> f. 124r *Let the heathen whych trust not in the Lord* B.G: [*UP* p. 90; *M3*, p. 404]
>
> f. 148r *pas fourthe my wountyd cries* [*T* 77; *M3* CLIX]
>
> f. 150r *Quondam was I in my Ladys gras* W [?] [*UP* XLVIII; *M3* CLX]
>
> f. 152r *Ryd of bondage free from Kaer seuen years space and mor*   : G B [*UP* p. 90; *M3*, p. 409]
>
> f. 162 r *Syns Loue ys founde wyth parfytnes* AA [*UP* LI; *M3*, p. 411]
>
> f. 175r *that tyme that myrthe dyd styrr my shyppe*   [*D* f. 17v; *M3* CLXXIII]
>
> f. 176r *degrese of Lyghtnes Lefte behynde* H [John Harington?]
>
> *He that spares to speak hathe hardly his entent* [John Harington?]
>
> f. 177r *A remembrance of the dethe of the Vertuis Lady Quiene Kateryne dowager. . .* B G. [Prose]

There are fifteen entries of poetry by Blage. He had a fondness

for the sign noted, sometimes with his initials and sometimes un-
accompanied. Aside from his own initials, he clearly assigned one
poem to "AA" (or "A"), which need not be considered seriously
as a Wyatt poem. Both poems on f. 176v are probably by John
Harington, as the "H" between them indicates.

One poem Blage clearly gives to Wyatt by ascribing it "TW."
Another, *Quondam was I*, may be ascribed simply "W." The difficulty here is that the last line is a variation on the refrain of the
poem, and all the refrains are written in the outer margin. The
"W" [?], therefore, also appears as a smaller letter beneath the refrain. It is not distinct, although in heavy inking. Both poems,
however, are probably by Wyatt and ascribed to him. The first is a
Stoic meditation, with the concluding sentiment: "Vayne ys all
trust of mans refuge." The second is ironic advice to a lover who
thinks he has succeeded the poet in a lady's grace.

Two other poems entered by Blage were included in *T* among
Wyatt's poems. Altogether, then, there are four Wyatt poems
among Blage's fifteen entries, and none also occurs in *E*. That is
understandable in view of the fact that Blage probably came into
possession of *B* three years after Wyatt had died. He had his own
interests and difficulties to record.

Another measure of Blage's care for Wyatt's poetry would be his
correction of earlier copies in *B*. This evidence, however, shows
mostly that he had no access to *E* and did not use it to perfect
Wyatt's poems. Blage's corrections appear in the following poems:

f. 67r *At Last withdraw* [*D* f. 4r. In *A* f. 24r, only the first line
is used in a different poem.]

f. 68r *At most myschyefe* [*E* f. 34r; *D* f. 12r. Here the correction in line 7 could come from either manuscript]

f. 87r *Sens that my Language withowt eloquence* [Of unknown
provenance]

f. 100r *Hate whome ye lyst* [*D* f. 78v]

f. 121r *Als your ffondnes* [Of unknown provenance; *M3*, p. 403]

f. 129r *Myght I as well* [Of unknown provenance]

f. 173r *the knott that furst* [*D* ff. 22v, 23rv, and 33rv]

Of these seven poems, only one is certainly Wyatt's, *At most
myschyefe*, and in that instance the correction could have come
from *D* as well as *E*, since the corrected reading is in both manuscripts. In view of the rest of the copy in *B*, the relation of *B* to *D*
is much better estabished, except in the case of hand B's entries.
However one looks at this group of corrected copies, they present
little or no evidence that Blage had any personal interest in Wyatt's

texts or their main sources, *E* and the copy that made up *E*.

In brief, there is no ground for assuming that *B* was intended as a collection of Wyatt's poetry or that George Blage personally was a collector or preserver of Wyatt's poems. Only one person who wrote in *B*, hand B, had both an interest in and access to Wyatt's poems in copies close to his personal manuscript. His activity was, however, much more limited than those of the other two copyists. If the quality of the sixty-nine or seventy (to include *M3* CXXVIII) poems printed by Muir were higher, it might suggest that *B* contained a collection of poems that had escaped the three major manuscripts extant, including Wyatt's own. By any critical standard, however, such a conclusion is untenable. The few poems from *B* that are probably or surely by Wyatt only support the conviction that the others cannot be my him and that the collection as a whole represents a number of contemporaries.

The Park-Hill Manuscript

History

The Park-Hill Manuscript (*P*) is now in the British Museum as Add. MS 36529, for its actual identity was not understood in the earlier part of the twentieth century. Again it was Ruth Hughey who demonstrated that in 1791 the manuscript belonged to Rev. William Sayle of Stowey in Somerset. Bishop Percy borrowed it from the Rev. Mr. Sayle. In 1800 it was purchased by Thomas Park, who used it for his edition of *Nugae antiquae* (1804). About this time Park sold his library, with the manuscript, to "the wealthy dry-salter Thomas Hill."[1] Hence, the manuscript had not been used for the earlier editions of *Nugae antiquae*. Alexander Chalmers borrowed it, however, from Hill for the preparation of Volume II of *The Works of the English Poets* (1810). Then G. F. Nott borrowed it for his work, although he was able to have possession of it for only a very short time. In 1811 Thomas Hill sold many of his manuscripts, including *P*, to Longmans, who used it for A. F. Griffiths' edition of the *Bibliotheca Anglo-Poetica*. The manuscript lost its Hill identity when Longmans catalogued it as from the library of Thomas Park. It passed successively from Richard Heber to Sir Thomas Phillipps, then to the British Museum as Add. MS. 36529.

Although *P* is important for the poetry of Surrey, it is less so for that of Wyatt. It is one of the Harington manuscripts of Tudor derivation, having the hand of Sir John Harington, and possibly of his two daughters, Frances and Ellina. It is made up almost entirely of poems composed before 1565, in addition to a Latin poem by Edmund Campion written before 1569. Unlike the other Harington manuscrips discussed so far, this one passed out of the hands of the Haringtons during the seventeenth century, for in 1663 it was in the possession of Sir James Tyrrell of Oxford.

There are only seven poems by Wyatt in *P*. They all occur between ff. 30r and 35v, with blanks at ff. 31v, 33v, 33rv, and 35r. The first four are confirmed by *E*. Then on f. 32v appear the three poems:

Luckes my faire falcon	[*T*, among Wyatt's poems]
A face that shuld content	[*T*, among Wyatt's poems]
The wandring gadling	[*E* f. 32r; *D* f. 35v]

The last four poems are those that have been discussed in relation to *Nugae antiquae* and *A*:

f. 33r *Playn ye my neyes*   [*Nugae antiquae*, 1769]
      I see my plaint with open eares [*Nugae antiquae*, 1769]
f. 35v *Vengaunce must fall on thee*   [*Nugae antiquae*, 1769]
      Spring of all woe   [*Nugae antiquae*, 1769]

As Hughey showed that these poems printed in *Nugae antiquae* were probably grouped with seven other Wyatt poems in *A*, they may be included among poems probably written by Wyatt. The grouping in *P* is not interrupted by the poems of any other poet; there were simply blank sides left for the later insertion of other poems. Thus, *P* fits neatly into the pattern formed by *E*, *A*, and *T*.

Minor Manuscripts

History

Versions of a few Wyatt poems appear in the Harleian MS 78 (*H*) and the Parker MS 168 (*C*). Only one of these manuscripts, *H*, is of any importance.

In *H* there is a distinct manner of indicating Wyatt's authorship that isolates two of the poems. On f. 23r in the upper left-hand corner is "Sir Th. W." and each of the three poems on that side of the leaf has an additional heading: "Sir T. W.," "Tho. W. to Bryan," and "Tho. W." Clearly the heading at the upper left refers to the poem at the top of the column. The verso contains one poem that fills the side and is again headed in the upper left "T Wyat of Love." Thus, one must conclude that on f. 24r the heading at the upper left refers only to the poem in the left-hand column, namely, *O goodly hande*, which is also in *E*. The poem in the right-hand column should have a similar heading if it is by Wyatt, and it has only the title *A balad of will*. There is no evidence that Wyatt ever used a title. Both facts cast suspicion on the *balad of will*, which must be placed in the doubtful category. Similarly, *An Epitaphe of Sir Thomas Grauener knyght*, on f. 24v, is signed merely "W." Since there is no record of a Sir Thomas Gravener who died before Wyatt, it is doubtful that this poem is Wyatt's. Also, the laconic manner of assigning the poem casts doubt on it.

C was given to John Jegon, master of Corpus Christi College, Cambridge, from 1590-1602, by Roger Cox, son of Bishop Richard Cox of Ely (1500-1581).[1] It was apparently assembled by Bishop Cox and is entirely suitable to his character, consisting largely of selections from the Church Fathers, prayers, proverbs, pious verse in English and Latin, and documents relating to ecclesiastical or public affairs.

Although M. R. James described the volume as containing about 200 folios, he was using the term "folio" in the modern sense of "page," one side of a leaf. By my own count there are 119 folio leaves, but only the opening section of *loci communes ex patribus* is numbered. The first folio recto displays two numbers, an old number 98 and a new number 1, showing that those leaves of the opening section were originally from another volume. The renumbered leaves 1-65 are followed by a blank and then a new section on Christian martyrs and other religious figures, whose folios are unnumbered to the end of the volume. All the folios except the last two, which would be ff. 118-119, are the same paper, water-marked by a hand with a flower extending from the middle finger. Folios 118-119 are conjugates of an older paper, unwatermarked, containing an account of Thomas Cromwell's speech and prayer at his execution on f. 118rv, and a Latin prayer and an indulgence on f. 119v. Folio 119r is blank.

On f. 118v Cromwell's concluding words to Wyatt from the scaffold are recorded thus: "& he turned him abowt & sayed fare-well Wyat. / & gentell Wiat praye for me." On f. 118r Cromwell asserts: "and now I pray you that you woll beare me recorde / that I dye in the Catholicke faith not doubtyng / of any article of my faithe, no nor doubtyng of / any Sacramentes of the churche. . . ." There is no heading or subscription to this item.

I can make no connection, by handwriting or habit, between these words and the Wyatt poems on what would be ff. 110r-111v, except that the verses are also moral or plaintive, hence suitable to the whole collection. On f. 110r are 28 lines of verse beginning *Like as the byrde in the cage enclosed*, subscribed "C [?]" or "F [?] telos." The Greek word may have been added later as a translation of "finis." But the exact nature of the single Tudor let-ter remains uncertain. M. R. James noted that it might also be an "R" or a "P."[2] In any case, the same letter appears on f. 111v at the end of *Myne owne Jhon poyntz*, in combination with a clear "W." I have tentatively transcribed these letters as "F. [finis] W." Wyatt's satire begins at the top of what would be f. 110v.

The poem *Like as the byrde* also occurs in *T* (271). The style of this poem is heavily Chaucerian, and a significant fact about the text is that there is no attempt to smooth out the meter. Since it is in the same hand as Wyatt's satire on the verso, it offers some assurance that the copyist did not habitually adapt a text to the standards of the mid-sixteenth century.

Since there is no other connection of *C* with either *E* or Wyatt's life and poetry, one must evaluate the text of Wyatt's satire entire-ly on the basis of its fidelity to the surviving portion in *E*, lines 52-103. The collation shows a surprising accuracy. The text of *D* is slightly better in this portion, but in lines 1-51, *D* suffers the un-fortunate omission of four lines. Lines 1-51, where *C* and *D* dis-agree substantially, is probably the record of Wyatt's own revi-sions, but it is impossible to say which reading is the later. The considerable number of variants in *A*, which is generally faithful to *E*, probably also indicates minor revisions.

The Court of Venus

History

The Court of Venus (*V*) is the generic title given to three individual volumes of verse published between 1537 and 1564. Each
survives in a unique, fragmentary copy. One fragment consists of
fifteen leaves now in the Douce Collection of the Bodleian Library.
It was probably published between 1537 and 1539. Another fragment consists of only two leaves now in the Miriam Lutcher Stark
Collection of the University of Texas Library, Austin. It was probably published between 1547 and 1549. The third fragment consists of eight leaves now in the Folger Shakespeare Library, Washington, D.C.. Only this fragment of the three has a title page:
"THE / Courte of / Venus. Newly / and diligently cor- / rected
with many pro- / per Ballades newly / amended, and also / added
thervnto / which haue not / before bene / imprinted." This edition
of the work probably appeared between 1561 and 1564.[1]

Any publication of a Wyatt poem in the 1537-1539 *V* would
immediately raise the question of Wyatt's possible cooperation
with a publisher in the last five years of his life. To begin with, the
surviving fragments of the 1537-1539 *V* include no poem confirmed by any of the manuscripts. Only one complete lyric survives, "Dryuen by dissyr to set affection," consisting of twenty
lines in quatrains. Despite the congruence of the opening words
with "Dryven bye desier I dede this ded," the *V* lyric is not at all
like the latter poem, which occurs in *D*, *B* and *T* as a single stanza
of rhyme royal. One other bit of verse in this edition resembles the
last ten lines, also in quatrains, of another Wyatt lyric, "which had
me in the snare". Fraser was of the opinion that both poems were
probably by Wyatt, but they provide no evidence above the level
of cliché. On the basis of style alone they must be put in the questionable category.

Nevertheless, the appearance of poems by Wyatt in at least one
of the later editions of *V* suggests the possibility that some leaves
of the first edition that no longer survive may have included poems
by Wyatt. For that reason one must consider what the other surviving leaves of the 1537-1539 *V* indicate about the nature of the
publishing venture.

The remaining leaves of the first edition contain a long pseudo-
Chaucerian poem called *The Pilgrim's Tale*. This crude poem is a
remarkably audacious comment on the religious and political situation of England at the time of the Pilgrimage of Grace, October

1536. The observations are put in the mouth of a "comely priest," met by a pilgrim to the shrine of Sempringham. Complaining that he has been muzzled by the bishops, the priest nevertheless attacks the system of orders, identifies the Pope as Antichrist, and asserts that the king is God's intended head of the Church on earth. He also uses the patriotic context to argue for the Protestant doctrine of justification by faith.

These positions are evident in the following quotations:

> suffisyth ynoghe to ther dome.
> to do as our elders haue don
> to mok & dissayue, men of there lyuelod
> in making beleue in thece brother hod
> wher we shold only beleue in christis name
> as we be taught, of the churche our dam
> ner a mogst ourselues or haue suche sectis.
> which the innocent people sore infectis
> deuyding christ as insufficient.
> to simple wyttis a great incomberment
> in dyuerse colors flekyd lyke a pye.

After this attack on monastic and mendicant orders, the priest makes a statement of Pauline doctrine:

> for paull him selue wold haue yet known
> that mans work is our own
> for wether it be he cephas or apollo
> that is our awn what euer we do.
> which is nought whan we do best.
> exceptyd only our faith in christ.
> the thing for good that we pretend.
> takis non effect as meritoriuse end.
> therfore merit in vs is non.
> but in our redemer crist alon.

The attack on religious orders and their exploitation of reliques— "rottyn bons"—culminates in a statement about the control of orders:

> thes wordis sayd he haue I caght
> whiche put me cleyn, owt of dowt
> that bisshopis to kingis shold lowt
> ner amongst them to haue no hed
> for christ him selue it for beyd
> and confirmid kingis in suche renown
> next him in erthe to haue dominion.

These "sects" or religous orders are accused of submitting to the

Whore of Babylon and of inciting insurrection against the princes whom God has appointed on earth. Several rebels who follow in the tradition of Cain and the first rebel angels are named: Perkin Warbeck, Jack Straw, and "now of lat owr cobler the dawe" or Nicholas Melton, one of the leaders of the Lincolnshire rebels. The poem closes with an "exclamation" by the author of the tale, including these words:

> O false pretens of gratinse [gracious] pilgrimage
> for the comyn welth which is the destrower.
> wyll thu neuer leue to bryng folke in dotage
> which of all lyes was the fyrst father.[2]

The author of these remarkable comments was very likely Robert Shyngleton, a priest, who according to Anthony Wood, "took occasion to reflect on the times, and certain persons in his sermons."[3] Shyngleton finally paid the penalty for his audacity by being hanged for treason. Moreover, the printer of the 1537-1539 edition of *V* was Thomas Gybson, another person noted for his strong anti-Catholic sentiment.

At this time in Wyatt's own life, he was recovering from the shock of Anne Boleyn's execution, along with those of her brother and her other accused lovers. Having recently been released from prison himself, Wyatt was not likely to have cooperated with so dangerous an undertaking as that represented by Shyngleton's poem. Probably, however, some of Wyatt's lyrics were included in the first edition as a mask for the propaganda contained in the pseudo-Chaucerian tale. From *D*, it is possible to guess where they came from, since that volume indicates that copies of Wyatt's poems were in circulation during the 1530s.

Clearly the writer of *The Pilgrim's Tale* thought he was flattering the king while expounding his own views of the true religion; but only a foolish subject could have been guilty of such presumption, and Wyatt was surely not such a man. He knew his place after the summer of 1536, if not well before that date. The person who put together the first edition of *V* must have been a reckless Protestant like Robert Shyngleton or John Bale, working with the printer Thomas Gybson. Wyatt, having inhabited the world of the court and international diplomacy since 1526, could not have been led into so crude and audacious a venture. It is a safe guess, therefore, that any of his verses which may have been printed in the volume were not included with his consent.

Whether *The Pilgrim's Tale* appeared in the second edition of *V*, 1547-1549, is unknown. With the Protestant party in control at court, the *Tale* could have been reprinted without fear of punishment. However, the running title that appears on the two surviving leaves is *A Boke of Balettes*, which suggests a collection of short lyrics. On these two leaves are printed five short lyrics, two of which are incomplete:

The fantasy of my harte Finis. [L. 22 of *If fansy would favor*; *E* f. 30r; *A* f. 75r; *D* f. 34v]

Loue whome ye lyst and spare not Finis [Of unknown provenance]

Shall she neuer out of my mynde Finis [Of unknown provenance]

My penne take payne a lytle space Finis. [*D* f. 3v, subscribed *fynys*]

My lute awake perfourme the last [*E* f. 43v, signed *Tho*; *D* f. 14v, subscribed *fynys qd Wyatt* ᴕ]

Since there are no significant variants between *E* and *D* for *If fansy would favor*, it is impossible to tell which manuscript was the source of the *V* version. Many significant departures are made in the *V* text from the text shared by *D* and *E*. In the case of *My lute awake* there are minor variants, suggesting that the source of the *V* versions is *D*. Of the five lyrics or fragments in the 1547-1549 edition, only two are Wyatt poems.

In the 1561-1564 edition of *V* there survives a *Prologue* to the *new court of Venus*, fifteen stanzas in rhyme royal, and twelve short lyrics. Both the *Prologue* and the group of lyrics were probably in the two earlier editions. Of the twelve lyrics, the following also occur in the 1547-1549 edition:

My penne take payne Finis [*D* f. 3v]

My lute awake Finis [*E* f. 43v; *D* f. 14v; *T* 87]

If fantasy would favour Finis [*E* f. 30r; *D* f. 34v; *A* f. 75r]

Loue whom you lyst and spare not Finis [Of unknown provenance]

Shall she neuer out of my mynd; Finis [B.M. Add. MS 18752]

Of these lyrics, *If fantasy would favour* also occurs in the 1537-1539 edition.

Four more poems are unique to the 1561-1564 edition of *V*:

To whom should I sue to ease my payne [*M3* CCLXV]

Fortune what ayleth the

I may by no meanes surmyse

Now must I lern to faine. [*M3* CCLXVIII]

One also occurs in *B*, with a variant first line:

During of payne and greuous smart [*B* f. 83r; *M3* CXXIV;
   UP p. 87]
One poem occurs elsewhere only in *T*, among the Wyatt poems,
Dysdaine me not without desert. The twelfth poem, printed only
in the last of the three *V* editions and in *T*, also occurs in
manuscripts:
   Meruaile no more al tho Finis [*E* f. 35r; *D* f. 16v]
   Among these poems, three are confirmed by *E* and one by *T*. Of
the poems unique to the last edition of *V*, not one has anything
like Wyatt's style. *Fortune what ayleth the* has a particularly mind-
less and awkward movement:

> She hath my hart and euer shal
> In this terrestial
> What can she more of me require
> Her whom I loue best
> God send her good rest
> And me hertely my whole desyre.

These lines could hardly have been written by Wyatt. In fact, they
sound like fifteenth century doggerel.
   In brief, the three editions of *V* offer no lyrics worthy of Wyatt
that were not previously available from the manuscripts or *T*. This
conclusion is fortified by the *Prologue*, extant in the 1561-1564
edition and probably included in the first edition. The *Prologue* is
an awkward imitation of Gower or Chaucer, with the conventional
background of a hunt in the forest. Left alone in despair for love,
the lover is confessed by Venus' clerk Genius, in order to prevent
his heart from breaking. The lover is also set to copy the poems
that follow in the printed volume. He asks for a description of
Venus' court. Genius gives him some physical details, which the
lover promises to add at the conclusion of the sequence. Genius re-
ports that Venus is angry at certain persons who through religion
are bound to Diana but actually serve Hecate. Venus therefore in-
tends to make Diana dismiss these hypocrites. In this context
seems to be an allusion to the insurrection attributed to evil religion in *The Pilgrim's Tale*:

> Ipocrysye is spyed for al his treasure
> That he spedeth as wel as the false foxe
> As that in armes, had many a bloudy boxe.[4]

   Since two of the nuns at Lichfield were found to be "not bar-
ren" by an ecclesiastical commission of 1535, the *Prologue* may
have been further intended as an attack on monastic institutions
for women in the trappings of a courtly romance. In style, the

Prologue is beneath criticism. In spirit, nothing could be farther from Wyatt's notion of the personal interplay between man and woman. No additional evidence is needed to prove that the work of Wyatt was alien to the guiding minds of *V*.

Tottel's *Miscellany*

The first edition of Tottel's *Miscellany* *(T)*, with a colophon dated 5 June 1557, contained 271 poems in all, among which were 97 attributed to Wyatt (nos. 37-127, 266-271). The second edition, with a colophon dated 31 July 1557, corrected this arrangement in only one instance. No. 82 was removed from Wyatt's poems and placed among those of uncertain authorship. This arrangement was preserved in all succeeding editions. As there is no evidence to the contrary, one may assume that the treatment of no. 82 in *T* indicated the sole correction in an otherwise accurate presentation.

When Hyder E. Rollins edited *T.* the 97 poems of Wyatt within its covers included 18 unique to the *Miscellany.* Since there was no manuscript evidence to impugn Tottel's authority for the grouping of the other 79 poems, his authority for the 18 unique poems was also accepted. All modern editors of Wyatt's poetry have followed his authority. There is no ground for challenging the tradition, even though not all 18 of those poems are today unique to the *T.* Muir's rediscovery of *B* supplied manuscript versions of some of them. Following are the numbers of the 18 poems, three of which are now extant in *B;* the other 15 remain unique to *T:*

T 74	*Accused though I be* [*B* f. 70r, hand A]
T 76	*Within my brest*
T 77	*Passe forth my wonted cryes* [*B* f. 148r, hand of George Blage]
T 78	*Your lokes so often cast* [*B* f. 104r, hand of George Blage]
T 80	*For want of will*
T 81	*If euer man*
T 84	*Svch is the course*
T 105	*Svffised not (Madame)*
T 106	*When first mine eyes*
T 107	*Synce loue wyll nedes*
T 108	*Mystrustfull mindes*
T 109	*It burneth yet*
T 113	*I see, that chance*
T 114	*For shamefast harm*
T 117	*Through out the world*
T 119	*In court to serue*
T 269	*Speake thou and spede*
T 270	*If thou wilt mighty be*

As shown for the entries of the three copyists and George Blage in *B*, the authority for including these poems among Wyatt's comes from *T* and not from *B*. However, since the editorial practice of *T's* editor was consistently one of revision toward metrical smoothness, it is probable that the three copies in *B* are a safer guide to Wyatt's original text than is *T*.

In *M3* Muir printed variants from the first and second editions of *T*. Although he did not so indicate, those variants were apparently based on the Rollins edition. However, in one instance (*M3*. XLVII, l. 12), the variant does not occur in the Rollins list of variants and misprints, namely: "bering] learnying". A check of this variant against photostats of the unique copy of the first edition in the Houghton Library, Harvard University, shows that Muir's variant is a ghost.

Notes

The Egerton Manuscript

1. Ruth Hughey, "The Harington Manuscript at Arundel Castle and Related Documents," *Library*, XV (1935), 388-444. Hughey (I, 11-62) confirmed and extended the argument.

2. Raymond Southall, *The Courtly Maker: An Essay on the Poetry of Wyatt and His Contemporaries* (Oxford: Basil Blackwell, 1964), Appendix A.

3. Hughey, "Harington Manuscript," p. 399n2.

4. Southall, *Courtly Maker*, p. 160, estimated the loss of eighteen complete leaves but did not enumerate them. His account of the foliation is puzzling, since he counted ff. 1-4 as modern, yet his Tudor hand A begins on f. 4.

5. Southall, *Courtly Maker*, p. 28.

6. Hughey, "Harington Manuscript," pp. 422-423.

7. Hughey, I, 45, and nn. 58, 59.

8. L. R. Merrill, *The Life and Poems of Nicholas Grimald* (New Haven: Yale University Press, 1925), pp. 20, 33.

9. All of Grimald's emendations of individual poems are recorded in my transcript of *E*.

10. Southall, however, assigned ff. 62v-63v to hand A.

11. Hughey, "Harington Manuscript," p. 415, first identified the hand of Nicholas Grimald in *E* by comparing it with the holograph of his *Archipropheta*, Royal MS 12 A. XLVI.

12. The same Wyatt signature occurs in his holograph letters. I have compared the *E* signature with that used by Wyatt in the original manuscript of the following documents: John S. Brewer *et al.*, eds., *Letters and Papers, Foreign and Domestic, of the Reign of Henry VIII* (London: 1830-1910), vol. XII, pt. 2, 931; vol. XIII, pt. 1, 1228; vol. XIII, pt. 2, 615.

The Arundel-Harington Manuscript

1. For my review of Hughey, see *JEGP*, LXI (April 1962), 378-381.

2. Hughey, I, 53-60.

3. Hughey, I, 13n10; II, 192.

The Devonshire Manuscript

1. Southall, *Courtly Maker*, Ch. II, App. B, p. 173.

2. Southall, *Courtly Maker*, pp. 18n1, 16.

3. Edward A. Bond, "Wyatt's Poems," *Athenaeum*, no. 2274 (27 May 1871), 654-655.

4. See Ethel Seaton, *RES*, VII (1956), 55-56; R. C. Harrier, "A Printed Source for 'The Devonshire Manuscript,'" *RES*, XI (1960), 54. These stanzas and others from *D* were included as probable Wyatt poems in Kenneth Muir, "Unpublished Poems in The Devonshire Manuscript,"

Proceedings of the Leeds Philosophical Society: Literary & Historical Section, VI, pt. 4 (May 1947), 253-282.

5. Edwin Casady, *Henry Howard, Earl of Surrey* (New York: Modern Language Association of America, 1938), pp. 22, 182.

6. Southall, *Courtly Maker,* p. 173.

7. Another caveat against the identification of handwriting with individuals is implicit in Edward Bond's view that the person who made these selective notations was Lady Margaret. See n.3.

8. Southall, *Courtly Maker,* pp. 16-22.

9. Cf. specimens of Anne's hand in Joseph Netherclift, *Autograph Letters. . .* (London, 1838), plate 12; John Gough Nichols, *Autographs of Royal, Noble, Learned, and Remarkable Personages. . .*(London, 1829), under "Queens"; Henry Savage, ed., *The Love Letters of Henry VIII* (London, 1949), pp. 111, 112.

10. See Richard Harrier, "Notes on Wyatt and Anne Boleyn," *JEGP,* LIII (1954), 581-582.

11. See Nott, I, 161, 251; II, vii-ix, 590-591.

12. See Charles Willison Eckert, "The Poetry of Henry Howard, Earl of Surrey" (Ph.D. diss., Washington University, St. Louis, 1960).

13. See Agnes K. Foxwell, *A Study of Sir Thomas Wyatt's Poems* (London: University of London, 1911), pp. 1-19.

14. Foxwell, *Study,* p. 133.

15. Foxwell, *Study,* p. 17.

16. Kenneth Muir, *Life and Letters of Sir Thomas Wyatt* (Liverpool: Liverpool University Press, 1963), p. 250; *Sir Thomas Wyatt and His Circle: Unpublished Poems* (Liverpool: Liverpool University Press, 1961), p. 73.

17. Muir, *Life and Letters,* p. 17.

18. Muir, *Life and Letters,* p. 224.

19. *Unpublished Poems,* p. xv.

20. Southall, *Courtly Maker,* p. 5.

21. Southall, *Courtly Maker,* p. 5.

22. J. C. Maxwell's comments on the poems in *B* are specially illuminating. As in the case of the *D* poems, however, his use of the term "superior" was purely esthetic, since he did not allow any particular "superiority" for *E.* See Maxwell's review of Muir's "Unpublished Poems in The Devonshire Manuscript," *Notes & Queries,* ns VIII (August 1961), 318.

23. At this point in the manuscript hand B corresponds almost exactly to hand B of Southall (*Courtly Maker,* p. 173), although I disagree with him that hand B also occurs on f. 3r.

24. See Russell A. Fraser, ed., *The Court of Venus* (Durham: Duke University Press, 1955).

25. Muir, *Life and Letters,* p. 17n6. This text, no. 119 in *M2,* was eliminated in *M3.* Its quality should put one on guard about accepting poems into the Wyatt canon simply because they sound masculine or vigorous.

26. Southall, *Courtly Maker,* p. 4.

27. The last word of this poem is "Causeles," but since it is placed in the center of the leaf, it was taken as a signature by Bond, "Wyatt's Poems," *Athenaeum* (27 May 1871), 655.

28. Southall, *Courtly Maker*, p. 173, was probably correct in interpreting the "ʕ" as "secundus" when at the head of an entry and as "sequitur" when at the foot.

29. See R. L. Greene, "Wyatt's 'I am as I am' in Carol-Form," *RES*, ns XV (1964), 175-180.

The Blage Manuscript

1. In *M3*, p. xii-xiii, there is very little about *B*, since Muir referred in a footnote to his earlier edition.

2. The information about the state and history of *B* was kindly supplied by William O'Sullivan, Assistant in Charge of Manuscripts, in a letter of 10 May 1960. O'Sullivan noted that *B* is catalogued no. 730 in Edward Bernard's *Catalogii MSS Angliae et Hiberniae* (Oxford, 1697), II, pt. 2, and is the third item of no. 160 in *Catalogue of Trinity College, Dubin, MSS.* (Dublin, 1900). See also Hugh Jackson Lawlor, *Primate Ussher's Library Before 1641* (Dublin, 1900).

3. Cf. *UP*, p. x.

4. *UP*, p. ix.

5. Muir, *Life and Letters*, App. C; *UP*, p. x.

6. *UP*, p. xi.

7. *UP*, p. xv in1. In *M3*, poem 20 of *M2* appeared under the same number and without any variants from *B*.

8. For a printed list of the poems as they occur in *D*, I refer to *M2* rather than *M3*, because in the later edition Muir replaced *D* texts with those of *B*.

9. The texts of these two poems, *(UP*, no. XIV) are reprinted as one entry in *M3* (no. CXXVIII) but with three stars separating the two metrical units.

10. See *UP*, p. ixn2.

11. See *V*, p. 125.

12. These twenty-two poems appear in *UP*, nos. I-XXII, and also in *M3*, between nos. CIX-CXLI but interspersed with additional poems from other parts of *B*.

13. *UP*, pp. xvi, 66.

14. R. H. Robbins, *Secular Lyrics of the XIV and XV Centuries* (Oxford: Clarendon Press, 1952), no. 20.

15. In a note to the incomple line 67 of no. CXLI in *M3* (p. 400), Muir suggested a possible rhyme word as "storms."

16. The poem appears in *M3*, pp. 394-395, where it is described as "some weak verses in octosyllabic terza rima." These verses, however, are decidedly stronger than almost any of the *B* poems in *M3* and are "possibly" by Wyatt.

17. The full first line is "Spytt off ther spytt whiche yᵗ in vayne." Since Muir missed the "r" on the third word, he edited the line, no. CLXIII, thus: "Spytt off the spytt whiche they in vayne."

The Park-Hill Manuscript

1. Hughey, "Harington Manuscript," 408-410. The history of *P* comes from this article.

Minor Manuscripts

1. Montague R. James, *A Descriptive Catalogue of the Manuscripts in the Library of Corpus Christi College Cambridge* (Cambridge, 1912), I, 378-380.

2. James, I, 380.

The Court of Venus

1. See *V*, Introduction. I disagree with Fraser, incidentally, as to Wyatt's contribution to the three editions.

2. Fraser, pp. 88-89, 90, 92, 99.

3. Fraser, p. 32.

4. Fraser, p. 117; see also pp. 148, 149.

Part Two.

The Egerton Manuscript

Editorial Principles

The aim of the transcript of Egerton MS 2711 (British Museum) is to represent all handwriting affecting the texts of the poems up to the publication of Tottel's *Miscellany* (1557). In each case the note supplies the additional data needed to understand the full significance of the text.

The variants are fixed within the terminal date of 1557. They refer primarily to substantial disagreement among the manuscripts and printed texts up to Tottel. Punctuation is not usually recorded, except for punctuation within the line that substitutes for the omission of a word. All punctuation within the variant phrase itself is recorded. Since there is no sure guide to pronunciation or to the systems of meter employed, it would be impossible to record all possible differences in syllabification. Variants are added that could allow for extra syllables as I read the line. For example, the final "eth" or "ed" rather than the spellings "es" or "de." The manner in which scribes dealt with Wyatt's more peculiar spellings, such as "trowgh" for "troth" or "trouth," is also followed. Where the first half of a variant is an entire line of the text I have not repeated that line, as has been the custom in Kenneth Muir's editions.

Although no attempt is made to record variants from modern editions, the notes point out the most important errors in the texts of Hughey and Muir. There would have been little point in collating the texts of Nott and Foxwell, except to give credit for certain readings.

In transcribing *E*, I was greatly aided by *Elizabethan Handwriting, 1500-1650: A Manual*, by Giles E. Dawson and Laetitia Kennedy-Skipton (New York: Norton, 1966). Two problems noted by them (p. 23) deserve special mention: initial letters and spacing. In an effort to preserve the capitalization of the manuscript, I frequently had to make a fairly arbitrary choice. This is true especially where the only difference between a minuscule and a capital is the size of the letter. When the scribe or writer clearly used a special form simply as an initial letter, I transcribe it as an ordinary minuscule.

A more subtle problem has to do with the spacing between words and between syllables of perhaps the same word, such as "into," or "in to," or "inward." Where there is no pen lift from letter to letter, the letters and words are joined together. But such instances, referred to in the notes, are rare. In most instances I had to decide whether extra space was left, perhaps for the insertion of later punctuation or wording that was never forthcoming. In such cases the problem is indicated, either in the text, the note, or both. An interesting example of wording if in *The furyous gonne* (f. 40v), line 8, where one must choose between "now hard" or "inwhard."

Dawson and Kennedy-Skipton also noted (p. 25) that some writers "represent an *e* or *r* or *s* indifferently by a mere hump." In the case of Wyatt's hand, I pay particular attention to his habit of frequently representing a hooked "e" by a mere hump in the middle of a word or by a tick of the pen at the end of a word. All these instances, whether by Wyatt or the scribes, are indicated by an italic "e." Since the question of Wyatt's metrical system or systems is not yet settled, I have treated his vaguer indications of "e" in this way so as to alert future students of his meter.

All poem and line numbers as well as folio numbers are editorial additions. Each note heading indicates all occurrences of a poem up to Tottel with the number for *T* in the Rollins edition. Deletions in the manuscripts are indicated by being placed within angle brackets.

The common Tudor abbreviations used by Wyatt and the scribes are:

$\mathcal{G}$ = "ur as in "our" or "your"

$\mathcal{e}$ = "es" as in "hertes"

$\mathcal{J}$ = "er" as in "vndeserued"

$\mathcal{C}$ = "re" as in "prepare"

$\mathcal{p}$ = "er" as in "peraduenture"

$\mathcal{p}$ $\equiv$ "pro" as in "propertie"

$\mathcal{q}$ = "quod"

$\sim$ = "m" or "n" or simply scribal fourish

The sign $\mathfrak{s}$ is a terminal "s" frequent in the Devonshire MS as an isolated mark but also in Egerton. I have recorded inconsistencies such as "m$^{\mathfrak{c}}$cy" where one would expect "m$^{\mathfrak{J}}$cy" for "mercy." The long "s" has been transcribed the same as the short "s."

Poems

1

Behold love thy power how she dispiseth
  my great payne how litle she regardeth
  the holy oth wherof she taketh no cure
  broken she hath and yet she bideth sure   4
  right at her ease & litle she dredeth

Tho.   Wepened thou art and she vnarmed sitteth
  to the disdaynfull her liff she ledeth
             th
  to me spitefull w oute cause or mesur   8
        Behold love

I ame in hold if pitie the meveth
  goo bend thy bowe that stony herte breketh
  and with some stroke revenge the displeasur   12
     e
  of y & him that sorrowe doeth endur
  and as his lorde / the lowly entreath
        Behold love

E f. 4r, hand A. *D* f. 69v. *T* 69. In *D* the refrain lines are written on the inner margin, with an extra refrain to follow the fourth line. Beneath the last line in *D* is "fs".

    The only scribal punctuation in *E* is the / (l. 14). In this line the final "e" in "lorde" was made simply by capping the downward stroke of the letter "d." I am not sure whether the "ffinnis / [?]" written and deleted after line 15 in *E*, is by the scribal hand A or a later hand.

    E was elaborately emended by Nicholas Grimald, (*G*), whose pen can be distinguished from the scribe's by comparison with the specimen of Grimald's holograph on the lower half of f. 7v. Grimald's ink was slightly darker and his pen point a bit finer.

G: Looue
1. Behold love] Beholde, love, she dispiseth] shee dispiseth: 2. my]
My she regardeth] shee regardeth· 3. the] The oth] oth, taketh]
  takes
taketh∧ cure] cure: 4. broken she hath] Broken shee hath: yet she]
                                   thee
yet, shee sure] sure, 5. right] Right ease] ease: she]∧shee dredeth]
dredeth· 6. Wepened] Wepen⟨e⟩d art] art: she vnarmed sitteth] shee
                                       all
vnarm⟨e⟩d sitteth: 7. to the disdaynfull] Too thee disdaynfull,/ liff she
ledeth] liffe shee ledeth: 8. to me spitefull] Too mee spitefull, cause
                                      Looue:
or mesur] cause, or mesure. 9. Behold love] Beholde, love: 10. ame in
hold] am⟨e⟩ in holde: the meveth] thee meveth: 11. goo] Go⟨o⟩ bowe]
bowe: breketh] breketh: 12. and] And, stroke] stroke, 13. of y &
                                          e
     ee
him] Of y, & him: endur] endure: 14. and] And, lorde / the lowly

entreath] lorde, / thee low/ly,/<u>entreath</u> ^e ^{here,} entreateth·   15. Behold love]
^{Looue·}
Beholde, love·∧

Although *G* seems to have had an indirect effect on *T*, it was not such as
to suggest that Grimald was Tottel's editor. For example, *G* preserves the
rondeau form in *E*, while in *T* the poem becomes a fourteen-line lyric,
perhaps intended as a sonnet. *G*'s fondness for doubled letters, as in "Looue"
"shee," is ignored in *T*, although *T* reads "thee" (l. 5, 13, 14). Whereas much
of *G*'s punctuation is imitated in *T*, including the full stops at the ends of
lines 5, 8, and 14, there are independent signs in *T*. *G*'s medial colon is
preserved in line 4 of *T*, but the colon becomes a comma in lines 5 and 6.

Some of *G*'s most striking metrical adjustments are adopted. However,
while *T* reads "takes" (l. 3) rather than "taketh," as in *E*, the form "takis"
also crept into the corrupted *D* version, probably because the copyist felt
the pressure of metrical regularity at that point. *T* has the added "thee"
(l. 5), the "all" (l. 7), and the concluding phrase "here entreateth." Line 14
in *T* thus becomes an italianate hendecasyllable; while the line in *E*, as the
scribe wrote it, had nine syllables, which perhaps accounts for the / dividing
the line.

D T: 2. great] greuous *T*   payne] greef *D*   3. the] thy *D*   holy] solemne
T   taketh] takis *D*] takes *T*   4. *D adds* beholde love   5. she] thee she *T*
6. thou haste weapon vnarmid she syttith *D*   7. her] all her *T*   8. spitefull]
dispitefull *D*   cause] iust cause *T*   9. *T adds* <u>how</u> proudly she triumpheth
10. if] but if *T*   pitie the] thee pitie *T*   meveth] me with *D*   12. displeas-
ur] great displeasure *T*   13. sorrowe] sorrowes *D*   14. lowly entreath]
lowlye entreathe *D*] lowly here entreateth *T*   15. Behold love] beholde &
ꝯ *D*] *om. T*

2

What vaile͡th trou͡th or by it to take payn
    to stryve by stedfastnes for to ⟨be⟩ ∧^{at}tayne
    to be iuste & true & fle from dowblenes

    sythens all alike where ruele͡th craft∧ⁱnes   4
    rewarded is boe͡th fals & plain
    sonest he spede͡th that moost can fain
    true meanyng hert is had in disdayn
    against deceipt & dowblenes   8
            What vaile͡th trouth

    Deceved is he by crafty trayn
    that meane͡th no gile & doe͡th remayn
    wth in the trap͡p wou^tte redresse   12
    but for to love lo suche a maisteres
    whose crueltie nothing can refrayn
            What vaile͡th trouth

E f. 4rv, hand A. *T* 70. A special problem arises with this text, for the scribe made corrections that must be distinguished from *G*. A later hand also left its record on the leaf.

The scribe hand A had to insert an "i" omitted from "craftiness" (l. 4) and another "i" omitted from "vaileth" (l. 9). What may appear to be a / after "hert" (l. 7) is actually the deletion of a false start.

The following revision appears: "⟨sythens⟩_∧," (l. 4). While this sort of change in spelling is characteristic of *G*, the hand does not appear to be his unless it is another kind of script he sometimes employed. *T* reads "Since" here, so this word may be the record of another hand directly or indirectly influential on *T*.

G: troũth or by it to] tro⟨u⟩th? or, by it, too   payn] payne?   2. to stryve by stedfastnes] Too stryve, by stedfastnes, ∧ at tayne] ∧ ob at tayne: 3. to be iuste & true] Too bee iust⟨e⟩, & true: fle] flee   dowblenes] dowblenes: 4. alike] alike,   5. rewarded] Rewarded   boeth fals] bo⟨e⟩the fals,   plain] plaine: 6. sonest he spedeth] soonest hee speedes⟨eth⟩,   moost] mo⟨o⟩ste fain] faine· fayne: 8. deceipt] decei⟨p⟩te,   dowblenes] dowblenes: 0. trouth] tro⟨u⟩th?   10. Deceved is he] Deceyued is he Deceyude is hee,   trayn] trayn: 11. meaneth] meaneth meanes   gile] gile: 12. trapp] trapp,   redresse] redresse: 13. but] but,   love lo] love, lo,   a] à   maisteres] maist⟨e⟩res: 14. crueltie] crueltie   refrayn] rest⟨f⟩rayn: 15. trouth] tro⟨u⟩th?

A comparison of these emendations with *T* shows the same mixed pattern of indirect influence. *G* abandoned his habit of capitalizing initial letters of lines after the fourth line. Once again, this rondeau became a kind of sonnet in *T*, dropping the fifteenth line and filling out the ninth.

Some of *G*'s most important emendations are ignored. *T* does not follow him in line 2, where *T* reads "attayn." Further, his suggestion to guide the meter by accenting the "a" of line 13 is ignored for the insertion of an additional word. *T* followed a similar policy in line 14, perhaps because the meaning of the underlining of the word "crueltie" was as mysterious to him (or his editor) as to me.

T, however, shows the emended forms of "troth" (l. 1) and "flee" (l. 3). *T* reads "Soonest" and "spedes" (l. 6), both reflecting *G*'s preferences, although not exactly for the second word. Again, the kind of heavy pointing that *G* wanted shows up in *T*, but not following his particular preferences for colons, commas, and full stops.

T: 3. to . . . true] How to be iust   4. sythens] Since   5. fals] crafty False 6. spedeth] spedes   fain] lye and fayn   7. disdayn] hye disdain 8. dowblenes] cloked doublenesse   9. *T adds* or parfit stedfastnesse 10. Deceved] Deceaud   by] by false and   11. meaneth] meanes   and] and faithfull   12. woute] without ^t help or   13. maisteres] sterne maistresse 14. Where cruelty dwelles, alas it were in vain   15. *om. T*.

3

Cesar when that the traytoᵇ of Egipt
witͪ thonourable hed did him present

covering his gladnes did represent

      th

playnt w his teeres / owteward as it is writt   4

and Hannyball eke when fortune him shitt

clene from his reign & from all his intent

laught to his folke / whome sorrowe did torment

his cruell dispite / for to disgorge & qwit   8

so chaunceth it oft that every passion

the mynde hideth by colo⁹ contrary

with fayned visage now sad now mery

Whereby if I laught any tyme or season   12

it is for bicause I have not her way

to cloke my care but vnder spo⟨r⟩rt & play

E ff. 4v, 5r, hand A. *D* f. 70r. *T* 45. Beneath the last line is "fs⸗" in *D*. This
text presents a major and minor problem. *M1-3* read "nother way" (l. 13)
where the scribe of *E* wrote "not her," which was deleted. It is clear that the
deletion was by *G*, who added "nother" above it. At this point both *T* and *D*
read "none other." Wyatt is relating the political psychology of this sonnet to
his amorous experiences, but Tottel apparently found the association unaccept-
able or puzzling, as did those hands that produced the highly corrupted version
in *D*. Indeed, Wyatt's most discussed poem, *They fle from me*, opens with a
stanza totally ambiguous as to whether the loyalties being lamented are either
political or amorous. The minor question (l. 14) is: what was the letter deleted
in the word "sport" and who did it? Here *M1* and *2* read "sport," while *M3*
reads "spoort." But the deleted letter was more likely an extra "r" put in by
hand A and then deleted by him.

G: 1. Cesar] Caesar   2. hed] hed,   present] present: 3. gladnes] gladnes:
4. playnt] playnt,   teeres / owteward] teeres⟨/⟩owteward: writt] writt:

5. and Hannyball eke] and, Hannyball, eeke,   6. clene] cleᶜne   reign] reign:

intent] intent: 7. folke 6] folke, ⟨/⟩ torment] torment: 8. cruell
dispite /] cruell dispite⟨/⟩   to disgorge & qwit] too disgorge, & qwite   9. so
chaunceth it] so, chaunceth it   oft] oft: every] every   10. hideth] hideth,

colo⁹ contrary] co/lo⁹ contrary: 11. visage] visage,   sad] sad,   mery]
mery.   12. Whereby] Whereby,   laught] laught,   tyme] tyme,   season]
                              nother
season: 13. is] is: not her way] no⟨t her⟩ waye,   14. to] too   care but]
care: but,   spo⟨r⟩rt & play] spo⟨r⟩rt, & playe

    Once again *T* shows a good parallel to *G*'s idea of terminal and medial punc-
tuation, but not necessarily with *G*'s choice of comma and colon. The crucial
emendation of "nother" is adopted in spirit but not letter, since *T* reads "none
other." Tottel was not likely to make public Wyatt's personal twist to the political theme of the sonnet.

D T: 1. when that] whan *D*   3. gladnes] hartes gladnesse *T*   5. and . . . eke]
Eke Hannibal *T*   him shitt] ded flitt *D*] him outshyt *T*   6. from him and to
Rome ded her whele relente *D*   7. ded laugh among thim whom tearis had

besprent *D*   8. her cruell dispight inwardelye to shitt *D*   9. it oft] me *T*
12. if I laught any tyme or] If I laugh at eny *D*] if that I laugh at any *T*
13. for bicause] by cause *D*]   because *T*   not her] none other *D T*

4

<blockquote>

The longe love that in my thought doeth harbar

   and in myn hert doeth kepe his residence

   into my face preseth with bold pretence

   and therin campeth spreding his baner   4

She that me lerneth to love & suffre

   and will that my trust & lust negligence

   be rayned by reason shame & reverence

   with his hardines taketh displeasur

Wherewithall vnto the hert̲e forrest he fleith

   leving his entreprise with payn & cry

   and ther him hideth & not appereth

What may I do when my maist̲͛ fereth   12

   but in the feld with him to lyve & dye

   for goode is the liff ending faithfully

</blockquote>

E f. 5rv, hand *A*. *A* f. 63r. *T* 37. This is one of the *E* texts unsigned by Wyatt, which no doubt indicates that he did not examine the work of hand *A*. As a result, the ending on "lust" (l. 6) indicating the genitive case was left unsupplied. *G* added the necessary letters.

G:

    1. love] love,   harbar] harbaͭr: 2. myn] my⟨n⟩   residence] residence:

3. into] intoo   preseth] preseͣth,   pretence] pretence: campeth] campeth,

baner] baner·   5. me lerneth] mee lerneth̲ (lerns)   to love & suffre] too love, &

suffre: 6. will] will: (wills)   lust negligence] lustis negligence   trust] trust,

7. rayned] ray̲ned   shame & reverence] , shame, & reverence: 8. taketh

displeasur] taketh displeasur· (takis)   9. Wherewithall] Wherewithall,   he fleith]

he fleith: 10. entreprise] entreprise,   payn & cry] payne, & cry: 11. there]

there,   hideth] hideth: appereth] appereth·   12. do] doo: fereth] fereth?

13. feld] fᵢelde,   to lyve & dye] too lyve, & dy⟨e⟩·   14. liff] liffe,   faithfully]
faithfully·

    Cf. these notations with Ruth Hughey, "The Harington MS at Arundel Castle," *Library* XV (1935), 442-443. Our disagreements are minor, but Hughey omitted the underlining of ned is the word "rayned" (l. 7). She and Muir read *G*'s needed completion of "lust" (l. 6) as "lustes" rather than "lustis." Hughey represented *G*'s revision of "lerneth" (l. 5) as "lernz," while I take the "z" to be his peculiar form of the final "s." Actually, this "z" is written with a descending tail stroke. Hughey's facsimile nicely illustrated how the two halves of "Wherewithall" (l. 9) are linked by an extended stroke on the second "w."

Both *T* and *A* read "learns" (l. 5), so this is an instance where the copyist of *A* picked up a hint from *G*. *A* again follows the "wills (l. 6) of *G*, which becomes "willes" in *T*. Most of *G*'s medial and terminal punctuation appears in *T*, though not with exactly the same marks; while *A* makes no effort to reproduce them.

A T: 1. doeth] *T*   2. myn] my *A T*   4. therin] there *T*   spreding] displaying *T*   5. lerneth] learns *A T*   suffre] to suffer *T*   6. will] wills *A*] willes *T*   lust] lustes *A T*   8. taketh] takes *A T*   9. Wherewithall vnto] Wherwith loue to *T*   fleith] flieth *A*] fleeth *T*

5

Alas the greif and dedly wofull smert
   the carefull chaunce shapen afore my shert
   the sorrowfull teres the sighes hote as fyer
   that cruell love hath long soked from myn hert   4
   and for rewerd of o^9 great desire
   disdaynfull dowblenes / have I for my hier
O lost s^{9}uis O payn ill rewarded
   o pitifull hert with payn enlarged   8
   o faithfull mynde to sodenly assented
   retourn Alas sethens thou art not regarded
   to great a prouf of true faith presented
   causeth by right suche faith to be repented   12
O cruell causer of vndes^{9}ued chaunge
   by great desire vnconstantly to raunge
   is this yo^9 way for prouf of stedfastenes
   (perdy you knowe the thing was not so straunge   16
   by former prouff) to muche my faithfulnes
   what nedeth then suche coloured dowblenes
I have wailed thus weping in nyghtly payn
   in sobbes & sighes Alas & all in vayn   20
   in inward plaint & herte wofull torment
   and yet Alas lo crueltie & disdayn
   have set at noght a faithfull true intent
   and price hath priuilege trouth to prevent   24
But though I sterve & to my deth still morne
   and pece mele in peces though I be torn
   and though I dye yelding my weried goost

shall never thing again make me retorn̄
I qwite thentreprise of that that I have lost
to whome so ever lust for to proffer moost

E ff. 5v-6rv, hand A. *D* f. 2v (fragment). *B* f. 74r. Neither the *D* nor the *B* text
has any indication of authorship. Beneath the last line in *B* is "ffinis". The
quality of *D* and *B* can be compared on the basis of lines 13-30 only, which
reveal little superiority in either. Lines 1-12 in *B* show considerable corruption, including the smoothing out of the rhyme in line 8 not noted in *M3*. I
include the variant "myghtly" (l. 19) in *D* because *M3* incorrectly notes it as
"myghty".

G:

1. greiff] grei⟨f⟩fe,   smert] smert: 2. chaunce] chaunce,   shert] shert :
3. teres] téres: hote as fyer] hote, as fy/er :   4. cruell] cruell   long]
,long,   hert] hert. 5. and] and,   rewerd] rew/erd   o͡ɔ̃ desire] desire:
6. dowblenes /] dowblenes⟨/⟩ I]I,   hier] hier· 7. s⟩uis] s⟩uis: rewarded]
rewarded: 8. hert] hert,   enlarged] enlarged: 9. to] , too   assented]
assented: 10. retōurn Alas sethens] retōurn: Alas: sethens   regarded]
regarded 11. to] too   a prouf] à proofe 12. suche] such⟨e⟩   be repented]
be/ repented 13. causer of] causer of   chaunge] chaunge: 14. raunge]
raunge: 15. way] waye: prouf] proofe   stedfastenes] stedfastenes,
16. ⟨perdy] ⟨perdye   knowe] knowe: 17. faithfulnes] faithfulnes?
18. then suche] , then, such⟨e⟩   dowblenes] dowblenes? 19. I have] I have
thus] , thus,   payn] payn: 20. & sighes Alas] ,& sighes: Alas: vayn]
vayn: 21. plaint] plaint: torment] torment· 22. Alas lo crueltie] ,Alas,
lo, crueltie, 23. a] à   intent] intent: 24. trouth] tro⟨u⟩th   prevent]
prevént· 25. But] But,   sterve] sterve: morne] morne: 26. torn̄] torn̄:
27. dye yelding] dy⟨e⟩, y/elding   goost] go⟨o⟩ste: 30. moost] moost·

D B 1-12. *om. D.* 3. the sighes] sethes *B* 4. soked] stykyd *B* 6. have I]
I haue now *B* 7. ill] evyll *B* 8. enlarged] enlardyd *B* 9. to] so *B*
10. sethens] syns *B* 11. prouf] sorrowe *B* 12. repented] repeteyd *B om.*⁓
13. chaunge] chaunce *B* 14. raunge] rain *D* 16. you] I *D* ye *B*
19. thus] this *B* nyghtly] myghtly *D* 24. prevent] present *D*] p⟩sent *B*
25. sterve] s⟩ue *B* 26. mele] me *B* 28. retorn] to torne *B* 30. lust] liste
D] lyste *B*

6

But sethens you it asay to kyll
by crueltie & dowblenes
that that was yowers you seke to spill
against all right & gentilnes   4
and sethens you will even so I will

And then Helas when no redresse
   can be to late ye shall repent
   and say yo^rself with woorde expresse   8
Helas an hert of true intent
   slain have I by vnfaithfulnes

E f. 7r (fragment), hand A. One or more folios are missing at this point in E.
These lines occur nowhere else in manuscript or print. They were carefully
edited by G, as were the other lines on the opening folios of E. However, beneath them on the same side of the leaf, is a distinctly different and no doubt
later hand:

   I plede, and reason, my selffe emonge
   agaynst reason, howe I suffer
   but she that doethe me all the wronge
   I plede and reason my sealffe emonge

These words were untouched by G, probably because they were not in the
manuscript when he worked on it.

G: But] But,   asay] asaye   2. crueltie] crueltie,   dowblenes] dowblenes:

3. yowers] yowers,   seke] se/ke   spill] spill;   4. right] right,   gentilnes]
gentilnes: 5. you will] you will: I will] I will: 6. then Helas] ,then,
Helas,   7. be to late] bee: too late,   repent] repent: 8. say] saye   self]
self,   expresse] expresse: 9. Helas] Helas: 10. I] I,   vnfaithfulnes]
vnfaithfulnes·

7

Who so list to hounte I know where is an hynde
   but as for me helas I may no more
   the vayne travaill hath weried me so sore
I ame of theim that farthest cometh behinde   4
   yet may I by no meanes my weried mynde
   drawe from the Diere but as she fleeth afore
   faynting I folowe I leve of therefor
sethens in a nett I seke to hold the wynde   8
Who list her hount I put him owte of dowbte
   as well as I may spend his tyme in vain
   and graven with Diamonde in letters plain
There is written her faier neck rounde abowte   12
   Noli me tangere for Cesars I ame
   and wylde for to hold though I seme tame

E. f. 7v, hand A. A f. 63r. B f. 185r. The text in E was either not checked by
Wyatt or, if he did examine the work of hand A, he found it perfect and did

not leave his usual signature in the margin. Instead, the outer margin has the
name "Wyat" written in the same pen and ink as that used for a heading
"Sonet 2 ent⁾ ." to the poem: The same pen and ink classified as "Sonet ⟨2⟩
1 ent⁾ ." the stanza copied by *G* beneath Wyatt's sonnet. Thus, the person
who made this system of classifications in *E* must have worked after *G* had
edited the poems that interested him.

 G copied here the first stanza of Wyatt's *The restfull place*, which occurs
elsewhere in *D* and *T*. Since at least one folio is missing from *E* at this point,
it is likely that hand A had copied the poem here on a leaf now lost. Perhaps
G wished to illustrate *in extenso* his system of spelling and punctuation. *G*'s
specimen follows:

Too hiz bedde .

O restfull place : reneewer of my smart:
O laboorz salue: encreasing my sorowe:
O bodyez eaze: ô troobler of my hart:
Peazer of mynde: of myne unquyet fo:
Refuge of payene: remembrer of my wo:
Of care coomefort: where I dispayer my part:
The place of slepe: wherin, I doo but wake:

t
Bysprent w tearez, my bedde, I thee forsake·

G: 1. hounte] h⟨o⟩unt⟨e⟩:   know] know,   hynde] hynde·   2. but] but,

a
me helas] me: helas,   more] more·   3. sore] sore·   4. am⟨e⟩ of the⟨i⟩m, that
furdest cume
farthest cometh behinde·   5. yet may I] yet, may I,   meanes] meanes,
6. Diere] D⟨i⟩ere: 7. folowe] folowe·   therefor] therefore: 8. sethens]
sithens   a] à   wynde] wynde·   9. hount] h⟨o⟩unt: dowbte] dowbte:
10. as I], as I: vain] vain.   11. and] and,   Diamonde] Diamonde,   plain]
plain: 12. written] written,   abowte] abowte;   13. tangere] tangere:
ame] am⟨e⟩:   14. hold] holde: tame] tame·

A B: 1. an] a *B*   2. helas] alas *A B*   4. farthest] furthest *A*   cometh] come
A] cume *B*   5. fleeth] flyth *B*   7. leve] must leve *B*   8. sethens] sens *B*
9. her] to *A*   11. and graven] and grave *A*] Igravyn *B*   14. and . . . hold]
wyld to be caught *B*

8

O small hony much aloes & gall
   in bitternes have my blynde lyfe taisted
   his fals swetenes that torneth as a ball   24
   with the amourous dawnce have made me traced
   and where I had my thought & mynde ataced
   from all erthely frailnes & vain pleasur
   he toke me from rest and set me in errox   28
He hath made me regarde god muche lesse then I ought
   and to my self to take right litle heide
   and for a woman have I set at nought

all othre thoughte in this onely to spede   32
and he was onely counceillog of this dede
alwayes wheting my youthely desyere
on̄ the cruell whetstone tempered w th fier
But (helas) where nowe had I ever wit   36
or els any othre gift geven me of natur
that souner shall chaunge my weryed sprite
then the obstinate will that is my rueler
so robbeth my libertie with displeasur   40
this wicked traytog whom I thus accuse
that bitter liff have torned me in pleasaunt vse
He hath chased me thorough dyvers regions
thorough desert wode & sherp high mountaignes   44
thoroughe froward people & strait pressions
thorrough rocky sees over hilles & playnes
with wery travaill & labourous paynes
alwayes in trouble & in tediousnes   48
in all errour and daungerous distres
But nother he nor she my tother ffoo
for all my flyght did ever me forsake
that though tymely deth hath ben to sloo   52
that as yet it hath me not overtake
the hevynly goodenes of pitie do it shake
and not this his cruell extreme tyranny
that fedeth hym with my care & mysery   56
Syns I was his owre rested I never
nor loke for to do and eke the waky nyghte
the bannysshed slepe / may no wyse recouer
by decept and by force over my sprite   60
he is rueler and syns there never bell strike
where I ame that I here not my playnte to renew
and he himself he knoweth that that I say is true
ffor never wormes have an old stock eaten   64
as he my hert where he is alwaye resident
and doeth the same with deth daily thretyn
thens com̄ the teres and the bitter torment
the sighes the worde and eke the languisshem̄et 68
that annoye boeth me / and ₚaduentur othr
iudge thou that knowest thone & thothr

Myn aduersary with grevous reprouff
   thus he began here lady thothr part   72
   that the plain trueth from which he
              draweth a⟨loff⟩lowff
   this vnkynd man shall shew ⟨h⟩ere that I part
   in yonge age I toke him from that art
   that selleth worde and maketh a
          clattering knyght   76
   and of my welth / I gave him the delight
Now shameth he not on me ʌfor to complain
   that held him evermore in pleasaunt game
   from his desire that myght have ben his payne   80
   yet onely thereby \ I broght him to som frame
   which as wretchednes he doth greatly blame
   and towerd honos I qwickened his wit
   where els as a daskard he myght have sitt   84
He knoweth that Atrides that made Troye frete
   and Hannyball to Rome so trobelous
   whome Homere honoured Achilles that grete
   and the Affricane Scipion the famous   88
   and many othr by much vertue glorious
   whose fame and hono   did bryng theim above
   I did let fall in base dishonest love
And vnto him though he no dele worthy were   92
   I chose right the best of many a mylion
   that vnder the mone was never her pere
   of wisdome womanhode & discretion
   and of my grace I gave her suche a facon   96
   and eke suche away I taught her for to teche
   that never base thought his hert myght have reche
Evermore thus to content his maistres
   that was his onely frame of honeste   100
   I sterred him still towerd gentilnes
   and caused him to regard fidelitie
   patiens I taught him in aduersite
   suche vertues he lerned in my great schole   104
   wherof he repenteth the ignoraunt ffole
These were the decepte & the bitter gall
   that I have vsed the torment & the anger

sweter then for to inIoye eny othr in all   108
of right goode seed ill fruyte I gather
and so hath he that thunkynd doeth forther
I norisshe a Serpent vnger my wyng
and of his nature nowe gynneth he to styng   112
And for to tell at last my great sᴊuise
from thousand dishoneste I have him drawen
that by my meanes in no maner of wyse
never vile pleasur him hath overthrawen   116
where in his dede shame hath him alwaies gnawen
dowbting repoort that should com to her eere
whome now he accuseth he wounted to feere
What soever he hath of any honest custume   120
of her & me that holdeth he every wit
but lo there was never nyghtely fantome
so ferre in errour as he is from his wit
to plain on vs he stryveth with the bit   124
which may ruell him & do hym pleasur & payn
and in oon Oure make all his greif remayn
But oon thing there is above all othr
I gave him wynge wherew^th he myght fly   128
to honoᵍ & fame and if he would farther
by mortall thinge above the starry sky
considering the pleasur that an Iye
myght geve in erthe by reason of his love   132
what should that be that lasteth still above
And he the same himself hath sayed or this
but now forgotten is boeth that & I
that gave her him his onely welth & blisse   136
and at this worde with dedly shright & cry
thou gave her me ẝ I but by & by
thou toke her streight from me that wo worth the
not I ẝ he but price that is well worth   140
At last boeth eche for him self concluded
I trembling but he with small reverence
lo thus as we have nowe eche othr accused
dere lady we wayt onely thy sentence   144
she smyling after thissaid audience
it liketh me (ꝙ she) to have herd yoᵍ question
but lenger tyme doth aske resolution

E ff. 8r-10v (om. ll. 1-21), hand A. *A* f. 102rv (om. ll. 80-147). *T* 64. The *E* text was elaborately edited by *G*, some of whose changes show up in *T*, notably those listed as variants for line 54. In many other instances, however, *T* reflects emendations recorded in *A* and having no relation to *G*'s changes in *E*. Note, for example, the variants for lines 23, 25, 28, 29, 34, 40, 61, 62, 63, and 64, to cite only about half the important instances in which *G*'s punctuation was superceded by recasting a phrase or most of the line.

The variants for the word "through" are listed here to show that *T* is not quite so consistent in spelling as noted in *M3*, especially in lines 43-45. According to Rollins, *T* printed "thorough" (l. 43), following *E* exactly, although in lines 44 and 45 *T* follows the spelling of *A* without the final "e." The variants for lines 125 and 132 were not listed in *M3*.

G: 22. hony] hony: aloes & gall] aloes, & gall,   23. bitternes] bitternes,   24. swetenes: that torneth, as à ball   25. dawnce] dawnce, traced] traced·   26. thought] thought,   ataced] ataced,   27. frailnes] frailnes,   pleasur] pleasur: 28. rest] rest: erroᵍ] erroᵍ·   29. god] god, ought] ought: 30. heede] heede: 31. and] and,   woman] woman, 32. thoughte] thoughte;   spede] spede·   33. dede] dede: 34. always wheting] alwayes, whetting   35. whetstone] whetstone;   36. (helas) where
nowe] (h͟e͟las) where, nowe,   wit] wit?   37. nature] nature?   38. sprite] sprite: 39. will] will: rueler] r͟u͟eler·   40. libertie] libertie,   displeasur] displeasure,   41. traytoᵍ] traytoᵍ·   accuse] accuse: 42. liff] liffe 43. me] me,   regions] regions: 44. wode] wode;   mountaignes] mountaignes: 45. . . . people: & straite pressions: 46. sees] sees: hilles & playnes] hilles, & playnes: 48. trouble] trouble,   tediousnes] tediousnes: 49. errour] errour,   50. nor she] ,nor she,   ffoo] ffoo,   51. flyght] flyght, forsake] forsake: 52. slo] slo: 53. as yet] ,as yet,   overtake] overtake:
54. goodenes of pitie] g͟o͟o͟denes, of pitie,   shake] s͟(͟h͟)͟ake slake·   55. not] note   tyranny] tyranny: 56. fedeth hym] feedeth hym,   & mysery] ,& mysery·   57. his] his: never] never: 58. do and eke] do: and, eke, 59. slepe /] slepe⟨/⟩   recouer] recouer·   60. decept] decepte,   61. rueler] rueler: strike] strike: 62. ame] am⟨e⟩:   not] not: renew] renewe 63. himself he knoweth] himself, hee knoweth: say is true] saye, is true· 64. old stock eaten] olde stocke eaten: 65. hert] hert: resident] resident: 66. thretyn] thretyn·   67. teres] teres: torment] torment: 68. the sighes: the worde: and eke, the languisshemet: 69. me / and] me, / and, 70. thou] thou,   thone & thothr] thone, & thothre   71. aduersary] aduersary,   reprouff] reprouff,   72. . . . began: here lady   thothr part 73. trueth] trueth,   lowff] lowff: 74. shew] shew: part] part.   75. age] age,   art] art: 76. worde] worde: a] à   77. welth /] welth⟨/⟩   delight] delight·   78. Now] Nowe,   complain] complain·   79. game] game· 80. desire] desire,   payne] payne: 81. frame] frame: 82. as wretchednes] ,as wretchednes,   blame] blame: 83. wit] wit: 84. as a daskard] ,as a daskard,   sitt] sitt·   85. that Atrides] :that Atrides,   frete] frete: 86. Hannyball] Hannyball,   trobelous] trobelous: 87. honoured] honoured,   grete] grete: 88. Scipion the famous] Scipion, the famous: 89. othr] othr,   glorious] glorious: 90. fame] fame,   above] above: 91. fall] fall,   love] love·   92. him] him,   were] were: 93. a mylion] à mylion: 94. that] that,   mone] mo/ne,   pere] pere: 95. womanhode] ,womanhode,   discretion] discretion: 96. suche a facon] such⟨e⟩à facon: 97. teche] teche: 98. reche] reche·   99. thus] ,thus,   maistres] maistres:

100. honeste] honeste·   101. still] ,still,   gentilnes] gentilnes:
102. fidelitie] fidelitie   103. aduersite] aduersite·   104. lerned] lerned,
schole] sch/ole: 105. repenteth] repenteth,   ffole] ffo/le   106. decepte]
decepte, gall] gall: 107. . . . vsed: the torment, & the anger:
108. sweter] sweter,   109. gather] gather·   110. he] he: thunkynd doeth
forther] thunkynde doeth forther·   111. a] à   vnger] vnger   wyng] wyng:
112. and] and,   nature nowe] nature, now⟨e⟩,   styng] styng·   113. And]
And,   at last] ,at last,   s⟩uise] s⟩uise: 114. drawen] drawen: 115. that]
that,   meanes] meanes,   wyse] wyse,   116. overthrawen] overthrawen·
117. where] where,   dede] dede,   118. repoort] repo⟨o⟩rte: should com]
shoulde com   eare] eare·   119. now he accuseth] ,now, he accuseth:
feere] feere·   120. custume] custume: 121. & me] ,& me,   122. lo] ,lo,
123. errour] errour: wit] wit·   124. vs] vs: bit] bit: 125. him] him:
& payn] ,& payn: 126. in oon] ,in oon   greif remayn] greefe remayne
127. But] But,   is] is,   othr] othr: 129. & fame] ,& fame: farther]
farther,   130. sky] sky: 131. pleasur] pleasure: 132. erthe] erthe:
love] love: 133. be] be,   above] above·   134. or this] ,or this·   135. & I]
,& I: 136. him] him: & blisse] ,& blisse·   137. and] and,   worde]
worde,   & cry] ,& cry: 138. . . . me: I: but, by, & by,   139. me] me:
the] thee   140. not I: he: but price: . . . worth   141. . . . :boeth, . . . self,
concluded: 142. I, trembling: but, he,   143. lo thus] lo, thus,   nowe]
now⟨e⟩,   othr] othr,   144. dere lady: we wayte . . . sentence   145. smyling]
smyling: 146. question] question: 147. but] but,   resolution] resolution·

A T   1-21. om.] A T   3. our om. A] T   22. O] So A T   23. have . . .
taisted] my blynde Lif hath ytasted A T   24. swetenes] semblaunce A T
25. the] faire and A T   have made me] made me be A T   26. ataced]
araced A T   27. from all] from A T   &] and from A T   28. he . . . rest]
Me from my rest he toke A T   set me] sett A T   29. He . . . lesse] God
made he me regard, lesse A T   30. take right] take A   34. alwayes wheting]
Whetting all wayes A T   desyere] frayle desyre A T   35. on the] On A T
36. But] But oh A T   where nowe] wheare A T   37. or els any] Or A T
geven] geuen to T   38. chaunge] be chaunged A T   40. my libertie] he my
freedome A T   42. have torned me] hath turned A T   43. chased me] me
hasted A T   44. thorough] throughe A T   45. thoroughe] Throughe A T
strait pressions] through bitter passions A T   46. thorrough] Throughe A T
over] and over A T   47. &] and with A T   49. in all] All in A T
52. though] thoughe my A T   53. as] me as A T   hath me] hath T
54. goodenes] Godds em. G] gods A] goddes T   shake] slake em. G A T
55. not] note em. G] note they A T   cruell extreme] cruell A T
56. fedeth] feedes A T   57. owre] hower A T   58. for to] to A T   59. no]
in no A T   60. decept] guyle A T   and by] and A T   my] my thralled A T
61. and . . . strik] / syns whiche bell never strykes A T   62. That I heare not,
as sownding to renewe A T   63. My playntes / hym self, he knowes, that I
say true A] . . . knoweth . . . T   64. have an old stock] olde rotten stocke
have A T   65. is alwaye] is A T   67. and] / and thence A T   69. annoye]
noye A T   70. thone & thothr] the one and eke the tother A T
71. aduersary] aduersair T   with] with suche A T   72. thothr] thother A T
73. trueth] trothe A T   74. this] Thus A   shall shew ⟨h⟩ere] may shew / err
A T   75. in] In his A T   76. maketh] makes A T   77. my] the A T
78. shameth] shames A T   79. game] gayne A T   80-147. om.   81. onely
thereby] therby alone T   82. as] now, as T   greately] so T

83. I qwicken] quickned I *T*   84. where . . . myght] Where:as a daskard els
he mought *T*   85. that Atrides] how grete Atride *T*   88. the Affricane]
Thaffricane *T*   89. vertue] nurture *T*   92. no dere worthy] vnworthy *T*
93. right the] the *T*   94. the mone was never] sonne yet neuer was *T*
95. &] and of *T*   97. away] way *T*   98. myght have reche] so hye might
reche *T*   101. sterred] stirred *T*   102. caused] causde *T*   104. he lerned]
learned, he *T*   105. he repenteth] repenteth, now *T*   106. the decepte &
the] the same deceites, and *T*   108. for . . . all] euer dyd to other fall *T*
109. I] loe thus I *T*   110. hath] shall *T*   thunkynd] the vnkinde *T*   I . . .
Serpent] A Serpent nourish I *T*   vnger] under *corr. G*   112. of . . .
nowe] now of nature *T*   114. I have] haue I *T*   115. in . . . of] him in no
maner *T*   116. him] once *T*   119. accuseth he wounted] blames, her
wonted he *T*   120. soever] euer *T*   121. holdeth] holdes *T*   122. there was
never] yet neuer was there *T*   125. pleasur] ease *T*   126. Oure] hower *T*
remayn] his gayn *T*   127. there] yet there *T*   128. fly] vpflie *T*
129. farther] to higher *T*   130. by] Than *T*   132. his] the *T*   133. or] ere
T   137. shright] shreke *T*   138. me] once *T*   139. streight] ayen *T*
140. ghe . . . worth] but price : more worth than thou (quod he.) *T*
141. boeth eche] eche other *T*   142. trembling] trembling still *T*   143. have
. . . othr] eche other haue *T*   144. we . . . thy] now we waite thyne onely *T*
145. after thissaid] at the whisted *T*   147. aske] ask a *T*

9

Was I never yet of yo^9 love greved
    nor never shall while that my liff doeth last
    but of hating myself that date is past
    and teeres continuell sore have me weried   4
I will not yet in my grave be buried
    nor on my tombe yo^9 name yfixed fast
    as cruell cause that did the sperit son hast
    ffrom thunhappy bonys by great sighes sterred   8
Then if an hert of amourous faith & will
    may content you withoute doyng greiff
    please it you so to this to do releiff
    yf othre wise ye seke for to fulfill   12
    yo^9 disdain ye erre & shall not as ye wene
    and ye yo^9 self / the cause therof hath ben

E f. 11r, hand A. *A* f. 63r. *T* 38. Hughey (II, 131-132) illustrated the emendations of *G* in *E* and traced their effect on *A* and *T*. The copyist of *A* was sensitive to *G*'s revisions of spelling but not his punctuation. I have minor disagreements with Hughey about *G*'s work. Hughey omitted the full stop added by
G to the last word. I am also quite sure that *G* placed a full stop at the end of
line 8.

G: 1. yet] ,yet,   greved] gre^{e}ved: 2. shall] shall: liff] liffe   last]
last: 3. but] but,   past] past: 4. weried] weried·   5. buried] buried;

6. fast] fast: 7. cause] cause,   8. bonys] bon⟨y⟩s: sterred] sterred·
9. Then] Then,   amourous] amo⟨u⟩rous   & will] ,& will,   10. you] you:
greiff] greefe: 11. so] so,   do releiff] doo releeffe·   12. yf othre wise] yf,
othre wise,   13. disdain ye erre] disdain: ye erre: not] not,   wene] we/ne:
ye^{ow} ben] be/ñe·   ben] be/ñe· ^{beene·}

A T: 1. Was . . . yet] Yet was I neuer *T*   2. greved] yet greevid *A*] agreued
T   6. yfixed] haue fixed *T*   7. the sperit] the spirite *A*] my sprite *T*
9. may . . . withoute] Content your minde withouten *T*   12. ye] you *T*
13. disdain] wrath *T*   ye . . . ye] you . . . you *T*   14. ye] you *A T*   hath]
haue *T*

10

> Eche man me telleth I chaunge moost my devise
>> and on my faith me thinck it goode reason
>> to chaunge propose like after the season
>> ffor in every cas to kepe still oon gyse   4

Tho   ys mytt for theim that would be taken wyse
>> and I ame not of suche maner condition
>> but treted after a dyvers fasshion
>> and therupon my dyvernes doeth rise   8
> but you that blame this dyvernes moost
>> chaunge you no more but still after oon rate
>> trete ye me well & kepe ye in thesame state
>> And while with me doeth dwell this weried goost   12
>> my word nor I shall not be variable
>> but alwaies oon yor owne boeth ferme & stable

E f. 11v, hand A. *A* f. 63v. *D* f. 75v. *T*46. The *D* text is subscribed merely "fs".
It also includes six variants, which look simply like corruptions. Wyatt's signature "Tho" appears reassuringly in the outer margin of the leaf in *E*. The
reading "word" (l. 13) was accepted in *M3*, whereas *M2* had read "wordes."
In this instance hand A did add a downward hook to the final "d," but it was
not the sign for "es." Two ghosts were perpetuated in *M3* for *A*: the variants
for "now" (l. 13) and "you" (l. 14) But *A* clearly reads "nor" (l. 13) and
"your" (l. 14).

A D T: 1. me telleth] telle me *D*] me telth *T*   moost] of *D*   3. propose]
purpose *A T*] po^r pos *D*   like] even *D*   4. every] ech *T*   7. after a] after /
aft' a *D*   8. dyvernes] dyversnes *A D T*   9. that . . . dyvernes] that . . .
dyversnes *A D*] this diuersnesse that blamen *T*   11. ye me] you me *T*   ye
in the same] ye y same *D*] you in that *T*   13. word] wod^reD   not] never *D*
14. oon] as *D*

11

ffarewell the rayn of crueltie
                t
   though that w pain my libertie
   dere have I boght yet shall surete
   conduyt my thoght of Ioyes nede   4
Of force I must forsake pleasure
   agoode cause iust syns I endure
   thereby my woo which be ye sure
            th
   shall therew goo me to recure   8
I fare as oon escaped that fleith
   glad that is gone yet still fereth
   spied to be cawght and so dredeth
   that he for nought his pain leseth   12
In ioyfull Pain reioyse myn hert
   thus to sustain / of eche apt
   let not this song from the estert
   welcom emong my plaisaunt smert   16

E f. 12r, hand A. *T* 61. In this instance   *G*'s inking is much like that of the
scribe, which suggests that he returned to work on *E* after at least one break.

G: 3. boght] boght· 7. woo] woo· 11. cawght] cawght:

T: 1. rayn] hart 3. yet shall surete] and wofully 4. Finisht my fearfull
tragedy 5. pleasure] such pleasure 10. that] he yet] and yet 14. apt]
a part

12

Yf amours faith an hert vnfayned
   a swete languo⁹ a great lovely desir
   yf honest will kyndelled in gentill fier
Wyat   yf long erro⁹ in a blynde maze chayned   4
yf in my visage eche thought depaynted
   or els in my sperklyng voyse lower or higher
   which nowe fere nowe shame wofully doth tyer
   yf a pale colour which love hath stayned   8
yf to have an othre then my self more dere
   yf wailing & sighting continuelly
   th
   w sorrowfull anger feding bissely

yf burning a farre of and fresing nere   12
ar cause that by love my self I distroye
yours is the fault & myn the great annoye

E f. 12v, hand A. *A* f. 65r. *T*98. The heavy deletion and overwriting of the *E*
text has led to minor disagreements among editors. I agree with *M2* that line
10 has "&" rather than "or" (*A T*), and that the first word in line 13 is "ar."

G: 12. of] of:

A T: 1. amours] amorous *A T*   an] or if an *T*   5. depaynted] distayned *T*
6. els in] if *T*   7. nowe . . . shame] fear and shame, so *T*   8. a] *om. T*
love] loue alas *T*   10. &] or *A T*   sighting] Sighing *A T*   12. farre] fall *A*
13. ar] or *A*   distroye] stroy *T*

13

ffarewell Love and all thy lawes for ever
thy bayted hooke shall tangill me no more
Senec and Plato call me from thy lore
to ℘faict welth my wit for to endever   4
In blynde erroᵍ when I did ℘seuer

Tho.   thy sherpe repulce that pricketh ay so sore
hath taught me to sett in tryfels no store
and scape fourth syns libertie is lever   8
Therefore farewell goo trouble yonger herte
and in me clayme no more authoritie
with idill yeuth goo vse thy ℘pertie
And theron spend thy many britill derte   12
                                    lost
for hetherto though I have ⟨spend⟩ all my tyme
me lusteth no lenger rotten boughes to clyme

E f. 13r, hand A. *A* f. 65v. *D* f. 75r. *T* 99. The text in *D* is subscribed "fs", and
the numerous variants suggest corruption. The difficulty of reading the *D*
text has produced at least one ghost variant and one error. Hughey (II, 140)
read "when last" (l. 5), which should be "whylist." Again Hughey reads
"longe & rottyn (l. 14) where the scribe wrote "lengre ⟨b⟩ rottyn", antici-
pating the word "bowes" to follow. Both these readings are repeated in *M3*.
The variant listed in *M3* for *E* in line 11 does not exist.

A D T 1. ffarewell . . . thy] Nowe fare well love and thye *D*   3. Senec . . .
call] to sore a profe hathe called *D*   4. to . . . to] to surer ⟨selthe⟩ welthe
my wyttis to *D*   5. when] whylist *D*   6. ay] *om. D*   7. hath . . . store]
Taught me in trifles that I set no store *T*   8. and] but *D T*   sysn] for *D*]
thence: since *T*   12. theron] therevpon go *D*   many] *om. D*   13. though]
om. D   all] *om. D T*   14. lusteth] liste *D T*

14

Wyat

My hert I gave the not to do it payn
but to presʃue it was to the taken
I sʃued the not to be forsaken
but that I should be rewarded again   4

                        a
I was content thy sʃunt to remain
but not to be payed vnder this fasshion
nowe syns in the is none othre reason
displease the not if that I do refrain   8
Vnsaciat of my woo and thy desire
assured be craft to excuse thy fault
but syns it please the to fain a default
farewell I say ꝑting from the fyer   12
for he that beleveth bering in hand
[   ] weth in the sand

E f. 13v hand A. *A* f. 65v. *D* ff. 3r (*D1*), 75v (*D2*). *T* 100. The lower left corner of the leaf in *E* is torn away. In *D* are two versions, both incomplete. The
first is recorded in two hands, but the completing hand failed to include lines
10-11. On the inner margin of f. 3r, on a level with the first word of the text,
is a large terminal "s" (ꝋ), of the style that appears elsewhere in *D* but usually
after the sign "fs". The second version in *D* omits line 11. Beneath the last
line on f. 75v is written only "fs".

A D T: 2. it . . . the] ⟨was⟩yt was to the *D1*] lo it to thee was *T*   3. to be]
that I should be *T*   4. be rewarded] recieue reward *T*   5. thy sʃunt]
they slave *D1*   6. this] suche *D1 D2*   And, not to be repayd after this fashion
                                  t
T   7. nowe syns] no sens *A*] now sins y *D2*   none othre] no maner of
D1] there none nother *T*   8. displease] De Displease *D1*   if that I] tho y
D1   refrain] restraine *D2*   9. thy] my *D1*   10. *om. D1*   be] by *A D2 T*
to excuse] texcuse *D2*] for to excuse *T*   11. *om. D1 D2*   please] pleaseth
T   a] *om. T*   12. ꝑting] departing *T*   the] this *A*   13. beleveth] beleves
D1] doth beleue *T*   14. [   ] weth in the sand] Plowithe in water and sowith
in sand *A D2*] Ploweth in the water: and soweth in the sand *T*] ploues in the
water and sows in the sand *D1*

15

ffor to love her for her loke lovely
my hert was set in thought right fermely
trusting by trought to have had redresse
but she hath made an othre ꝑmese   4

and hath geven me leve full honestly
yet do I not reioyse it greatly
for on my faith I loved to surely
but reason will that I do sesse   8
     for to love her
Syns that in love the paynes ben dedly
me thincke it best that reddely
I do retorn to my first adresse   12
for at this tyme to great is the prese
and ᵽilles appere to abundauntely
     ffor to love her

E f. 14r. *D* f. 75r. The *D* text is complete but has no subscription.

D:
   3. trought] ⟨tusthe[?]⟩ trouthe   redresse] ⟨releffe⟩ & redresse   4. an othre] anodre   6. reioyse] refuse   7. to] so   8. will] woll   sesse] leesse   10. ben] be   11. thincke] thincke   14. ᵽilles] parells

16

There Was never ffile half so well filed
to file a file for every smythes intent
as I was made a filing instrument
to frame othre while I was begiled   4
But reason hath at my follie smyled
Tho.   and ᵽdon me syns that I me repent
of my lost yeres & tyme myspent
for yeuth did me lede & falshode guyded   8
Yet this trust I have of full great aᵽaunce
syns that decept is ay retourneable
of very force it is aggreable
that therew all be done the recompence   12
then gile begiled plained should be never
and the reward litle trust for ever /

E f. 14v, hand A. *A* ff. 60v (*A1*), 65v (*A2*). *D* f. 19v. *B* f. 174r. *T* 39. The *E* text is signed "Tho." in the outer margin. It was revised by the same hand that entered the "Wyat" designations on f. 15v and elsewhere and the name "Petrarke" at the top of f. 22v, as the inking clearly shows. The revisions of *E* were "⟨every⟩" (l. 2), "othr⟩s" (l. 4), and "ᵽdond" (l. 6).
    The *D* text is headed "To my [*blank*]" and subscribed "ffynyss".
Hughey (II, 142), following Foxwell, read the s as "tv" interlaced, as if it

D: 1. that] that eke   2. reason] good reason   3. for as the *ρ*verbe
saithe right notable   4. eche] everye   5. thy] thy owne   6. on] vppon
7. nor] nother   of myn] is my   8. thyn] thi   is] is thus   10. thought]
demid   11. fasshion] fasten   mutable] so dobtable

20

Goo burnyng si͡ghes Vnto the frosen hert
   goo breke the Ise with pite paynfull dert

Wyat   my͡ght never perse and if mortall prayer
   in hevyn may be herd at lest I desir   4
   that de͡th or mercy be ende of my smert
       th
Take w the payn wherof I have my *ρ*t
   and eke the flame from whi͡ch I cannot stert
   and leve me then in rest I you require   8
      Goo burning si͡ghes
I must goo worke I se by craft & art
   for true͡th & fai͡th in her is laide a*ρ*t
   Alas I cannot therefor assaill her   12
   wi͡th pitefull plaint & scalding fyer
   that oute of my brest doe͡th straynably stert
      Goo burning si͡ghes

E f. 16v, hand A. *D* f. 61v. *T* 103. Beneath the last line of the *D* text is
"finis". In *T* this rondeau was changed into a kind of sonnet, as were poems
1 and 2. The *E* text has one correction and punctuation by the same hand
that copied the verses on the lower half of f. 24v. These are: 2 with pite]
   whiche
⟨with⟩ pites   3. perse] perse: 4 herd] herd: Although the colons are not
certain, they were probably entered by the same hand that corrected line 2.
Wyatt did not personally check this text.

D T:
           t
     2. with pite] w piteus *D*] which pities *T*   3. if] yf that *T*   4. may . . .
I] be herd, at lest yet I *T*   5. be . . . my] end my wofull *T*   6. the] you *D*]
thee *T*   9. *T adds* fulfil that I desire   13. plaint] complaint *T*   14. That
from my brest disceiuably doth start *T*   15. om. *T*

21

It may be good like it who list
   but I do dowbt who can me blame
   for oft assured yet have I myst
   and now again I fere thesame   4

The wyndy worde the Ies quaynt game
of soden chaunge maketh me agast
for dred to fall I stond not fast
Alas I tred an endles maze   8
that seketh to accorde two contraries
and hope still & nothing hase
imprisoned in liberte
as oon vnhard & still that cries   12
alwaies thursty & yet nothing I tast
for dred to fall I stond not fast
Assured I dowbt I be not sure
and should I trust to suche suretie   16
that oft hath put the prouff in vre
and never hath founde it trusty
nay sir In faith it were great foly
and yet my liff thus I do wast   20
for dred to fall I stond not fast

E f. 17r, hand A. *B* f. 98r. *T* 58. I cannot find the "Wyat" noted for *E* in
M3.

B T: 1. It] Hit *B throughout*   3. for ofte as sure I haue hit myste *B*   5. The
wordes, that from your mouth last came *T*   Ies] yeche *B*   6. maketh]
makes *B*] make *T*   8. an] a *B*   9. seketh . . . two] seeke to accorde to *B*]
seke taccord two *T*   10. hope] hopith *B*] hope thus *T*   nothing] naught
elke *B*   13. yet nothing I] yet naught *B*] naught doth *T*   16. and . . . to]
Should I then trust vnto *T*   17. hath] haue *T*   18. hath founde] yet proved
B] yet haue *T*   19. great] but *B*   20. I do] doo I *B T*   21. I] that *B*

22

Resound my voyse ye wode that here me plain
    boeth hilles and vales causing reflexion
    and Ryvers eke record ye of my pain
Wyat   which have ye oft forced by compassion   4
    as Iudges to here myn exclamation
    emong whome pitie I fynde doeth remayn
    where I it seke Alas there is disdain
Oft ye Revers to here my wofull sounde   8
    have stopt yo^g course and plainly to expresse
    many a tere by moysto^g of the grounde

the erth hath wept to here my hevenes
   which causeles to suffre without redresse   12
   the howgy oke have rored in the wynde
   eche thing me thought coplayning in their kynde
Why then helas doeth not she on me rew
   or is her hert so herd that no pitie   16
   may in it synke my Ioye for to renew?
O stony hert ho hath this Ioyned the
   so cruell that art cloked with beaultie
   no grace to me from the there may procede   20
   but as rewarded deth for to be my mede

E f. 17v, hand A. D f. 72r. T 59. The D text is subscribed "fs:s". Three
colons were inserted in the E text, after "Revers" (l. 8), "course" (l. 9), and
"art" (l. 19). They are probably by the same hand that wrote "Wyat" in
the margin.

D T: 1. here] herithe D   2. vales causing] valeis causers of D   3. record
ye] record⟨er o⟩ye D   4. have . . . forced] hathe . . forced D] haue oft
forced ye T   5. to] lo to T   6. pitie I fynde] I finde pitye D] such (I finde)
yet T   7. seke] sought D   9. to expresse] texpresse D __10. a tere] atree D
12. to suffre] I endure T   14. coplayning in their] movig in the D   17.
Ioye] Ioyes D   18. O stony hert] o⟨s⟩ tygres herte D   this Ioyned] so
clokid D] thus framed T   19. so . . . cloked] that arte so cruell / cou⟩ d D
20. no . . . may] there is no grace frō the that maye D] That from thee may
no grace to me T   21. rewarded] rewarde D T

23

In faith I wot not well what to say
   thy chaunces ben so wonderous
   thou fortune with thy dyvers play
   that causeth Ioyful dolours   4
   and eke thesame right Ioyus
   yet though thy chayn hathe me enwrapt
   spite of thy hap hap hath well hapt
Though thou me set for a Wounder   8
   and sekest thy chaunge to do me payn
Tho.   mens mynde yet may thou not order
   and honeste & it remayn
   shall shyne for all thy clowdy rayn   12
   in vayn thou sekest to have trapped
   spite of thy hap hap hath well happed

In hindering thou diddest fourther
and made a gap where was a stile   16
cruell willes ben oft put vnder
wenyng to lowre thou diddist smyle
lorde how thy self thou diddist begile
that in thy cares wouldest me have lapped   20
but spite of thy hap hap ⟨hap⟩ hath well happed

E f. 19r, hand A. *T* 60. In *E* are three instances of inserted virgules, thus:
"/ hap / hap" (l. 7), "hap / hap /" (l. 14), and "/ hap /⟨hap⟩" (l. 21). These
do not sufficiently match either hand A or "Tho." signed by Wyatt in the
margin.

T: 1. well] om.   4. causes] makst the   dolours] dolourous   8. me set]
hast set me   9. thy] by   10. may thou not] mayst thou not so   11. and]
For   &] if   13. trapped] me trapt   15. thou diddest] me, me didst thou
18. lowre thou diddist] lower, then didst thou   20. lapped] wrapt

24

Som fowles ther*e* be that have so ρfaict sight
agayn the Sonne their Iyes for to defend
and som bicause the light doeth theim offend
do never pere but in the darke or nyght   4
Wyat   Other reioyse that se the fyer bright
and wene to play in it as they do pretend
and fynde the contrary of it that they intend
Alas of that sort I may be by right   8
for to withstond her loke I ame not able

and yet can I not hide me in no darke place
remembraunce so foloweth me of that face
so that with tery yen swolne & vnstable   12
my destyne to behold her doeth me lede
yet do I knowe I run into the glede

E f. 19v, hand A. *A* f. 66r. *T* 47. The single correction in line 8 of *A* made
it a perfect copy, in substance, of *E*. The fact is striking because of the
metrical intricacy of the *E* text, involving many monosyllables.

A T: 2. agayn] Against *T*   4. do never pere] Neuer appeare *T*   5 that]
to *T*   fyer] fire so *T*   6. do] om. *T*   7. and fynde the] But find *T*   8. I
may] may I *T*   by] ⟨of⟩by *A*   10. and yet] Yet *T*   11. remembraunce . . .
me] So foloweth me remembrance *T*   12. so . . . tery] That with my
teary *T*   14. yet do] And yet *T*

25

Bicause I have the still kept fro lyes & blame
  and to my power alwaies have I the honoured
  vnkynd tong right ill hast thou me rendred
  for suche deserft to do me wrek & shame   4

Wyat   In nede of succoꝰ moost when that I ame
  to aske reward then standest thou like oon aferd
  alway moost cold & if thou speke towerd
  it is as in dreme vnꝑfaict & lame   8
And ye salt teres again my will eche nyght
  that are with me when fayn I would be alone
  then are ye gone when I should make my mone
And you so reddy sighes to make me shright   12
  then are ye slake when that ye should owtestert
  and onely my loke declareth my hert

E f. 20r, hand A. A f. 66rv. T 48. In E is one revision by a later hand:
   k
"(t)owerd" (l. 7). This appears to be the work of the hand of the specimen
on the lower half of f. 24v.

A T: 1. have the still] still kept thee T   2. alwaies have I] alwaies have A]
alwayes T   3. right ill] right well A] to yll T   6. then . . . like] then . . . as
A]: thou standst like T   7. if . . . towerd] if . . . aworde A] if one word be
sayd T   8. as in ... .] in a . . . A] As in a dreame, vnperfit is the same T
9. again] agaynst A T   10. fayn] om. T   12. you] ye T   14. my loke]
my Love A] doth my loke T   declareth] declare T

26

I fynde no peace and all my warr is done
  I fere & hope I burn & freise like yse
  I fley above the wynde yet can I not arrise
  and noght I have & all the worold I seson   4
Wyat   That loseth nor locketh holdeth me in prison
  and holdeth me not yet can I scape no wise
  nor letteth me lyve nor dye at my devise
  and yet of deth it gyveth me occasion   8
Withoute Iyen I se & withoute tong I plain
  Idesire to ꝑisshe and yet I aske helthe
  I love an othre and thus I hate my self

I fede me in sorrowe & laught in all my pain   12
likewise displeaseth me boeth lyff & deth
and my delite is causer of this stryff

E f. 20v, hand A. D f. 82rv. P f. 32r. T 49. The D text is subscribed "fs."
The P text is headed "Pace non trouo" in italic script. The E text is headed
"petrarke," probably by the same hand that inserted three colons, after
"se" (l. 9), "pisshe" (l. 10), and "othre" (l. 11). The final "t" on "laught"
(l. 12) is probably a scribal error for the final "e", since there is no preter-
ite tense in the Italian source.

D P T: 3. above the wynde] aboute the heaven D] aloft T   can I not arrise]
can not ryse P   4. and] yet P   5. loseth nor locketh] loosithe⟨and⟩ₐlockithe
D] lockes nor loseth T   holdeth] holdᷔP   6. holdeth] holdᷔ P T   scape]
escape P   7. letteth] letᷔ P T   8. me occasion] me⟨necassyon[?]⟩ occasion
D] none occasion P   9. Iyen] yes D] eye P T   se &] se, T   10. desire]
wish T   and yet I aske] yet aske I P] , yet I aske for T   11. thus I hate]
yet I have P   12. me] om. P   laught] lawghe D P T   13. likewise] Lo,
thus T   displeaseth] pleaseth P   lyff & deth] deth and lyf D P T   14. this
stryff] my gryef P

27

Though I my self be bridilled of my mynde
retorning me backewerd by force expresse
if thou seke honoᷓ to kepe thy promes
who may the hold my hert but th⟨y⟩ou thy self
                        vnbynd   4
Sigh then no more syns no way man may fynde
thy vertue to let though that frowerdnes
Tho.   of ffortune me holdeth and yet as I may gesse
                though othr be present thou art not all behinde   8
Suffice it then that thou be redy there
at all howres still vnder the defence
of tyme trouth & love to save the from offence
Cryeng I burne in a lovely desire   12
with my dere maisteres that may not followe
whereby his absence torneth him to sorrowe

E f. 21r, hand A. A f. 66v. A later hand inserted four colons into the E
text, after "let" (l. 6), "holdeth" (l. 7), "present" (l. 8), and "maisteres"
(l. 13). I take "maisteres" to mean "master's" rather than "mistress." The
single variant in the A text is therefore a misinterpretation.

A: 13. maisteres] mystres

28

My galy charged with forgetfulnes
 thorrough sharpe sees in wynter nyghte doeth pas
 twene Rock and Rock & eke myn ennemy Alas
 that is my lorde sterith with cruelnes   4
Wyat And every owre a thought in redines
 as tho that deth were light in suche a case
 an endles wynd doeth tere the sayll a pase
 of forced sighte and trusty ferefulnes   8
 A rayn of teris a clowde of derk disdain
 hath done the wered corde great hinderaunce
    th
 wret⟨c⟩hed w erro⁾ & eke with ignoraunce
The starres be hid that led me to this pain   12
 drowned is reason that should me confort
 and I remain dispering of the port

E f. 21v, hand A. *A* f. 66v. *T* 50.

A T: 2. thorrough] throughe *A T* 3. myn ennemy] my fo *T* 4. sterith]
stirreth *A* 5. owre] houre *A T* 6. light] ⟨light⟩*A* 8. sighte] ⟨sighte⟩*A*
10. hath] Haue *T* 11. and eke] ,and *T* 12. led] leade *T* 13. drowned]
Drownde *T* me confort] me compforte *A*] be my comfort *T*

29

Auysing the bright bemes of these fayer Iyes
 where he is that myn oft moisteth & wassheth
 the werid mynde streght from the hert depteth
 for to rest in his woroldly padise   4
And fynde the swete bitter vnder this gyse
Wyat what webbe he hath wrought well he pceveth
 whereby with himself on love he playneth
    th
 that spurreth with fyer and bridilleth w Ise 8
Thus is it in suche extremitie brought
 in frossen though nowe and nowe it stondeth in flame
 twyst misery and welth twist ernest & game
 But few glad and many dyvers thought   12
 with sore repentaunce of his hardines
 of suche a rote cometh ffruyte fruytles

E f. 22r, hand A. *A* f. 67r. *T* 51. The *E* text shows one colon inserted by a later hand, after "fyer" (l. 8). The scribal error "though" for "thought" (l. 10), is followed exactly in *A*. The *A* text is also slightly more accurate than indicated by Hughey (II, 146), who created a ghost variant out of the change from "webbe" (l. 6) in *E* to "webbs" in *A*. Here Hughey read "webb," which was picked up in *M3*.

A T: 1. Auysing] Advysing *A*   these] those *T*   2. is] abides *T*   moisteth] moistes *T*   3. depteth] parteth *A*   4. for] *om. T*   in] within *T*   woroldly] worldlye *A T*   5. And . . . bitter] And bitter findes the swete *T*   6. he] there he *T*   7. whereby] Wherby then *T*   8. spurreth] spurs *T*   bridilleth] brydleth eke *T*   9. In such extremity thus is he brought *T*   10. Frosen now cold, and now he standes in flame *T*   11. misery] wo *T*   twist] :betwixt earnest *T*   12. But few] With seldome *T*   13. with] In *T*   14. rote] roote lo *T*

30

Ever myn happ is slack & slo in comyng
   desir encresing myn hope vncertain
   that leve it or wayt it doeth me like pain
Wyat   and Tigre like swift it is in pting   4
Alas the snow shalbe black & scalding
   the See waterles fisshe in the moyntain
   the Tamys shall retorn back into his fontain
   and where he rose the sonne shall take lodging   8
Ere that I in this fynde peace or quyetenes
   o⟨n⟩ that love or my lady rightwisely
   leve to conspire again me wrongfully
And if that I have after suche bitternes   12
   any thing swete my mouth is owte of tast
   that all my trust & travaill is but wast

E f. 22v, hand A. *A* f. 67r. *T* 94. A later hand inserted one colon in the *E* text, after "swete" (l. 13). The scribal error in line 10 of *E* is noted as uncorrected in *M3*.

A T   1. myn] mye *A T*   2. myn] my *A*] ay my *T*   3. leve it] loue *T*   doeth me like] alike doth me *T*   4. swift] so swift *T*   5. shalbe black] black shal it be*T*   6. fisshe in] ,and fishe vpon *T*   7. retorn back] backe returne *T*   8. take] take his *T*   9. that] *om. T*   10. rightwisely] rightuouslye *T*   11. again] against *T*   12. that] *om. T*

31

Love and fortune and my mynde remembre
   of that that is now with that that hath ben

<pre>
                do torment me so that I very often
Wyat   envy theim beyonde all mesure   4
            Love sleith myn hert fortune is depriver
                of all my comfort the folisshe mynde then
                burneth & plaineth as one that sildam
                lyveth & rest still in displeasure   8
            My plaisaunt dayes they flete away & passe
                but daily yet the ill doeth chaunge into the wours
                and more then the half is run of my cours
            Alas not of steill but of brickell glasse   12
                I see that from myn hand falleth my trust
                and all my thoughte are dasshed into dust
</pre>

E f. 23r, hand A. *A* f. 67rv. *T* 95. A later hand set off one phrase within
colons, thus: ":with that:" (l. 2). And another revision, from "&" to "in"
(l. 8), shows up in the variants of *A* and *T*. It looks like the work of the hand
that wrote the verses on the lower half of f. 24v.

A T   1. and fortune] ,Fortune *T*   mynde] minde which do *T*   2. of that
that] Eke that *T*   with that that] and that that once *T*   3. do . . . I]
Torment my hart so sore that *T*   4. envy] I hate and enuy *T*   5. myn hert]
my hart *A*] my hart while *T*   8. &] in *A T*   10. but] And *T*   yet the ill
doeth] doth myne ill *T*   into the] into *A*] to the *T*   11. and] While *T*   the
half] halfe *T*   run] runne now *T*   13. myn] my *A T*

32

<pre>
            How oft have I my dere & cruell foo
                with those yoᵍ Iyes for to get peace & truyse
                profferd you myn hert but you do not vse
                emong so high thinge to cast yoᵍ mynde so lowe   4
Wyat   Yf any othre loke for it as ye trowe
                there vayn weke hope doeth greately theim abuse
                and thus I disdain that that ye refuse
                                        no
                it was ones mine it can more be so   8
            Yf I then it chase nor it in you can fynde
                in this exile no manner of comfort
                nor lyve allone nor where he is called resort
            He may wander from his naturall kynd   12
                so shall it be great hurt vnto vs twayn
                and yoᵍ the losse and myn the dedly pain
</pre>

E f. 23v, hand A. *A* f. 67v. *T* 96. The *E* text was heavily deleted and overwritten, so that minor differences in transcription are likely to occur among
modern editors. In two places colons appear to have been inserted, after
"hert" (l. 3) and "allone" (l. 11). However, I cannot find the final "s" where
one would expect it to occur in "yoꝰ" (l. 14). The correction in line 8 is clearly
scribal.

A T: 2. those . . . &] my great pain to get som peace or *T*   3. profferd you
myn] Geuen you my *T*   4. emong] in *T*   5. ye] you *T*   6. weke] weite *A*
7. thus . . . ye] that thus I disdayne that you *T*   8. can] may *A*   9. I . . . nor]
you it chase, that *T*   14. youꝰ] yours *A T*

33

      Like to these vnmesurable montayns
         is my pain full lyff the burden of Ire
         for of great height be they & high is my desire
         and I of teres and they be full of fontayns   4
      Vnder Craggy rocke they have full barren playns
Tho.   herd thoughte in me my wofull mynde doeth tyre
         small fruyt & many leves their toppes do atyre
         small effect with great trust in me remayns   8
      The boyseus wynde oft their high bowghes do blast
         hote sighes from me continuelly be shed
         cattell in theim and in me love is fed
      Immoveable ame I and they are full stedfast   12
         off that restles birdes they have the tone & note
         and I always plainte that passe thorough my throte

E f. 24r, hand A. *A* f. 67v. *T* 97. Five colons were inserted in the *E* text, after
"they" (l. 3), "teres" (l. 4), "me" (l. 6), "theim" (l. 11), and "I" (l. 12).
In two of these instances the insertion by a later hand is noticeable for special
reasons. In line 3 the colon is imposed on the back sweep of the final "y." In
line 6 the colon is crowded and oddly angled. None of the inking matches
Wyatt's signature in the margin.

A T: 1. to] vnto *T*   2. is] So is *T*   3. of great height] hye *T*   5. full] *om. T*
8. small effect with] With small effect *T*   9. boyseus] boyst'ous *A*] boystous
T   10. from] in *T*   11. cattell] Wilde beastes *T*   and in me love] ,fierce
love in me *T*   12. Immoveable] Vnmoueable *T*   are full] *om. T*   13. that
restles] singing *T*   tone] tvne *A T*   14. that passe] passing *T*   thorough]
through *A T*

34

           th
     Madame w outen many worde
       ons I ame sure ye will or no

and if ye will then leve yor borde
and vse yor wit and shew it so   4
And with a beck ye shall me call
and if of oon that burneth alwaye
ye have any pitie at all

Tho.   aunswer him faire with & · or nay   8
Yf it be & · I shalbe fayne
if it be nay frendes as before
ye shall an othre man obtain
and I myn owne and yor no more   12

E f. 24v, hand A. B f. 128r. T 53. The E text has only one inserted colon, after "wit" (l. 4). The marks after "&" (ll. 8 and 9) are scribal. Beneath the E verses are another set, headed "Aunswer" and composed from a woman's point of view. Both the heading and the verses are copied in an italic hand, which was responsible for minor emendations elsewhere in E. There is no mark of punctuation within the text of these verses, and the italic hand is distinctly different from that on f. 70r. For example, the dotted "y," common in Wyatt's script, does not appear here. These verses were printed in M3 (p. 298). They also occur in B on f. 128r. Muir did not observe that these verses are copied in the same hand that copied Mestris what nedis, as if the two poems were composed together as a pair by the same author. There are considerable variants, however.

Aunswer
2 ent$^{)}$
Of few wourdes $\overset{r}{s}$ you seme to be
and wher i doutyd what i woulde doo
your quik request hathe causyd me
quikly to tell you what you shawl trust too   4
for he that wyl be cawlyd wythe a bek
makes haste sute on Lyght desier
is euer redi to the chek
and burnythe in no wastynge fyer   8
therfor whyther you be lywe or lothe
and whyther it giue you Lyght or soer
I am at a poynt I haue made a othe
Content you wythe nay for you get no moer   12

Title Aunswer] the Aunswer B   1. you] ye B   2. i doutyd] ye dobtyd B
4. quikly to tell you what you] shortlye to tell what ye B   6. makes haste
sute on] and make hot swet of B   8. and] om. B   9. but chese ye whether
ye be leue or loth B   10. or whether ye take yt lyght or ⟨trth⟩e B   11. I haue
sworne and mad A nothe B   12. you wythe nay for you] ye $\overset{t}{w}$ A nay for
ye B

B T:

1. Madame wth outen] Mestris what nedis B   2. ye] you T   3. and]
om. B   ye] you T   5. And] For T   ye] you T   shall] may B   6. burneth]
borns B] burns T   7. any pitie] pity or ruth T   8. &·] ye B] yea T   9. &·]
ye B] yea T   11. obtain] Retayne B   12. myn] my B

35

Ye old mule that thinck yoͬ self so fayre
   leve of wi͡th craft yoͬ beautie to repaire
   for it is true withoute any fable
   no man setteth more by riding in yoͬ saddell   4
   to muche travaill so do yoͬ train apaire
       ye old mule

Tho.   With fals savoure though you deceve thayer
   who so tast you shall well ꝑceve yoͬ layer   8
   savoureth so͡m what of a Kappurs stable
       ye old mule

Ye must now serve to market & to faire
   all for the burden for pannyers a paire   12
   for syns gray heres ben powdered in yoͬ sable
   the thing ye seke for you must yoͬ self enable
   to pourchase it by payement & by prayer
       ye old mule   16

E f. 25r, hand A. The text is heavily deleted and overwritten.

36

Suche happe as I ame happed in
   had never man of true͡th I wene
   at me fortune list to begy͡n .
   to shew that never ha͡th ben sene   4
   a new kynde of vnhappenes
   nor I cannot the thing I mene
   my self expres

My self expresse my dedely pain   8
   that can I well if that myg�ht sͨue
Tho.   but why I have not helpe again
   that knowe I not vnles I starve
   for honger still a myddes my foode   12
   so graunte me that I desͨue
   to do me good

To do me good what may prevaill
   for I deserve & not desir   16
   and still of cold I me bewaill

and raked ame in burnyng fyer
for tho I have suche is my lott
in hand to helpe that I require   20
it helpeth not
It helpeth not but to encrese
    that that by prouff can be no more
    that is the hete that cannot cesse   24
    and that I have to crave so sore
    what wonder is this gredy lust
    to aske & have and yet therefor
    refrain I must   28
Refrain I must what is the cause
    sure as they say so hawke be taught
    but in my case laieth no suche clause
    for with suche craft I ame not caught   32
    wherefore I say and good cause why
    with haples hand no man hath raught
    suche happe as I ·

E ff. 25v-26r, hand A. The lines on f. 25r were deleted and the leaf was over-written. Two inserted colons appear, after "have" (l. 19) and "say" (l. 30). The full stop at the end of the poem is scribal.

37

They fle from me / that sometyme did me seke
    with naked fote stalking in my chambre
    I have sene theim gentill tame and meke
    that nowe are wyld and do not remembre   4
    that sometyme they put theimself in daunger
    to take bred at my hand & nowe they raunge
    besely seking with a continuell chaunge
Thancked be fortune it hath ben othrewise   8
    twenty tymes better but ons in speciall
Tho.   in thyn arraye after a pleasaunt gyse
    when her lose gowne from her shoulders did fall
    and she me caught in her armes long & small   12
    therewithall swetely did me kysse
    and softely saide dere hert howe like you this
It was no dreme I lay brode waking
    but all is torned thorough my gentilnes   16

into a straunge fasshion of forsaking
and I have leve to goo of her goodenes
and she also to vse new fangilnes
but syns that I so kyndely ame s⁾ued   20
I would fain knowe what she hath des⁾ued

E f. 26v, hand A. D ff. 69v-70r. T 52. The D text is subscribed only "fs".
Punctuation has been an issue with this poem, arising from both its quality
and its peculiar meter or rhythm. The D text contains several more marks of
punctuation not falling within the scope of the variants. Virgules follow "my
chambre" (l. 2), "chaunge" (l. 7), "fortune" (l. 8), "bettre" (l. 9), "arraye"
(l. 10), and "des⁾ued" (l. 21).

M3 listed two variants for "They" (ll. 1, 5). These, however, were based
on a misreading of the hand in D, which tends to slight the medial "e." Thus,
the spelling in D is "theye" (ll. 1, 5, 6). M3 did not list the reading "she ded"
(l. 13) in D, nor "awakyng" (l. 15) in T. The reading "did my" (l. 13) in M3
is a misprint for "did me."

D T: 2. in] within T   3. I have] Once haue I T   gentill] both g̃etill D
4. remembre] once remember T   5. put theimself] haue put them selues T
7. with a] om. D] in T   9. in speciall] in esspiall D] especiall T   11. from
. . . did] did from her shoulders T   13. therewithall] but therewall D] And
therwithal, so T   did] she ded D   15. dreme I] dreame · for I D] dreame:
for I T   waking] awakyng T   16. torned thorough] tornd thorowe D]
turnde now through T   17. straunge] bitter T   18. goo] parte D   19. also]
like wise D   20. so kyndely] so g̃etillye D] vnkyndly so T   21. I . . . hath]
what think you bye this y̅ she hat D] How like you this, what hath she now T

38

There was never nothing more me payned
nor nothing more me moved
as when my swete hert her complayned
that ever she me loved   4
           Alas the while
With pituous loke she saide & sighed
alas what aileth me
Tho.   to love and set my welth so light   8
on hym that loveth not me
           Alas the while
Was I not well voyde of all pain
when that nothing me greved   12
and nowe with sorrous I must complain
and cannot be releved
           Alas the while

My restfull nyghtes & Ioyfull daies   16
   syns I began to love
   be take from me all thing decayes
   yet can I not remove
         Alas the while   20

              t
She wept and wrong her hande w all
   the teres fell in my nekke
   she torned her face & let it fall
   scarsely therewith coulde speke   24
         Alas the while
Her paynes tormented me so sore
   that comfort had I none
   but cursed my fortune more & more
   to se her sobbe and grone
         Alas the while

E f. 27rv, hand A.

39

Patience though I have not
the thing that I require
I must of force god wot
forbere my moost desire   4
        can
for no ways ∧⟨not⟩ I fynde
to saile against the wynde
Patience do what they will
   to worke me woo or spite   8
   I shall content me still
   to thyncke boeth daye & nyte
Tho.   to thyncke and hold my peace
   syns there is no redresse   12
     t
Patience w outen blame
   for I offended nought
   I knowe they knowe thesame
   though they have chaunged their thought   16
   was ever thought so moved
   to hat⟨h⟩e that it hath loved
Patience of all my harme

for fortune is my foo   20
patience must be the charme
to hele me of my woo
patience withoute offence
is a painfull patience   24

E f. 28r, hand A. *A* f. 75v. *D* f. 13v. *B* f. 146r. The *D* text is subscribed
"fynys q^d Wyatt⌒" The order of stanzas in *E* is followed in *A* and *D*, but in *B*
it becomes 3, 1, 2, 4. The correction in line 5 of *E* may be scribal or it may be
by Wyatt himself. In line 14 the scribe may have started to add a final "e" to
"offended."

A D B: 2. require] desyryd *D*   3. god] good *B*   4. my moost desire] y^t I
Requiryd *D*   5. ways] way *B*   7. they] she *D*] ye *B*   10. boeth . . . nyte] y^t
ons I myght *D B*   13. w^t outen] without *A*] off all my *B*   15. I . . . knowe]
I know she knows *D*] I wyshe she knoyth *B*   16. they . . . their] she have
changed her *D B*   18. that it] where yt *D*] wher hyt *B*   20. for] seth *B*
21. must be] shalbe *B*   22. hele] ease *D*

40

Paciens for my devise
  Impaciens for your part
  of contraries the gyse
  is ever the overthwart   4
  paciens for I ame true
  the contrary for yew
Paciens a good cause why
  you have no cause at all   8
  therefore your standeth awry
  ℘chaunce sometyme to fall
  paciens then take him vp
  and drynck of paciens Cupp   12
Pacience no force for that
  but brusshe yo^9 gowne again
  pacience spurne not therat
  let no man knowe your payne   16
  pacience evyn at my pleasure
  when yo^9 is owte of mesure
Thothr was for me
  this pacience is for you   20
  chaunge when ye list let se

for I have taken a new

pacience wth a good will

is easy to fulfill   24

E f. 28v. A f. 75v (fragment, ll. 1-8 only). D f. 71r. B f. 147r. The D text is subscribed only "fs", but it has the following heading:

> patiens tho I had nott the &c^) / to her y^t
>
> saide this patiens was not for her but y^t
>
> the cõt^rye of myne was most metiste for her po^g posse /

The variants to poem 39 indicate that the pronoun "she" (ll. 7, 15, 16) was introduced into the D text to suit this fictional background. In neither text of E is there a direct feminine mode of address or reference. Although the handwriting in E became smaller at this point, as if conserving space, it is the same hand A.

A D B: 3. contraries] contrarye D   4. is ever the] must nede be D] ys euer B   overthwart] overtharte D   5. ame true] am⟨try⟩tue^r D   8. you have] yos^r hathe D] ye haue B   9. your standeth] yowrs stande B   truste me that stonde awrye D   9-24. *om. A*   10. pchaunce] may chance B   sometyme to] maye some tyme D   11. then . . . vp] the saye and supp D   12. and drynck] a taste D   14. but] yet D   16. let . . . knowe] lest folke pceyve D   17. evyn] *om.* D   18. is owte of] hathe no D   19. Thothr] the tother D B   22. taken] tane D] tayne B

41

all to my harme

sending suche flame from frosen brest

against all right for my vnrest

And I knowe well how frowerdly

ye have mystaken my true Intent   28

and hetherto how wrongfully

I have founde cause for to repent

but dẽth shall ryd me redely

yf yo^g   hert do not relent   32

and I knowe well all this ye knowe

That I and myne

and all I have

ye may assigne   36

to spill or save

Why are ye then so cruel ffoo

vnto yo^g owne that loveth you so

E f. 29r (fragment, ll. 24-39 only), hand A. *D* f. 73v. The *D* text is subscribed "fs". In *E* a later hand, probably the hand of the verses on the lower
half of f. 24v, inserted one word, thus: "yf_∧ yo^ϛ" (l. 32). Although lines 1-23
are supplied by *D*, their accuracy is questionable. The variants show that lines
32-34 are very different in *D*. Another minor difference is that lines 21-22,
34-35 are copied as one line in *D*, as are lines 36-37.

D: 1-23. *om. E*   26. all right] nature *D*   27. frowerdly] sconefullye *D*

28. mystaken] mistane *D*   31. *om. D*   32. but if yo̊ herte doth not relente *D*
33. sins I do kno that this ye kno / ye shall sle me all wilfullye *D*
34. That I] for me *D*   39. loveth] lovis *D*

42

Vij

:Who hath̃ herd of suche ⟨tyranny⟩ before?
that when my plaint remembred her my woo
that caused it/she cruell more & more
wisshed eche stitche as she did sit & soo   4

Tho   had ⟨pricked⟩ myn hert/for to encrese my sore ·
and as I thinck/she thought it had ben so·
for as she thought this is his hert in dede/
she pricked herd/& made her self to blede ·   8

E f. 29v, hand A. *A* f. 68r. *D* f. 73r. *T* 68. The *D* text is subscribed "fs",
but in the outer margin is a large terminal ϛ which may be intended to identify the copyist of three poems crowded into the outer of the two columns
on the leaf. The inking in *E* indicates that Wyatt examined the text twice. The
ink of his signature is pale brown, while that of his corrections within the text
is dark black. The opening marginal colon preceding "Who" is scribal.

A D T: 1. Who hath̃] What man *T*   of suche] such *T*   ⟨tyranny⟩] crueltie
A T] ⟨crultye⟩ *D*   2. remembred her] remebreher *D*   5. ⟨pricked⟩ myn]
pricked my *A D*] prickt my *T*   to encrese] tencrese *D*   8. herd] her *D*

43

x If fansy would favoϛ
as my dsᵒuing shall
my love my ℓamoϛ
should love me best of all   4
But if I cannot attain
the grace that I desir
then may I well complain
my sᵒuice & my hier   8

ffansy doeth knowe how
   to fourther my trew hert
   if fansy myght avowe
   with faith to take pt   12
But fansy is so fraill
   and flitting still so fast
   that faith may not prevaill
   to helpe me furst nor last   16
ffor fansy at his lust
   doeth rule all but by gesse
   whereto should I then trust
   in trouth or stedfastnes   20
Yet gladdely would I please
   the fansy of her hert
   that may me onely ease
   and cure my carefull smart   24
Therefore my lady dere
   set ons your fantasy
   to make som hope appere
   of stedfastnes remedy   28
ffor if he be my frend
   and vndertake my woo
   my greife is at an ende
   if he continue so   32
Elke fansy deth not right
   as I des)ue and shall
   to have you daye & nyght
   to love me best of all   36

E f. 30rv, hand A. *A* f. 75r (*om.* ll. 1-8). *D* f. 34v (*om.* 11. 13-16). *V1*
pp. 124-125; *V2* (fragment ll. 22-36 only) p. 111. In line 33 of the *E* text it
is not entirely clear whether hand A intended to write "deth" or "doeth."

A D V   1-8. *om. A*   1-21. *om. V2*   1. fansy] fantasy *V1*   2. my des)uing
shall] I deserue and *V1*   3. my] my lady *V1*   5. But] And *V1*   cannot]
not *V1*   9. ffansy doeth knowe] Fantasy knoweth *V1*   10. fourther]
forbeare *V1*   12. to] for to *D*   13-16. *om. D*   13. fansy is so] fantasy is *V1*
14. flitting] fletynge *V1*   17. ffor fansy] Since fantasy *V1*   18. but] *om. V1*
19. then] put *V1*   20. or] and *V1*   21. gladdely] *om. A*   22. the fansy]
That fantasy *V1*] The fantasy *V2*   her] my *V1 V2*   24. cure] helpe *V1 V2*
26. set ons] Let se *V1 V2*   27. hope] *om. V1*   28. stedfastnes] stedefast *D*]
helpe and *V1 V2*   29. he] ye *V1 V2*   32. he] ye *V1 V2*   33. Elke fansy]
Els fantasy *V1 V2*   34. I] *om. D*   35. have] *om. V1*   you] her *V1 V2*

44

stelyng

: Alas madame for ⟨robbing⟩ of a kysse /

have I somuch yoᵉ mynd ther offended?

Tho.   have I then done so greuously amysse /

that by no meanes it may be amended?   4

then⟨to⟩ revenge you / ⟨then⟩

the next way is this

and ⟨sure ye shall not mysse⟩

an othr kysse shall have my liffe endid ·

⟨to have my liff with an othr ended⟩

first

for to my mowth the ⟨ton⟩ my hert did suck

next   clene

the ⟨tothre⟩ shall ∧ oute of my brest it pluck   8

E f. 31r, hand A. A f. 63v. T 54. All of the deletions, revisions, and additions shown in my text were made by Wyatt. Of the punctuation, only the question mark looks scribal. What may appear to be a full stop after "done" (l. 3) turns out to be a flaw in the paper. The marginal colon preceding the first word "Alas" is scribal. The inking shows that Wyatt worked on this text twice. The ink of his work on the first three lines, a pale brown, matches his signature "Tho." The ink of his revisions in lines 5-8 is black.

There are two sets of later revisions in two distinct hands. Hughey (II, 133-134) presented these as the work of one hand. However, the revisions
in   the matt'may
"the ⟨r⟩ offended?" (l. 2) and "⟨it may⟩ be ⟨a⟩ mended?" (l. 4) are in one
through amysse
lif⟨f⟩e endid·   throughe endid
hand, while the revisions "⟨othr ended⟩   (l. 6) are in another hand. M3 regarded what I read "through" (l. 6) as a later insertion by Wyatt himself, then his deletion. But there is surely another word after "through", of which the "ysse" is clearly visible.

stelyng
A T: 1. ⟨robbing⟩] stealing A T   2. ther] thearin A T   3. have I then] Or haue I T   4. it may be amended] the matter may be mendid A] it may not be amended T   5. then revendge you and the next way is this A] Reuenge you then, the rediest way is this T   6. an other kisse shall haue my lief

first
throughe endid A] Another kisse my life it shall haue ended T   7. ⟨ton⟩]
next   clene
first A T   8. ⟨tothre⟩] next A T   ∧oute] cleane out A T

45

What no ꝑdy ye may be sure

thynck not to make me to yoᵉ lure

with worde and chere so contrarieng

swete and sowre contrewaing   4

to much it were still to endure

trouth is tryed where craft is in vre

but though ye have ha⟨ve⟩ my hert͟e cure

Tho   trow ye I dote withoute ending   8

What no ℘dy

Though that with pain I do procure

for to forgett that ons was pure

w in my hert shall still that thing   12

vnstable vnsure and wavering

be in my mynde withoute recure

What no ℘dye

E f. 31v, hand A. *D* f. 19r. Beneath the last line in *D* is "fynys q̃ Wyatt͞ɤ."
In the *E* text Wyatt added line 15 and corrected the verb in line 7, both in
the same ink he used to sign the leaf. The pictograph in *M3* for the variant of
"hert" fails to indicate that the *D* drawing looks more like a heart than a face.
The variant adopted by *M3* from *D* for line 6 is misspelled.

D: 3. contrarieng] contraryng   6. tryed] trayde   7. ha⟨ve⟩ had
12. hert]

46

Viij

gadlyng

The wandering ⟨galdyng⟩ in the sommer tyde /

that fynd͟e the Adder/with his recheles fote /

start͟e not dismayd, so soudenly a side

Tho.   as Jalous dispite did tho there war*e* no bote /   4

when that he sawe me sitting by her side /

that of my helth/is very croppe & rote ·

it pleased me then to have so fair a grace /

to styng that hert that would have my place ·   8

E f. 32r, hand A. *D* f. 35v. *P* f. 32v. *T* 55. Beneath the last line of the *D* text
is a "w" in the same hand as the text. The *E* text is one of the most interesting for studying Wyatt's relation to his copyist. In line 8 are two deletions of
punctuation by Wyatt, thus: "hert⟨·⟩ that" and "my place·⟨:⟩" The ink of the
corrections matches the signature and the Roman numeral in the head margin.
This fact raises doubt that the two colons now visible were there when Wyatt
went over the text. They are "did: tho" (l. 4) and "me: sitting" (l. 5).
Although the ink does not contrast clearly with the scribal handwriting, these
colons may be the same as those inserted elsewhere in *E*. As the virgule in the
middle of line 2 was probably inserted by Wyatt himself, it is likely that all
similar signs were also inserted by him. It is not possible to tell whether the
comma in line 3 is scribal or by Wyatt. The corrected spelling "gadlyng" (l. 1)

is in the same ink and in Wyatt's hand, so it appears that the whole text was corrected only once.

D P T: 1. ⟨galdyng⟩] gadlyng *D P T*   4. as . . . did] As I Alous dyspyte Dyd *D*] as did gelosy *P*   7. then] *om. P*   8. that hert that] the wight that *P*] the hart, that *T*   have] have had *P T*

(superscript above line 1: gadlyng)

47

The lyvely sperke that issue from those Iyes
    against the which ne vaileth no defence
    have prest myn hert and done it none offence
    with qwaking pleasure more then ons or twise   4
Was never man could any thing devise

    the sonne bemes to torn wth so great vehemence
Tho   to dase mans sight as by their bright presence
    dased ame I muche like vnto the gyse   8
Of one I stricken with dynt of light⟨e⟩ning
    blynded with the stroke / erryng here & there
    so call I for helpe I not when ne where
The pain of my fal⟨s⟩ patiently bering   12
    for after the blase / as is no wounder
    of dedly nay here I the ferefull thounder

E f. 32v, hand A. *A* f. 67 (*bis*) r. *D* f. 36v. *T* 40. In the *E* text are three colons that do not contrast with the scribal inking, but which I treat here as later insertions because the evidence of such insertions is strong elsewhere in *E*: "hert: and" (l. 3), "helpe: I" (l. 11), and "I: the" (l. 14).

In the variants from *D* for line 14 in *M3* is an error copied from Hughey (II, 150), who read the first word of the deletion in *D* as "Geue." But it is "here" written exactly as the same word is copied in the second half of the corrected line. Further, Hughey showed the deletion under the correction, when it is actually above it. This is important, because it shows that the copyist made a false start with "here I the nay" before he checked his copy, which must have been accurate. He then deleted the false start and wrote the full line accurately below it, "of dedly nay here I the ferefull thondyr."

I cannot account for the variant listed in *M3* for line 12, thus: "bering] learnying *T1*." This reading from *T* is not available in Rollins(I, 33) nor in his list of variant readings and misprints. The photostat of *T1* used by Rollins indicates that *T1* here reads "bearyng".

A D T: 2. ne] there *T*   3. prest myn] prest my *A*] perst my *T*   6. the] *om. T*   9. I stricken] ystreeken *A*] I strekyn *D*] striken *T*   10. blynded] Blind *T*   stroke /] stroke, and *T*   11. ne] nor *T*   12. fal⟨s⟩] fall *A T*] faute *D*   13. after] streight after *T*   14. of dedly nay] of dedly nay *D*] Of deadly noyse *T*

(superscript above line 14 variant: ⟨here I the nay⟩)

48

What nedeth these threning worde & wasted wynde
all this cannot make me restore my pray
to robbe yo^c good I wis is not my mynde

Tho.   nor causeles yo^c faire hand did I display   4
let love be Iudge or els whome next we meit
that may boeth here what you & I can say
she toke from me an hert & I a glove from her
let vs se nowe if thon be wourth thothre   8

E f. 33r, hand A. A f. 68rv. T 56. In the E text is one colon, thus: "nowe:
if" (l. 8).

A T: 1. nedeth] nedes A T   threning] threatning A T   3. I wis] ywis T
5. meit] finde T   7. toke . . . an] reft my T   8. nowe] then T   thon]
thone A] one T   thothre] th'other A] the other T

49

Ryght true it is and said full yore agoo
take hede of him that by thy back the claweth
for none is wourse then is a frendely ffoo

Tho.   though they seme good all thing that the deliteth   4
yet knowe it well that in thy bosom crepeth
for many a man such fier oft kyndeleth
that with the blase his berd syngeth

E f. 33r, hand A. A f. 67 (bis) r. T 57. In E is one scribal correction that is
difficult to show in print because the correct letter was written directly upon
the wrong one: the word "thy" (l. 2) was first written as "the."
    The poem of eight lines on the upper half of the same leaf in E (no. 48)
contained only one colon. This poem of seven lines on the lower half has five
colons: "is: and" (l. 1), "him: that" (l. 2), "wourse: then" (l. 3), "good: all"
(l. 4), and "well: that" (l. 5). Many other poems, even longer, have none at
all. The erratic appearance of such marks adds to the doubt about their origin
and value, except as they relate to the habits and theories of Nicholas Grimald.

A T: 2. thy] the T   4. though they] Thought he T   6. such fier oft] oft
tyme suche fyre A] such fire oft times he T   7. berd syngeth] berd him self
he singeth T

50

What wourde is that / that chaungeth not
though it be tourned and made in twain

	it is myn aunswer god it wot	
Tho.	and eke the causer of my payn	4
	a love rewardeth with disdain	
	yet is it loved what would ye more	
	it is my helth / eke and my sore	

E f. 33v, hand A. A f. 67 (bis) r. T 266. The E text contains only the
scribal punctuation marks favored by Wyatt himself. The A text of this poem
was copied continuoisly with no. 49, as shown in Hughey (I, 155). As
Hughey noted, the cause of this error was probably not the heading to no.
49 now visible in E: "Sonet." Rather, it was probably the haste and weari-
ness of the scribe, who had already copied four sonnets in A, then turned the
leaf in E without thinking and managed to leave out words basic to the sense.
His error suggests that when he turned the leaf, the name "anna," now half
visible in the head margin of E, was not then there.

A T: 3. it] yf A   aunswer] Anna T   4. and . . . causer] and the cause A]
The only causer T   5. a love rewardeth] A Love A] My loue that medeth T
6. would ye] will you T   7. helth / eke and] salue, and eke T

51

	At moost myschief	
	I suffre greif	
	for of relief	
	syns I have none	4
	My lute & I	
	continuelly	
	shall vs apply	
	to sigh & mone	8
	Nought may prevaill	
	to wepe or waill	
Tho.	pitie doeth faill	
	in you Alas	12
	Morning or mone	
	complaint or none	
	it is all one	
	as in this case	16
	ffor crueltie	
	moost that can be	
	hath soveraynte	
	within your hert	20
	Which maketh bare	
	all my welfare	

nought do ye care
  how sore I smart   24

torn the leiff

No Tigres hért
  is so overt
  withoute dess⁾ t
  to wreke his Ire   28
And you me kyll
  for my good will
  lo how I spill
  for my desire   32
There is no love
  that can ye move
  and I can prove
  none othre way   36
Therefore I must
  restrain my lust
  banisshe my trust
  and welth away   40
ffor in myschief

E f. 34rv, hand *A*. *D* f. 12r. *B* f. 68r. The *D* text is subscribed "ffynys q⁽ᵈ⁾ Wyatt◦." Line 30 was inserted into the *E* text between two scribal lines by Wyatt at the same time that he signed f. 34r. *M3* incorrectly noted that lines 42-48 are in *B*. They are only in *D*, but *M3* repeated the *E* text of lines 2-8 rather than printing the text of *D*. The small correction in line 19, however, is scribal, where a "y" was written on top of the "u" in "soveraunte."

D B:
    4. syns] sith *B*   8 sigh &] ⟨wele⟩ and *B*   9. may] doth *B*   10. wepe] sighe *B*   11. pitie] sens pety *B* [sythor above]   12. Alas] al [*torn away*] *B*   15. it] hit *B* all one] Alone *D*] alOoone *B*   18. can] may *B*   19. soveraynte [*corr. of* "soveraunte"] suffraynte *D*] sufferaunte *B*   21. Which] and *B*   23. ye] you *B*   29. you] ye *B*   34. ye] you *B*   36. none othre] no nother *B*   37. Therefore] Wherfor *D*] Wherfore *B*   38. restrain my] Refrayn me *D*] refrayne my *B*   39. banisshe my] banysshe me *D*] and banyshe *B*   40. and welth away] from me alway *B*   41. ffor in myschief] thus in myscheffe *D*] Thus in my schyef &c⁾ *B*   42-48 *om. E B*] I suffer greffe / ffor off releffe / syns I have none / my lute & I / contynually / shall vs apply to / syght & mone *D*

52

Marvaill no more all tho
  the songe I syng do mone

　　　　　　for othre liff then wo

　　　　　　I never proved none　　　　　　　　　　　4

　　　　　And in my hert also

　　　　　　is graven with lr͞es diepe

　　　　　　a thousand sig͞hes & mo

　　　　　　a flod of teeres to wepe　　　　　　　8

　　　　　How may a man in smart

　　　　　　fynde matter to reIoyse

Tho.　　　how may a morning hert

　　　　　　set four͡th a pleasaunt voise　　　　　12

　　　　　Play who that can that ꝑt

　　　　　　nedє must in me appere

　　　　　　how fortune overthwart

　　　　　　doet͡h cause my morning chere　　　16

　　　　　Perdy there is no man

　　　　　　if he never sawe sig͡ht

　　　　　　that ꝑfaictly tel͡l can

　　　　　　the nature of the lig͡ht　　　　　　　20

　　　　　Alas how should I then

　　　　　　that never tasted but sowre

　　　　　　but do as I began

　　　　　　continuelly to lowre　　　　　　　　24

tor͡n

　　　　　But yet ꝑchaunce som chaunce

　　　　　　may chaunce to chaunge my tune

　　　　　　and when suche chaunce doet͡h chaunce

　　　　　　then shall I thanck fortune　　　　　28

　　　　　And if I have chaunce

　　　　　　ꝑchaunce ere it be long

　　　　　　for suc͡h a pleasaunt chaunce

　　　　　　to syng som plaisaunt song　　　　　32

E f. 35rv, hand A. *D* f. 16v. *V* 127-128. *T* 65. The *D* text is subscribed
"ffynys q̇ Tas Wyatt꜖". A word omitted in *E* is inserted thus: "And if I have
souche
chaunce" (l. 29). The hand that inserted "souche" is the same that copied
the verses on the lower half of f. 24v. It is impossible to tell whether this
insertion came before or after *T* gave the word topical value as a play on a
mistress' name.

D V T: 7. *E* And many thousands no *V*   8. a flod] The flouds *V*   11.
morning] wofull *V*   13. that can] can *D V*] so can *T*   part] depart *V*   14.
nede... me] In me must nedes *V*   16. *om. V*   18. never sawe] saw neuer
T   21. Alas] *om. D V*   I then] I do than *D*   22. tasted] tast *D T*   25.
ọchance
But yet⌃sum chance ⟨may chace⟩*D*] Such chaunce perchaunce may chaunce
V   26. may chaunce to] To cause me *V*   27. suche] shuche *D*] ⟨Souch⟩ *T*
29. I have chaunce] suche chance do chawnce *D V*] I haue ⟨Souch⟩ chance *T*
31. such] ⟨Souch⟩ *T*

53

Where shall I have at myn owne will
 teres to complain where shall I fett
 suche sighes that I may sigh my fill
 and then again my plainte ⟨to⟩ repete   4
ffor tho my plaint shall have none end
 my teres cannot suffice my woo
 to mone my harme have I no frend
 for fortunes frend is myshappes ffoo   8
Comfort (god wot) els have I none
Tho. but in the wynde to wast my worde
 nought moveth you my dedly mone
 but all you torn it into borde   12
I speke not now to move yo⁹ hert
 that you should⌃ᵣᵘᵉ vpon my pain
 the sentence geven may not revert
 I know suche labo⁹ were but vayn   16
    that
But syns⌃⟨for you⟩ I for you my dere
 have lost that thing that was my best
 a right small losse it must appere
 to lese thes worde and all the rest   20
But tho they sparkill in the wynde
 yet shall they shew yo⁹ falsed faith
 which is retorned vnto his kynde
 for like to like the proverbe saieth   24
ffortune and you did me avaunce
 me thought I swam & could not drowne
 happiest of all but my myschaunce
 did lyft me vp to thrawe me downe   28
And you with yo⁹ owne cruelnes

did set yo^g fote vpon my neck
me & my welfare to oppresse
withoute offence yo^g hert to wreke   32
Wher*e* are yo^g plaisaunt word*e* alas
wher*e* your faith yo^g stedfastnes
there is no more but all doeth passe
and I ame left all comfortles   36
But forbicause it doeth you greve
and also me my wretched liff
have here my trouth shall not releve
but deth alone my very striff   40
Therefor*e* farewell my liff my deth
my gayn my losse my salve my sore
farewell also with you my breth
for I ame gone for ever more /   44

podra esser che no es ·

E f. 36rv, hand *A*. *A* f. 78r. *T* 66. The *E* text has corrections by both Wyatt
and the scribe. Wyatt inserted "rue" (l. 14) and added the Spanish or Italian
tag beneath the last line. The black ink of the motto matches Wyatt's on f.
37r, when he revised poem 54. The deletions and the insertion in lines 4 and
17 are scribal.

    Several emendations were made by the hand of the verses on the lower
half of f. 24v: "yo^g owne cruelnes] ⟨yo^g owne⟩ ∧hir of cruelnes" (l. 29), "wher*e*
your] wher*e* ∧is your" (l. 34), "But forbicause] But ⟨forbicause⟩ synce somuche" (l. 37),
"trouth shall] trouth ∧naught shall" (l. 39), and "liff my] liff: my" (l. 41). As Hughey noted (II, 171), all these emendations except that for line 29 appear in
A and *T*. She therefore concluded that these emendations were in *E* when
the copy for *A* and *T* was prepared. However, it is just as likely that they
were made in *E* after *T* was printed. The exception of line 29 seems especially significant in this connection.

A T: 3. that] as *A*   12. all] stil *T*   22. yo^g] thie *A*   23. retorned vnto]
return'de vnto *A*] returned to *T*   24. saieth] saith *A*   25. avaunce]
advaunce *A*   29. yo^g owne] [*blank*] of *A*] her, of *T*   34. wher*e*] wheare
is *A T*   37. forbicause] since so moche *A T*   39. shall not] nought shall *A T*
40. very] wretched *T*

54

IX
She sat and sowde / that hath done me the wrong /
wherof I plain and have done many a daye ·

and whilst she herd my plaint ⟨&⟩ pitious song /

Tho.   wisshed my hert the samplar as it lay ·

the blynd maister / whome I have s⁾ ued so long /

grudging to here that he did here her saye /

⟨with⟩ her owne wepon ⟨did make⟩ her fynger blede /

to fele if pricking were so good in dede · /

E f. 37r, hand A. A f. 68v. D f. 73r. T 67. The D text is subscribed "fs".
Wyatt's work on the E text is in two colors of ink, indicating two occasions.
Both the signature "Tho." and the Roman numeral in the head margin are in
pale brown ink. The revisions in lines 3, 7, and 8 were made by Wyatt in
black ink. In line 8, Wyatt wrote the word "in" on top of the scribal word
"a." One colon in the E text, "plain: and" (l. 2), may or may not be scribal.

A D T: 3. whilst] whylest A] while D ⟨&⟩ in A D T   4. wisshed] She
wisht T as] that T 5. so] ⟨so⟩ A 7. ⟨with⟩] Made A T] w D ⟨did make⟩]
doe A T] ded make D

55

A Robyn

Ioly Robyn

tell me how thy leman doeth

and thou shall knowe of myn   4

My lady is vnkynd ꝑde

alack whi is she so

Wyat   she loveth an othre better then me

and yet she will say no   8

Responce

I fynde no suche doublenes

I fynde women true

my lady loveth me dowtles

and will chaunge for no newe   12

le plaintif

Thou art happy while that doeth last

but I say as I fynde

that womens love is but a blast

and torneth lik the wynde   16

Responce

Suche folke shall take no harme by love

that can abide their torn

but I alas can no way prove

in love but lake & morn̄   24
le plaintif
But if thou w⟨ilt⟩ avoyde thy harme
lerne this lessen of me
at othr*e* fieres thy self to warme
and let theim warme with the   28

E f. 37v (om. ll. 17-20), hand A. *D* ff. 22v (*D1*, fragment, ll. 1-8 only), 24rv
(*D2*, om. headings). The two *D* texts are in two different hands. The hand of
the complete version (*D2*) is unusually ornate, and its style has caused minor
disagreements concerning the variants. Where *M3* read the variant "that" (l.
21), *D2* actually reads "shal" in agreement with *E*. On f. 24v of *D* the subscription to the poem may be a cipher for "Wiat."It reads "ffynys q 58i3."ᵈ

The omission of lines 17-20 from *E* caused confusion in placing the headings. Thus, the last two headings in *E* should be interchanged. But since the
spacing in *E* indicates that they were not added later as an afterthought, the
confusion must have occurred in making the copy from which hand A
worked. In line 16 of *E* hand A may have indicated a final "e" on "lik" by
adding a cap to the end of the "k." In line 22 the word "w⟨ilt⟩" is blurred
rather than revised by the scribe.

D: 1. A] He *D1*] Hey *D2*   2. Ioly] gentyll *D1*   3. leman] lady *D1 D2*
4. doeth] dose *D2*   6. alack] allas *D1 D2*   7. loveth] loves *D1 D2*   me] I
D1 D2   8. no] *om. D1*   Responce] *headings om. D1 D2*   9-28. *om. D1*
9. suche] shech *D2*   10. I] for I *D2*   13. while that] yf ytt *D2*
16. lik] as *D2*   17-20. *om. E*] Yf that be trew yett as thov sayst / that women
turn ther hart / then spek better of them thov mayst / in hope to han thy partt ⁱ
D2   21. harme] hurt *D2*   23. no way] noways *D2*   25. But] Ytt *D2* ᵉ
thy] the *D2*   27. othre] others *D2*   28. warme] warn *D2*

56

Suche vayn thought as wonted to myslede me
in desert hope by well assured mone
maketh me from compayne to live alone
in folowing her whome reason bid me fle   4

Wyat   She fleith as fast by gentill crueltie
and after her myn hert would fain be gone
but armed sighes my way do stoppe anon̄
twixt hope & drede lacking my ⟨lib⟩libertie   8
                              disdaynfull
Yet as I gesse vnder ⟨that scornefull⟩ browe
one beame of pitie is in her clowdy loke
which comforteth the mynde that erst for fere shoke
And therewithall bolded I seke the way how   12

to vtter the smert that I suffre w^tin

but suche it is / I not how to begyn

E f. 38r, hand A. *A* f. 67 (bis) v. *D* f. 31r. *T* 41. Hughey (II, 152) stated
incorrectly that the *D* text is unascribed. Beneath the last line is a clearly
formed "W" preceded by either a "T" or a flourish. However, Hughey
(II, 153) observed rightly that line 8 in *E* was not revised by Wyatt as noted
in *M3*. The word "lacking" is entirely scribal and unrevised. The reading
"locking" is an invention of *T*. The single instance of Wyatt's pen in this
text is in line 9. where his revision "disdaynfull" stands out in a pale brown
ink contrasting sharply with the name "Wyat" in the margin, which is not
his hand or ink.

A D T: 3. maketh] makes *T*   4. bid] bids *T*   5. She . . . fast] So fleeth
she *T* l. 8] She flyeth as fast *D*   6. myn] my *A*   7. do] doth *D*   8. lacking]
locking *T*   9. ⟨that scornefull⟩] disdaynfull *A T*] the skornfull *D*   10. pitie]
ruth *D*   11. conforteth] comfortes *T*   12. And . . . way] That bolded
straight the way then seke I *T*   13. vtter] vtter forth *T*   that I suffre] I
bide *T*   14. it] ⟨y⟩ ytt *D*

57

Tho I cannot yo^ꝰ crueltie constrain

   for my good will to favo^ꝰ me again

   tho my true & faithfull love

   have no power your hert to move   4

   yet rew vpon my pain

Tho I yo^ꝰ thrall must evermore remain

   and for your sake my libertie restrain

   the greatest grace that I do crave   8

   is that ye would vouchesave

Tho   to rew vpon my pain

Tho I have not des^ıued to obtain

   so high Reward but thus to s^ıue in vain   12

   tho I shall have no redresse

   yet of right ye can no lesse

   but rew vpon my pain

   but

⟨ffor⟩ I se well that yo^ꝰ high disdain   16

         ⟨that⟩

   wull no wise graunt that I shall more attain

   yet ye must graunt at the lest

   this my poure and small request

    reioyse not at

⟨to rew vpon⟩ my pain   20

E f. 38r, hand A. *A* f. 78v (*om.* ll. 18-20). *D* f. 37v. The *D* text is subscribed "ʃ." Hughey (II, 171) misread the "w" of "wytsave" (l. 9) in *D* as
"vo." Her variant for line 12 also implied incorrectly that the word "but" is
not in *D*. *M3* copied her variant.

The "&" in *E* (l. 3) was probably deleted by someone, but it is impossible
to say whom. All of the revisions in *E* for lines 16-20 were made by Wyatt,
in the same ink as that of the marginal signature. *M3* was incorrect in
noting that the word "that" (l. 17) was deleted by the scribe. Wyatt himself
canceled his own second thought.

A D: 9. ye] you *A*   vouchesave] wytsave *D*   12. so high Reward] so⟨re-
$\overset{hey}{}$
but
ward *D*   16. ⟨ffor)] But *A*] for *D*   17. wull] Will *A*   more] more *A D*
⟨that⟩
reioyse not at
18.-20. *om. A*   19. poure] power *D*   20. ⟨to rew vpon⟩my pain] to rewe
apon my ⟨pains[?]⟩ payne *D*

58

To wisshe and want and not obtain
  to seke & sew esse of my pain
  syns all that ever I do is vain
      What may it availl me   4
All tho I stryve boeth & howre
  against the streme w^t all my powre
  if fortune list yet for to lowre
      What may it availl me   8
If willingly I suffre woo
  if from the fyre me list not goo
Tho.   if then I burn to plaine me so
      What may it availl me   12
And if the harme that I suffre
  be run to farre owte of mesur
  to seke for helpe any further
      What may it availl me   16
What t⟨o⟩ho eche hert that hereth me plain
  pitieth and plaineth for my payn
  if I no les in greif remain
      What may it availl me   20
Ye tho the want of my relief
  displease the causer of my greif
  syns I remain still in myschief
      What may it availl me   24
Suche cruell chaunce doeth so me threte

```
        continuelly inward to fret
        then of relesse for to trete
                What may it availl me            28
    ffortune is deiff vnto my call
        my torment moveth her not at all
        and though she torn as doeth a ball
                What may it availl me            32
    ffor in despere there is no rede
        to want of ere speche is no spede
        to linger still alyve as dede
                What may it availl me            36
```

E f. 39r, hand A. A f. 77r (*om.* ll. 1.-10). D f. 71v. Hughey (II, 169) misread the word (or form) "hit" (l. 4) as "that" in D. M3 copied the error. The refrain may be checked in D only at line 36, "What mey yt auayle me" , since the refrain is abbreviated in the other refrain lines. The form "hit" for "it" also occurs in B. Hughey noted correctly that in D the scribe wrote "me soo" (l. 11) on top of "my foo."

An omission in E was supplied, thus: "boeth & howre" (l. 5). The insertion is in the hand of the verses on the lower half of f. 24v. Since there was
no direct connection between E and D, the insertion need not reflect the
influence of the D variant. The phrase clearly had to be formulaic or proverbial, which probably explains why the E scribe omitted one of its elements.
The correction in E line 17 is scribal. The E text contains one colon, thus:
"ere: speche is" (l. 34), and it is difficult to say whether or not it was
inserted by the same hand as that of line 5.

A D: 1.-10. *om.* A   4. it] hit D   5. *om.* & howre] daye & night D   7.
lowre] lower D   17. hereth] heares A] heris D   18. pitieth] petis D   27.
relesse] relef D   trete] entreat A] intrete D   30. moveth her not] moves
not her A

59

```
    X Some tyme I fled the fyre that me brent /
            see by
        by ⟨hilles⟩ land ⟨dales⟩ by water and by wynd ·
        and now I folow the coles that be quent /
Tho     from Dovo to Calais against my mynde ·        4
        lo how desire is boeth sprong & spent /
        and he may se that whilome was so blynd ·
        and all his labo now he laugh to scorne /
        mashed in the breers that erst was all to torne ·    8
```

E f. 40r, hand A. A f. 68v. D f. 38v. H f. 23r (ll. 1.-4. only). T 71. Hughey (II, 159) was technically correct in noting that the D text is "unsigned." But

it is subscribed "Wiat" by the same hand as that of the text. The revisions
in line 2 of *E* were made by Wyatt in the same pale brown ink as he used for
his marginal signature. The large "X" preceding the first word is scribal. The
E text contains one colon: "⟨dales⟩: by" (l. 2). It is impossible to tell whether
or not it was inserted later. All the rest of the punctuation looks scribal.

A D H T:
                    see by
1. brent] so brent *T*   2. by ⟨hilles⟩ land ⟨dales⟩] by Sea by lande *A*]
by hyllys by dales *D*] by see by lande *H*] By sea, by land *T*   3. I . . . coles]
the coales I folow *T*   4. against my] with willing *T*   5. sprong] furth sprong
T   5.-8. *om. H*   7. now he laugh] laughes he now *T*   8. mashed] Meashed
T   all to] onely *T*

60

                                   t   X
          he is   y   somtyme hath
    ⟨IHeame⟩ not ded ⟨all though I had⟩ a fall ·

       the Sonne retorn⟨es⟩th/that was vnder the clowd⟨e⟩·

Tho   and when fortune hath spitt oute all her gall //

       I trust good luck to me shalbe allow⟨e⟩d⟨e⟩ ·   4

       for I have sene a shipp into haven fall

       after the storme hath brok boeth mast & shrowd⟨e⟩

       and eke the willowe that stoppeth with the wynde

       doeth ryse again and greater wode doeth bynd ·   8

E f. 40r, hand A. *D* f. 74r. *P* f. 32r. *T* 72. The *D* text is subscribed "fs".
The colors of the inks in the *E* text indicate that Wyatt worked on it twice.
In pale brown ink he wrote the Roman numeral heading, his signature, and
the cancellations of the letter "e" in lines 2, 4, and 6. At that time he also
probably added the double bar at the end of line 3.
    All the revisions in wording and spelling in lines 1 and 2 he did in a heavy
black ink. First he converted the large ornamental "I" of the scribe that
opened the poem into an "H" and added an "e." Then he repeated "he"
above the same word, adding "is." In line 2 he wrote "th" over the letters
"es" in the scribal word "retornes." The virgule here is rather crowded and
may have been added by Wyatt when he canceled the letter "e" in "clowde."
    The *E* text contains one colon: "again: and" (l. 8), which was probably
inserted in a gap left by the scribe. Although the colon does not look like
Wyatt's work, it does not contrast sharply with the scribal text.

D P T:
        he is   y somtyme hath
1. ⟨IHeame⟩] I am *D P*] He is *T*   ⟨all though I had⟩] altho I had *D P*]
                                      r
that somtime had *T*   2. retorn⟨es⟩th] retonis *D P T*   that . . . the] that was
hid vnder *P*] that hid was vnder *T*   4. to me shalbe] shalbe to me *P*   5. into
haven] into the haven *P*] in hauen *T*   6. after the] when *P*] After that *T*
&] & also *P*   7. and . . . willowe] The willowe eke *T*   stoppeth] stowpith
D P] stoupeth *T*

61

        the furyous gonne
          ⟨bombard⟩
       ⟨Like as the cañon⟩ in his ra⟨g⟩Iing yre /

when that the bowle is ramed in to sore,

and that the flame cannot ⱡt from the fire, /

Tho.   cracketh in sonder: / and in the ayer doeth rore   4

the shevered peces · / right so doeth my desire

     whose flame
⟨which daily⟩ encreseth from more to more /

    wyche to let owt
⟨whose flame to open⟩ I dare not loke nor speke ·

so inwhard force my hert doeth all to breke ·   8

E f. 40v, hand A. *A* f. 68v. *T* 73. This text includes a specimen of the
double or triple punctuation that occurs in *E*. The virgules are scribal, but
the rest of the punctuation was inserted by one or more hands. Not all of it
is likely to be by Wyatt, since no similar kind of punctuation appears in his
holograph poems. Further, the ink of the punctuation does not match the
verbal revisions done by Wyatt in dark black ink in lines 1, 6, and 7, including
the "I" in "ra⟨g⟩ling" written on top of the "g."

   Hughey (II, 160) read "inwhard" (l. 8) as "now hard" and *M3* followed
her reading. Although there is no dot on the "i" in "inwhard," *E* clearly
agrees with *T* in intending the word to be "inward." Wyatt's writing style in
the word "bombard" is the same as that of the poem <u>Vulcane</u> <u>bygat</u> <u>me</u> on
f. 70r.

      the furyous gonne
         ⟨bombard⟩
A T: ⟨Like as the canon⟩] The furyous gonne *A T* ra⟨g⟩ling] most ragyng *T*
2..when that] when *A*   3. and . . . flame] and it the same *A*   4. cracketh]
Crackes *T*   doeth] doe *T*   5. peces . . . doeth] peces. So doth *T*
  whose flame   wyche to let owt
6. ⟨which daily⟩] whose flambe *A T*   from] ay from *T*   7. ⟨whose flame to
open⟩] whiche to lett out *A T*   8. inwhard] that of *A*

62

My hope Alas hath me abused

  and vain reIoysing hath me fed

  lust and Ioye have me refused

  and carefull plaint is in their stede

  to muche avauncing slaked my spede   4

  myrth hath caused my hevines

  and I remain all comfortles

Whereto did I assure my thought   8

  withoute displeasure stedfastly

  in fortunes forge my Ioye was wrought

  and is revolted redely

  I ame mystaken wonderly   12

  for I though nought but faithfulnes

  yet I remain all comfortles

In gladsom chere I did delite
    till that delite did cause my smert   16
    and all was wrong where I thought right
    for right it was that my true hert
    should not from trouth be set apt
    syns trouth did cause me hardines   20
    yet I remain all comfortles
Sometyme delight did tune my song
    and led my hert full pleasauntly
    and to my self I saide among   24
    my happ is comyng hastely
    but it hath happed contrary
    assuraunce causeth my distres

    and I remain all comfortles   28
Then if my note now do vary
    and leve his wonted pleasauntnes
    the hevy burden that I cary
    hath alterd all my Ioyefulnes   32
    no pleasure hath still stedfastnes
    but hast hath hurt my happenes
    and I remain all comfortles

E f. 41rv, hand A. *A* f. 77rv. *D* f. 74v. The *D* text is subscribed "fs."
Hughey (II, 169) contained two errors, copied in *M3*. There is no disagreement between *D* and *E* for line 8. Also, Hughey read the word "led" (l. 23)
as "leds." However, hand A first wrote "let," then added a "d" upon the "t,"
finishing with a downward loop. This downward loop is occasionally
employed elsewhere by hand A where it cannot possibly indicate an "s,"
and it is different from the abbreviated "es" as well as from the final "s."
The *E* text contains one colon: "note: now" (l. 29), which does not contrast
with the text.

A D: 6. avauncing] advauncing *A*   slaked] slakte *D*   12. wonderlye] won-
deruslye *D*   13. though] thought *A D*   16. my] me *D*   20. trouth]
trothe *A*   me] mye *A D*   28. and I remaine *D*   29. do] doth *A D*
35. and I Remayne / *D*

63

What deth is worse ⟨this⟩ then this
    when my delight
        wele my   my
my ⟨wordly⟩ Ioye & blys
    is from my sight   4
    boeth daye & nyght

                    my liff alas I mys
                ffor though I seme alyve
                    my hert is hens   8
                    thus botles for to stryve
                    oute of presens
Tho.   of my defens
                    towerd my deth I dryve   12
                Hertles alas what man
                    may long endure
                    Alas how lyve I then
                    syns no recure   16
                    may me assure
                    my liff I may well ban
                Thus doeth my torment gro
                    in dedly dred   20
                    alas who myght lyve so
                    alyve as deed
                    alyve to lede
                    a dedly lyff in woo   24

E f. 42r, hand A. *D* ff. 39v (*D1*), 74r (*D2*). The *D2* text is subscribed "fs".
Although the leaf in *E* was overwritten by later hands, the text is remarkably clear. The correction in line 1 is scribal. The revisions in line 3 are
by Wyatt in the same pale brown ink as his signature in the margin.

D: 3. *E*] my wordly Ioy my blysse *D1*] my wordelye Ioye and blisse *D2*
12. towerd] towarde *D2*   19. Thus] Thys *D1*   23. alyve] A lyffe *D1*]
alif *D2*

64

                Thenmy of liff/decayer of all kynde /
                          th
                    that w his could wethers away the grene /
                    this othre nyght me in my bed did fynde /
Tho.   and offered me to rid my fiever clene ·   4
                                                  ay
                    and I did graunt so did dispere me blynde ·
                          th   ∧
                    he drew his bowe w arrowe sharp & kene / ⟨:⟩ ·
                    and strake the place where love had hit before ·
                    and drave the first dart deper more & more   8

E f. 42v, hand A. *T* 85. Wyatt went over the scribal text in two colors of ink,
probably indicating two occasions. The emendation of spelling in line 4 is

by Wyatt in black ink. The signature and the punctuation marks are in brown ink. Note especially the deletion of the colon at the end of line 6.

T: 1. Thenmy] The enmy   2. could wethers] cold wythers   3. dispere]
dispayre   arrowe] arrowes

65

  Ons as me thought fortune me kyst
   and bad me aske what I thought best
Tho. and I should have it as me list
   therewith to set my hert in rest   4
  I asked nought but my dere hert
   to have for evermore myn owne
   then at an ende were all my smert
   then should I nede no more mone   8
  Yet for all that a stormy blast
   had overtorned this goodely day
   and fortune semed at the last
   that to her promes she saide nay   12
  But like as oon oute of dispere
   to soudden hope revived I
   now fortune sheweth herself so fayer
   that I content me wonderly   16
  My moost desire my hand may reche
   my will is alwaye at my hand
   me nede not long for to beseche
   her that hath power me to comaund   20
  What erthely thing more can I crave
   what would I wisshe more at my will
   no thing on erth more would I have
   save that I have to have it still   24
  ffor fortune hath kept her promes
   in graunting me my moost desire
   of my sufferaunce I have ⟨my⟩ redres
   and I content me with my hiere   28

E ff. 42v-43r, hand A. *D* ff. 71v (*D1*, fragment, ll. 1-8 only), 73v-74r (*D2*).
T 86. The deletion in line 27 of the *E* text is scribal.

D T: 1. as] *om. D1 D2*   5. nought . . . dere] but my ladies *T*   7. all] *om.*
D1   8. no more] to more *D2*   mone] to mone *D1 D2 T*   9.-28. *om. D1*
10. had] hath *D2*   16 wonderly] wondreslye *D2*] wondersly *T*   28.
sufferaunce] soueraigne *T*

66

X

My lute awake ꝑfourme the last
    laboꝰ that thou and I shall wast
    and end that I have now begon
    for when this song is song & past   4
    my lute be still for I have done
As to be herd where ere is none
    as lede to grave in marbill stone
    my song may perse her hert ⟨so⟩ as sone   8
    should we then sigh or syng or mone
    no no my lute for I have done
The Rokke do not so cruelly

Tho
    repulse the waves continuelly   12
    as she my suyte & affection
    so that I ame past remedy
    whereby my lute & I have done
Prowd of the spoyll that thou hast gott   16
    of simple herte thorough loves shot
    by whome vnkynd thou hast theim wone
    thinck not he haith his bow forgot
    all tho my lute & I have done   20
Vengeaunce shall fall on thy disdain
    that makest but game on ernest pain
    thinck not alone vnder the sonne
    vnquyt to cause thy lovers plain   24
    all tho my lute and I have done
          the lye
Perchaunce they lay wetherd & old
    the wynter nyght that are so cold
    playnyng in vain vnto the mone   28
    thy wisshes then dare not be told
    care then who lyst for I have done
And then may chaunce the to repent
    the tyme that thou hast lost and spent   32
    to cause thy lovers sigh & swoune
    then shalt thou knowe beaultie but lent
    and wisshe and want as I have done
Now cesse my lute this is the last   36
    laboꝰ that thou & I shall wast

and ended is that we begon
now is this song boeth song & past
my lute be still for I have done   40

E ff. 43v-44r, hand A. *D* ff. 14v-15r. *B* f. 125rv. *V* p. 114 (*V1*, *om*. ll. 26.-30.,
33.-40.), pp. 119.-120. (*V2*, *om*. ll. 26.-30.). *T* 87. The *D* text is subscribed
                           d
"fynys q Wyatt̶ṡ."
    On the inner margin of f. 43v in *E* is a note by Nott: "Ascribed to Lord
Rochfort in Nugae [/] Antiquae vol. 3d p. 286." The edition referred to is
that of 1779 (III, 286). In the earlier 1769 edition of *Nugae antiquae* (II,
252), the poem is headed "By the Earl of Rocheford." The ascription was
continued in Thomas Park's 1804 edition of *Nugae* (II, 400). Nott (II, 545)
reclaimed the poem for Wyatt.
    In *E* the "X" in the margin preceding the opening of the text is scribal,
as is the correction in line 8. The revision of spelling in line 26 is by Wyatt,
in the same hand and ink as is used on f. 70r. The first word in *E* line 16 is
"Prowd̨" indicating that the downward loop on the final "d" sometimes
added by hand A does not stand for a final "s." The unusual form "songyne"
(ll. 4, 39) occurs in *B*. The word appears in *M3* as "sung" in both text and
variants.

D B V T: 1. last] last labor *D*   3. now] new *V1 V2*   4. for] And *T*   is
song] ys songe *D*] is sung *V1*] is gon *V2*] ys songyne *B*   7. as] A *V2*   in]
                                                her
in a *V2*   8. her hert] ⟨thy⟩ hart *D*] ,heart *V2*   9. we] whe *B*   sigh or syng]
                   u̅   or
syng or syghe *D*] synge∧walle *B*] syng wepe *V1*] syng, wepe *V2*   10. no no]
No more *V2*   11. Rokk̨e do] Rokk dothe *D B V2*   14. past] past all *V1 V2*
16. spoyll] splen *V2*   gott] shot *V2̇*   17. hert̨e thorough] harts throw *B*]
hart, through *V2*] hartes through *T*   shot] got *V2*   18. by whome vnkynd]
                                                                oun
vnkynd althoughe *B V2*   wone] w⟨y[?]e⟩ *B*   19. bow] owne *V2*   21.
shall] may *D B V1 V2*   thy] such *V1 V2*   22. makest] mak̨e *D B*] maketh
V1 V2   on] of *D B V1 V2*   ernest] yernyst *B*   23. thinck] trow *D B V2*]
true *V1*   24. vnquyt] [V] ngentylly *V1*] Vngently *V2*   thy] the *V1*] to
V2   plain] payne *V1*   26.-30. *om*. *V1 V2*   26. Perchaunce] May chawnce
                        the
D B T   they] they *D*] the *B*] thee *T*   wetherd] whetheryd *B*   27. nyght]
nyght̨e *D B T*   30. care then] but care *B*   33.-40. *om*. *V1*   33. lovers]
lou̇' *B V2*   sigh] to sighe *V2*   swoune] sowne *B V2*   34. beaultie] beawte
D] bevtye *B*] beauty *V2 T*   36. Now . . . lute] My lute be styll *B*   38.
                                                haue now   t
ended] end *B V2*   is that we] ys that I∧begone *D*] y I haue now *B*] that
I haue *V2*   39. now is] ffor when *B*] Or when *V2*   boeth song] ys songyne
B] is song *V2*

67

If chaunce assynd
were to my mynde
by very kynd
of destyne   4

yet would I crave
nought els to have
but liff & libertie
Then were I sure   8
I myght endure
the displeasure
of crueltie

Tho.   where now I plain   12
alas in vain
lacking my liff for libertie
ffor withoute thone
thothre is gone   16
and there can none
it remedy
if thone be past
thothre doeth wast   20
and all for lack of libertie
And so I dryve
as yet alyve
all tho I stryve   24
with myserie
drawing my breth
lowking for deth
& losse of liff for libertie   28
But thou that still
maist at thy will
torn all this ill
aduersitie   32
for ye repare
of my welfare
graunt me but liff & libertie
And if not so   36
then let all goo
to wretched woo
and let me dye
for thone or thothre   40
there is none othre

                    th
my deth or liff w libertie

E ff. 44v-45r, hand A. *D* f. 70v. *B* f. 109r (fragment, ll. 1-4 only). The *D* text is subscribed "fs".

D B: 5.-42. *om. B*   7. but] but only *D*   15. thone] ton *D*   16. thothr*e*] tother *D*   19. thone] ton *D*   20. thothr*e*] tother *D*   40. thone or thothr*e*] ton or tother *D*

68

Nature, that ⟨gavce⟩ gave the bee so feet a gra⟨c⟩se, /
       fynd
    to ⟨get⟩ hony of so wond⟨e⟩rous fashion : /
    hath taught the spider owte of thesame pla⟨c⟩se,
Tho.   to fetche poyson, by straynge alteration ·   4
    tho this be stra⟨u⟩ynge⟨r⟩/, it is a stra⟨u⟩ynger case,/
    th   sse
    w oon ky⟨s⟩ by secret operation/,
    boeth th⟨o⟩ese at ons/, in those yo^{9} lippes to fynde:/
    in chaunge wherof/, I leve my hert behinde ·   8

E f. 45r, hand A. *D* f. 71v. *B* f. 129v. *H* f. 23r. *T* 88. The *D* text is subscribed "fs". The *H* text is ascribed "Sᵗ T. W." The variant "seche" listed in *M3* for *H* in line 2 is inexplicable.

My text shows Wyatt's careful emendations in spelling, punctuation, and wording. There are two colors of inking by Wyatt. The signature in the margin is in pale brown, while the emendations are in dark black. These emendations include the virgules added to the scribal commas and the spelling and word changes in lines 1-6. Exceptions are the correction of "⟨gavce⟩" (l. 1), which is scribal, and the two colons (ll. 2,7), which are crowded in before the two virgules at the ends of the lines. In this case Wyatt showed a definite preference for some spellings: "grase" rather than "grace" (l. 1), "wondrous" rather than "wonderous" (l. 2), "plase" rather than "place" (l. 3), and "straynge" rather than "straunge" (l. 5). The deletion of "e" in "wonderous" makes for a metrically exact line, but with an unnatural series of accents unless one imagines an unmarked caesura after "hony."
          fýnd   fýnd
It could be "to⟨get⟩honý of só wond⟨e⟩róus fashión /" or "to⟨get⟩hóny [caesura] óf so wónd⟨e⟩rous fáshion /" The absence of the medial virgule suggests the former.

                   fete   fynd
D B H T: 1. feet] ⟨swete⟩ *D*] fayre *B*] fatt *H*] feat *T*   2. ⟨get⟩] gett *D*] featch *B*] fynde *H*] find *T*   of] aftre *B*   wond⟨e⟩rous] strange a *B*   4. poyson] poysons *D*   5. case] ⟨thynge⟩ kase *B*   6. by] of *B*   7. th⟨o⟩ese] theise *D*] these *B*] theys *H*] these *T*   yo^{9}] thy *B*] o^{9} *H*

69

              th
I have sought long w stedfastnes
    to have had som ease of my great smert
    but nought availleth faithfulnes

        ^t
to grave w^t in your stony hert   4
But happe and hit or els hit not
  as vncertain as is the wynde
  right so it fareth by the shott
  of love alas that is so blynd   8
Therefore I plaid the foole in vain
  with pitie when I first began
  yor cruell hert for to constrain

Tho.   syns love regardeth no doulfull man   12
But of yor goodenes all yor mynde
  is that I should complain in vain
        is
  this ∧ the favo^r that I fynde
  ye list to here how I can plain   16
But tho I plain to please yor hert
  trust me I trust to temper it so
  not for to care which do revert
  all shalbe oon in welth or woo   20
ffor fansy rueleth tho right say nay
  even as the goodeman kyst his kowe
  none othre reason can ye lay
  but as who saieth I reke not how   24

E f. 45v, hand A. *D* f. 71v. The *D* text is marked after the last word: "how /ᴇ"
(l. 24), and beneath the last line is "fs". The word "is" (l. 15) was inserted by
Wyatt in the italic script he used on f. 70r.

D: 12. regardeth] regardᵉ   17. please] eese   19. do] side   21. rueleth] Rulis
22. none othre] no nother

70

X   Lyke as the Swan
    doeth strayn her v
    right so syng I w
    I dy I dy and yo   4
  I shall enforce my
    that all that her
    shall knowe th
    I dy I dy and y   8
Yo^r vnkyndnes ha

Tho   and chaunged
             to paynfull
             I dy I dy a   12
        Consumeth my
             your fawte
             melting in
             I dy I dy   16
        My faith
             bured sh
             I do bequ
             to cry I   20

E f. 46r, hand A. *D* f. 73r. *B* f. 122r. The *D* text is subscribed "fs͡s." The leaf in
E was torn away vertically, leaving only the opening words of each line. The text
must be completed from *D* or *B*. Since there is no complete *E* version, the editorial
choices must be made on critical grounds. In line 19 I prefer the more pointed
adjective "verye" (*D*) to the formulaic "wery" (*B*).

D B: 1. . . . towardis her dethe *D B*   2. . . . voyse w^t dolefull note *D B*   3. . . . w
waste of brethe *D B*   4. . . . you regarde yt note *D B*   5. . . . faynting brethe *D B*
6. . . . heris this delye note *D*] . . . dedlye note *B*   7. . . . that you dothe cause my
deth *D*] . . . do cause my dethe *B*   8. . . . & ∂ *D*] and you regard yt not *B*   9. . . .
hath swone my dethe *D B*   10. . . . hathe my ple^asunte note *D B*   11. . . . sighis y^t
stoppis my brethe *D*] . . . stoppe my brethe *B*   12. dy a] dye / *D*] dy and you
regard yt not *B*   13. . . . lif faileth my brethe *D B*   14. . . . is forger of this note
D B   15. . . . tearis a cruell dethe *D B*   16. I dy] I dye *D*] I dy I dy and you
regard yt not *B*   17. . . . w^t me aft^r my dethe *D B*   18. byrrid shalbe / and to this
note *D B*   19. . . . bequeth my verye brethe *D*] . . . wery brethe *B*   20. . . . I
dyede & you reg^arde yt note *D*] . . . regardid not *B*

                        71

             rmed
             mynde affermed
             ould be confermed   3
                                                           4
             that I myght like   5
             arme her hert alike
             not se the like   7
                                                           8
             my self in prese   9

I should not cese

hold my pease   11

                                 12

d me a pase   13

  had taken place

  de in her grace   15

                                 16

        had found   17

        unde

        ever sovnde   19

                                 20

    st   21

      est

        doeth rest   23

                                 24

E f. 46v, hand A. *D* f. 72v. The *D* text is concluded "Ineternum / fs☌" (l. 24). The leaf in *E* was torn away vertically, leaving no trace of each refrain line and only concluding portions of other lines. All the lines must be completed from the only other text, *D*.

D: 1. Inet⁾ nũ I was de⟨d⟩termmid   2. for to have louid and my ...   3. that wᵗ my herte it shuld ...   4. Ineternũ   5. forthwᵗ I founde the thing ...   6. and sought wᵗ loue to warme ...   7. for as me thought I shuld ...   8. Ineternum   9. To trase this daunse I put ...   10. vayne hope ded lede and bad ...   11. to s⁾ue / to suffer / & still to ...   12. Ineternum   13. Wᵗ this furst Rule I fordred ...   14. that as me thought my trowghthe ...   15. wᵗ full assurans to stond ...   16. in eternum   17. It was not long or I by proofe ...   18. that feble bilding is on feble grounde   19. for in her herte this wode ded neverʳ ...   20. Ineternum   21. Ineternũ then frõ my herte I keste   22. that I had furst det⁾ mind for the best   23. nowe in the place anotheʳ thought ...   24. Ineternum

                    72

  Syns ye delite to knowe
    that my torment & woo
    should still encrese
    withoute relese   4
    I shall enforce me so
    that liff & all shall goo
    for to content yoᵍ cruelnes

          And so this grevous trayne   8
          that I to long sustayn
          shall sometyme cese
          and have redresse
Tho   and you also remain   12
          full pleased with my pain
          for to content yoᵍ cruelnes
     Onles that be to light
          and that ye would ye myght   16
          se the distresse
          and hevines
          of oon slain owte right
          therewith to please yoᵍ sight   20
          and to content your cruelnes
     Then in yoᵍcruell mode
                          th
          would god fourthw   ye woode
          with force expresse   24
          my hert oppresse
          to do yoᵍ hert suche good
          to se me bathe in blode
          for to content yoᵍ cruelnes   28
     Then cowld ye aske no more
          then should ye ease my sore
          and the excesse
          of myn excesse   32
          and you should evermore
          defamed be therefore
          for to repent yoᵍ cruelnes /

E f. 47rv, hand A. D f. 72v. B f. 156r (*om.* ll. 8-14). The D text is subscribed "fs".
In addition to omitting the second stanza, the B text conflated lines 31-32, which
probably happened because of both the identical rhyme and the fact that the third
and fourth lines of each stanza were copied as one.

D B: 3. should] shall B   relese] redres B   8-14. *om.* B   16. that] yf B   19. oon
slain] on I slayne D] me your slaue B   21. your cruelnes] & c⁾ D   24. expresse]
exprest B   26. suche] some B   27. me] *om.* D   28. yoᵍcruelnes] & c⁾ D] your
heuynes B   31-32. and . . . excesse] & exsese of my B   32. myn] my D   33. you]
ye B   34. defamed] disdayned B   35. for] for for D] so B

73

Hevyn and erth & all that here me plain
　　do well pceve what care doeth cause me cry
　　save you alone to whome I cry invain
　　mercy madame alas I dy I dy   4
　　Yf that you slepe I humbly you require
Tho.　　forbere a while & let yo⁹ rigo⁹ slake
　　syns that by you I burn thus in this fire
　　to here my plaint dere hert awake awake   8
Syns that so oft ye have made me to wake
　　in plaint & teres & in right pitious case
　　displease you not if force do now me make
　　to breke your slepe crieng alas alas /   12
It is the last trouble that ye shall have
　　of me madame to here my last complaint
　　pitie at lest yo⁹ poure vnhappy slave
　　for in dispere alas I faint I faint   16
It is not now but long and long ago
　　I have you s⁾ ued as to my powre & myght
　　as faithfully as any man myght do
　　clayming of you nothing of right of right   20
Save of your grace only to stay my liff
　　that fleith as fast as clowd afore the wynde
　　for syns that first I entred in this stryff
　　an inward deth hath fret my mynde my mynd   24
Yf I had suffered this to you vnware
　　myn were the fawte & you nothing to blame
　　but syns you know my woo & all my care
　　why do I dy alas for shame for shame   28
I know right well my face my lowke my teeres
　　myn Iyes my worde & eke my drery chiere
　　have cryd my deth full oft vnto yo⁹ eres
　　herd of belefe it doeth appere appere   32
A better prouff I se that ye would have
　　how I ame dede therefore when ye here tell
　　beleveit not all tho ye se my grave
　　cruell vnkynd I say farewell farewell   36

E ff. 47v-48r, hand A. D f. 11r (fragment, ll. 25-36 only). The D text is subscribed "ffynys q Wyatt_s". The *E* text has two examples of the scribe linking two words together, "invain" (l. 3) and "believeit" (l. 35). There are several instances of the downward loop on the final "d": clowd" (l. 22), "mynd" (l. 24), and "cryd" (l. 31). The *E* text also contains two colons, thus: "apere: apere" (l. 32) and "farewell: farewell" (l. 36), which do not contrast with the rest of the text. The variants for lines 29 and 31 in *M3* were errcneous, and the one *D* variant for line 31 was omitted.

D: 1-24. *om. D*   30. drery] dere   31. have] hathe

74

Comfort thy self my wofull hert
   or shortly on thy self ⟨d⟩ the wreke
   for lenght redoubleth dedly smert
   why sighe thou hert & woult not breke   4
To wast in sight were pitious deth
   alas I fynd the faynt & weke
   enforce thy self to lose thy breth
   why sighe thou hert & woult not breke   8
Thou knowest right well that no redresse
   is thus to pyne and for to speke

Tho.   pardy it is remediles
   why sighe thou then & woult not breke   12
It is to late for to refuse
   the yoke when it is on thy neck
   to shak it of vaileth not to muse
   why sighe thou then & woult not breke   16
To sobb and sigh it were but vain
   syns there is none that doeth it reke
   alas thou doyst prolong thy pain
   why sighe thou then & woult not breke   20
Then in her sight to move her hert
   seke on thy self thy self to wreke
   that she may knowe thou sufferdst smert
   sigh there thy last and therewith breke /   24

E f. 48v, hand A. *D* f. 74r. The *D* text is subscribed "fs". The *E* text contains two colons, thus: "thy self: thy self" (l. 22) and "last: and" (l. 24), which do not contrast with the text. The correction in line 2 of *E* is scribal.

D: 1. Comfort] ⟨Cawerde⟩ ^{coforte}   3. lenght] lengthe   4. woult] will   5. sight] sighis   7. lose] loose   8. woult] will   12. woult] will   15. vaileth] vaylis   16. & woult not breke] *om.*   19. doyst] dost   20. why sighe thou then & woult not breke *E*] why sighe   23. sufferdst] suffird

75

Praise him for counceill that is droncke of ale   52
    grynne when he laugheth that bereth all the swaye
    frown when he frowneth & grone when is pale
On othres lust to hang boeth nyght & daye
    none of these poynte would ever frame in me   56
    my Wit is nought I cannot lerne the waye
And much the lesse of thinge that greater be
    that asken helpe of colours of devise
    to Ioyne the mene with eche extremitie   60
With the neryst vertue to cloke alwaye the vise
    and as to pourpose like wise it shall fall
    to ⟨ex⟩presse the vertue that it may not rise
As dronkenes good felloweshipp to call   64
    the frendly ffoo with his dowble face
    say he is gentill & courtois therewithall
And say that favell hath a goodly grace
    in eloquence and crueltie to name   68
    zele of Iustice and chaunge in tyme & place
And he that sufferth offence withoute blame
    call him pitefull & him true & playn
    that raileth rekles to every mans shame   72
Say he is rude that cannot lye & fayn
    the letcher a lover and tirannye
    to be the right of a prynce reigne
I cannot I no no it will not be   76
    this is the cause that I could never yet
    hang on their slevis that way as thou maist se
A chipp of chaunce more then a pownde of witt
    this maketh me at home to hounte & to hawke   80
    and in fowle weder at my booke to sitt
In frost & snowe then with my bow to stawke
    no man doeth marke where so I ride or goo
    in lusty lees at libertie I walke   84
And of these newes I fele nor wele nor woo
    sauf that a clogg doeth hang yet at my hele
    no force for that for it is ordered so
That I may lepe boeth hedge & dike full well   88
    I ame not now in ffraunce to Iudge the wyne

with saffry sauce the delicate to fele
Nor yet in spaigne where oon must him inclyne
    rather then to be owtewerdly to seme   92
    I meddill not with witte that be so fyne
Nor fflaunders chiere letteth not my sight to deme
    of black and white nor taketh my wit awaye
    with bestlynes / they beeste do so esteme   96
Nor I ame not where Christe is geven in pray
    for mony poisen and traison at Rome
    a comune practise vsed nyght and daie
But here I ame in kent & christendome   100
    emong the muses where I rede & ryme
Where if thou list my poynz for to com
Thou shalt be Iudge how I do spend my tyme

E ff. 49rv, hand A (*om.* ll. 1-51). A ff. 64r-65r (*om.* ll. 18-19, 29-31). D ff. 85v-
87r (*om.* ll. 28-30). C (unfoliated). U ff. 5v-7r. P ff. 30r-31r (*om.* ll. 18-19, 29-
31). T 125. The D text is subscribed "fs." The C text is subscribed "T. W." The
U text is subscribed "finis T. Wyet" and is headed by a copy of *Venemous
thorns* as an unbroken part of the whole.

    Hughey (II, 138) agreed with Foxwell that D is probably the best source for
lines 1-51, based on the high quality of ll. 52-103. In fact, D is slightly better than
Hughey's variants indicate, since two of them are ghosts. In line 91, Hughey mis-
read "$\widetilde{o\gamma}$" as "ay" and "$\mathcal{D}$" as "so," whereas D here actually agrees with E in
reading "õn" and "him." Both these errors were copied in *M3*. Hughey' statement
that C is the manuscript closest to T is erroneous, but at the time she did not know
of U's existence.

    I shall compare the other manuscripts with E in lines 52-103, taking first the
instances in which they show independent departures. P is eliminated, since it is
most likely a close copy of A, even to the position of headlines on the leaves. A
departs notably from E in ll. 53 (omits a word), 55 (plural), 57 ("to" changes the
noun "waye" to the verb "weigh"), 59 (verb form), 59 ("to" again changes noun
to verb), 67 (omission of verb in parallel syntax), 76 (variation in rhetorical form),
80 (omission of "to" in infinitive form), 83 (variant form of phrase), 84 (either
number or actual word difference), 86 (redundant "still"), 89 (omission), 90
(plural), 95 (word re-emphasizes the negative), 95 (plural), 97 (omission avoids
double negative), 99 (wording), 101 ("in" for "&," not noted in Hughey or *M3*),
and 102 the initials "J. P." disturb the meter. These are considerable departures
from E, especially in view of the omission of lines that must have been extant
within ll. 1-51.

    D differs from E in ll. 52 (verb form affecting meter), 54 (alternate verb ending),
56 (alternate negative form), 65 (unaspirated form), 85 (pronoun), 92 (wording),
94 (alternate form?), and 101 (form affects meter).

    C departs notably in ll. 53 (verb ending), 56 (preposition "wyth" for "in"), 62
(auxiliary verb), 66 (pronominal reference), 77 (omission of conjunction disturbs
meter), 81 (added word disturbs meter), 86 (word distribution over the line), 90
(plural), 102 (word form), and 103 (wording).

The relationships among *A*, *D*, and *C* as revealed by their mutual differences with *E* are as follows:

53 (*A* and *D* share verb form)
54 (*A*, *D*, and *C* correct scribal omission, or do not commit it)
77 (*A* and *D* share auxiliary verb)
80 (*A*, *D*, and *C* omit "to," regularizing meter)
83 (*A* and *C* have rhetorical variations)
85 (*A*, *D*, and *C* have rhetorical variations)
88 (*A*, *D*, and *C* prefer "dytche" to *E*'s "dike")
90 (*A* and *D* share "what" for *E*'s "with")
94 (*A* and *D* share alternate verb form;
   A has "witte" and *C* has "wyt" where *E* reads "sight")
95 (*A*, *D*, and *C* share alternate verb form)
96 (*A*, *D*, and *C* have variations, but *D* and *C* both omit "so")

Thus, there are six instances in which all three manuscripts agree, but in the last instance perhaps the crucial difference relates *D* more with *C*. In four cases *A* agrees with *D*, and in two, with *C*. In sum, the evidence of lines 52-103 in *A*, *D*, and *C* shows that *A* has the largest number of differences with *E*, *C* next, and *D* probably the least overall. But the choice between *C* and *D* depends almost entirely on how one weighs lines 86, 94, and 103, for these readings set off *C* from *A* and *D*. In line 94 "wyt" may have been Wyatt's first choice, since "sight" was one of the "five wits."

If *A* and *D* were complete texts, there would be little problem in choosing a copy text for lines 1-51. However, all five lines missing from *A* and the three missing from *D* are printed in *T*. *C* and *U* show that these lines were extant in manuscript. All 51 lines would have fitted neatly into *E* on one leaf (now missing), since 27 lines are copied on f. 49r. That measure would have allowed three line spaces for head room at the beginning of the poem. It is very likely that all 51 lines were copied into *E*.

The texts in *A* are usually of very high quality when compared with those in *E*. This text is an exception. Given the fact that the tercets are neatly displayed in *E*, the omission of five lines in two places in *A* must be because the copy for *A* was not in this instance prepared from the fair copy of *E*. It probably was from rough copy with deletions and revisions, with perhaps one or two tercets inserted in the margin or not yet added to the text.

Within the first 51 lines, *A* and *D* have a common omission (*A* omits ll. 29-31, *D* omits ll. 28-30). In the latter portion of the poem they share four variant readings, in lines 53, 77, 90, and 94. It is reasonable to conclude, then, that they are based on the same rough copy directly or at one remove.

In contrast to *A* and *D*, *C* is complete. This fact argues either for greater care on the part of the scribe with rough copy, for better copy, or for later copy after one or two tercets had been added to the poem. In any of these cases, *C* may not be lightly dropped as copy text for lines 1-51, especially since five lines must come from *C*. (*U* is out of the question.)

In *M3 D* was much "improved" after being chosen as copy text:

1 Myne owne *A C*] My nowne *D*] Myne owne *M3*
15 touche *A C*] twyche *D*] touche *M3*   me list *A*] my lyst *D*] and me lust *C*]
   : me lyst *M3*
19 *om. A*] from me tūne *D*] frame my tonge *C*] frame my tonge *M3*
25 to do so great a *A*] to do so grete *A D*] nor do suche *C*] nor do so great a *M3*
28 *om. D*] with wordes *A*] wth my worde *C*] with my wordes *M3*
32 wyles *A C*] wille *D*] wyles *M3*
38 highe Cesar *A*] him Cesar *D*] him Caesar *C*] highe Cesar *M3*
42 his *A C*] is *D*] his *M3*

43 suche *A C*] shuch *D*] suche *M3*
45 lyon *A C*] lyond *D*] lyon *M3*   of Coward *A*] off coward *C*] of cowarde *D*]
of cowarde *M3*
47 dyeth *A*] diethe *C*] dithe *D*] diethe *M3*
50 Topas] thopas *C*] thopias *D*] Thopas *M3*

These emendations include the most dramatic and important decision to be made
in the entire text, in line 38. If *D* has any authority, it should be used there,
especially since it is backed by *C*. Wyatt must have dared to write "him—Caesar."

In only one instance does *D* offer the editor a literary "value" on its own
authority:

7 because *A*] bycawse *C*] for be cawsse *D*] for becawsse *M3* This is the only case
in which *D* offers a reading not available in either *A* or *C* and which may be
preferred by the modern editor (if he assumes that Wyatt aimed at ten syllables in
every line). The value of the *D* reading is simply that it regularizes the meter. One
may conclude, then, that the first 51 lines should be based on *C* and emended
from *A* and *D*, rather than taking *D* as the copy text. Since *C* is the only accept-
able manuscript authority for five of the lines, this is the more reasonable procedure.

In one more instance Hughey created a ghost variant, which was copied into *M3*.
Hughey (II, 136) noted for *D* (l. 40) the variant "can," where *D* actually reads "if
lyve donnot lye," agreeing with *A*. In addition in *E* is one instance of a colon in the
text, in the very last line of the poem at the bottom of f. 49v. This looks like the
insertion of someone leafing through the volume and looking for a likely
spot. In conclusion, whether one decides on *D* or *C* for lines 1-51, consistent
and courageous editing demands the word "him" rather than "highe" in
line 38.

A D C U P T: 1-51. *om. E*
1. Myne owne J. P. sins you delight to knowe *A*
   Myne owne] My nowne *D*   J. P.] Iohn poyntz *D C U T*   sins] sythe *U*
   you] ye *D C T*   delight] lyst *U*
2. the cawse whye that homeward I do me draw *A*
   cawse] causes *C T*   that] *om. U*   do] *om. D C U T*
3. and flye the prease of Coortes whearso they go *A*
   flye] fle *D C P T*   they[I *C*
4. Rather than to lyve thrall vnder the awe *A*
   the awe] woo *U*
5. of Lordlye lookes wrapped within my Cloke *A*
6. to will and lust, learning to sett a lewe *A*
   lewe] lawe *D C T*] loo *U*] lowe *P*
7. It is not because I scorne or mocke *A*
   because] for be cawsse *D*
8. the powre of them to whome powre hath lent *A*
   to whome powre] to whome fortune *D C U P*] whom fortune *T*   hath]
   here hath *T*
9. chardge over vs of right to stryke the stroke *A*
   to stryke the stroke] to stroke to strike *corr. in margin* to strik ẙ stroke *C*
10. but trew it is that I haue ever ment *A*
    ever] allwais *D C U P T*
11. lesse to esteeme them then the common sorte *A*
12. of owtward thinge that iudge in theire entent *A*
13. without regarde what dothe inward resorte *A*
    what dothe inward] that dothe inwarde *C*] what inward doth *T*
14. I graunt somtyme that of glorye the fyre *A*
    that of glorye] of glory that *T*

15. doth touche my hart me list not to reporte *A*
   touche] twyche *D*   me list] my lyst *D*] and me lust *C*] my luste *U*   to
   reporte] repent *C*
16. blame by honour and honour to desyre *A*
   blame] pleysure *U*
17. but how may I nowe this honour attaine *A*
   I] he *U*   nowe this honour] this honour now *D C T*
18-19. om. A P
                    t
18. y̌ cannot dy the coloure blake *A* lyer *D*
   blake] of blak *C*
19. My poyntz I cannot fro͂m me tu͂ne to fay͂ne *D*
   fro͂m me tu͂ne] frame my tonge *C*] frame theyre tune *U*]   frame my tune *T*
20. to cloke the truthe for prayse without desert *A*
21. of them that list all vyce for to retaine *A*
   list] lust *C U*   vyce for to] vices to *C*] nice for to *T*
22. I can not honour them that sett͡e their parte *A*
   them] them them *C*   sett͡e] sett *C U T*
23. with venus and Backus all their lif longe *A*
24. nor holde my peace of them though that I smart *A*
   though that] Allthoo *D C T*
25. I can not crowche nor kneele to do so great a wronge *A*
   nor] and *U*   to do so great a] nor do suche *C*] to doo so myche *U*] to such
   a *T*
26. to worship them as god on earthe alone *A*
   as] lyke *D C U P T*
27. that are as woolves theise sillie lambs among *A*
   that] they that *U*   as] like *C*] *om.* as and like *U*   theise] the *U*
28-30. om. D
28. I can not with wordes complayne and mone *A*
   wordes] my worde *C*] my word͡e *U T*
29-31. om. A P
29. and suffer nought nor smart wythout co͂playnt *C*
30. Nor torne the worde that from my mouthe is gone *C*
31. I cannot speke and loke lyke *A* saynct *D*
                 th
   and] w *C*   lyke] ryght as a *C*] like as a *T*
32. vse wyles for witt and make disceate a pleasure *A*
   wyles] will͡e *D*   make] vse *C*
33. and call crafte Counsaile for profitt still to paynt *A*
   and call] Call *T*   profitt] lucre *T*
34. I can not wrest the law to fill the Cofer *A*
35. with innocent bloud to feede my self fatt *A*
36. and do my self hurt wheare my self I offer *A*
   my self hurt] most hurt *D C U P T*   my self I] most help I *D C U*] that
   most helpe I *T*
37. I am not he that can allowe the state *A*
38. of highe Cesar and dampne Cato to die *A*
   highe] him *D C U*   and . . . die] ⟨and Catho deme to dye⟩ and deme cato
   to dy *C*
39. that with his death did scape out of the gate *A*
                      t
   with his] by his *C*] w is *D*   scape] escape *C*] steppe *U*
40. from Cesars hands if Livie do not lye *A*
   Livie] lyve *D*   do] did *C*] dothe *U P T*
41. and will not lyve wheare lybertie was lost *A*

will] wolld *D C U*] ⟨will⟩*P*] would *T*
             ^{would}
42. So did his hart the Common weale applie *A*
  his] is *D*   weale] welthe *C U T*
43. I am not he suche eloquence to boste *A*
  suche] shuch *D*
44. to make the Crowe singing as the Swanne *A*
  to make] to marke *C*   the Crowe singing] the singing crowe *C*] the
  crow in singyng *T*
45. nor call the lyon of Coward beastes the moste *A*
nor] or *U*   lyon] lyond *D*   of Coward] of cowarde *D*] cowarde of *U*]
of coward ∧*P*   the moste] most *U*
46. that can not take a mowse as the Catt can *A*
  take a] catche the *U*
47. and he that dyeth for hunger of the golde *A*
  dyeth] dithe *D*   the golde] gold *C*
48. call hym Alexander and say that Pan *A*
49. passeth apollo in mvsyke many folde *A*
  many folde] many a fold *C*
50. prayse Sir Topas for a noble tale *A*
  Topas] thopias *D*] Topias *P*
51. and scorne the storye that the knight tolde *A*
52. droncke] drounkin *D*   of ale] ⟨asale⟩ of ale *P*   53. laugheth] laughes
A D P T] lawyghe *U*   bereth] beres *C*   all] *om. A P*   54. frowneth]
frowne *D T*   is] he is *A D C U P T*   55. On] vpon *U*   lust] luste *A U P*
nyght & daye] ⟨day and⟩ night and day *A*] day and night *P*   56. would] will
A C P   ever] neu *D*   in] wyth *C U*   57. the] to *A P*   58. the] *om. U*
59. asken] aske *A P*] aske the *U*   of devise] to devyse *A P T*   60. eche]
om. U   61. With the] With *T*   to cloke alwaye] ay to cloke *T*   62. and]
om. U   shall] may *C*   63. ⟨ex⟩presse] presse *A D C P T*] oppresse *U*
vertue] vertu ⟨to cloke⟩ *C*   62-63. *repeated T*   64. dronkenes] dronknes *U*
65. his] is *D*   dowble] faire double *T*   66. he] this *C*   67. And say] and
that *A P*] Affirme that *T*   72. to every] vnto ech *T*   75. a prynce reigne]
Prynce Realmes *U*   76. no no it] no nor it *A*] no nor yet *P*   77. that] *om.*
C U   could] wold *A D P*   78. maist] may *D*   79. chipp] ⟨s⟩chip *P*   80. to
hawke] hawke *A D C U P T*   81. in] in the *C U*   to] I *U*   82. to stawke]
I staulke *U*] ⟨at my book to Sitt⟩ w^t my bowe to stalke *C*   83. where so]
wheare that *A P*] wher to *C*] where *U*   84. lees] leases *A P*] leit *U*   85.
And] and so *U*   of these] of theire *D*   newes] *om. U*   nor wele nor]
nother weale nor *A P*] no wele nor *D*] nor well ne *C*   86. sauf . . . yet]
Save . . . yet still *A*] saue of a clogg that yet doth hang *C*   87. is] was *U*
88. dike] dytche *A D C U P*   89. now] *om. A P*   90. with] what *A D P*
saffry] saverye *A D C U P*   sauce] sawces *C*   the] these *A D C P*   those *T*
91. oon must him] men most theym *U*   92. owtewerdly] vtterlye *D*   94.
letteth] lette *A D P T*   my] me *D*   sight] witte *A*] wyt *C*   deme]
deeme
⟨dymme⟩ *A*   95. and] nor *A P*   nor] ne *U*   taketh] takes *A D C P T*
wit] witte *A U P T*   96. they beeste do so] the beastes do so *A P*] theybeste
do *D*] those beastes do *C*] those beaste dothe so *U*] such do those
beastes *T*   97. Nor I am not] Nor am I *C*] Neyther am I *U*   Christe]
truth *T*   is] was *U*   98. at Rome] of some *T*   99. practise] pla⟨yce⟩gue *A*]
place *P*   100. here I ame in] I am in *U*] I am here in *T*   and] and in *U*
101. emong] amonge *D*   muse] ⟨musues⟩ muses *C*   &] in *A*   102. list]
lust *C*   my poynz] my J. P. *A P*] myne owne Iohn Poyns *T*   for] *om. T*

103. how I] ⟨I⟩ howe I *D*   do spend] ∧^{do}spend *P*] dispende *C*] spende *U*

76

Desire alas my master & my foo /

u
so sore alterd thi sellff how mayst y se?
some tyme sowght t y dryvys
u
⟨whome y⟩ I ⟨did se*k*e / now chaseth⟩ me to & fro
t
some tyme ledst y ledyth*e*
⟨whome⟩ thow ⟨didst reule / now rewlyth⟩ th*e* & me · 4
what reson
Tho ⟨tyranie it⟩ is to rewle thy subiecte so?
by forcyd law & mutabilite
for where by th*e* I dowtyd to have blame
evyn now by hate agayne I dowt th*e* same · 8

TV

E f. 50r, Wyatt's holograph. *D* f. 73r. *T* 112. The *D* text is subscribed "fs". Wyatt's marginal signature is in a pale brown ink matching that of the text below on the same leaf, *Venemus thornes*. The test of *Desire alas* and its revisions is in a dark black ink.

Only one line in the *D* text (l. 4) matches the earlier version in *E*. It is, therefore, impossible to claim that the whole *D* text represents an earlier version from a Wyatt working draft. It could just as well be someone else's "improvement" on Wyatt's work.

D T: 1. Desire alas] Cruell desire *D* 2. so . . . sellff] thy silf so chaũgid for shame *D* 3. ⟨whome . . . chaseth⟩] (some, dryvys) yt I have sought dothe chase *D* I sowght] thou sekest *T* 4. ⟨whome . . . rewlyth⟩] (some, ledyth*e*) whõ yu didist rule / nowe rulith *D* 5. ⟨tyranie it⟩] (what reson) what right *D* 6. by . . . &] and to be rulid bye *D* 7. for] lo *D* 8. hate] dred *D*

77

V

Venemus thornes that ar so sharp & kene
sometyme ber flowers fayre & fresh*e* of hue
poyson offtyme is put in medecene
Tho and cawsith*e* helth*e* in man for to renue 4
t t
ffyre y purgith*e* allthing y is vnclene
may hele/& hurt · and if thes bene true
I trust somtyme my harme may be my helth*e*
t
syns evry wo is Ioynid w some welth · 8

TV

E f. 50r, Wyatt's holograph. *D* f. 72v. *H* f. 23r. *P* f. 32r. *U* f. 5v. *T* 267.
The *D* text is subscribed "fs". The *H* text is headed "S̄ T. W." The *U* text, which lacks one line, forms the opening lines of a text of *Myne own Iohn poyns*.

   The *E* text is a fair copy in Wyatt's holograph, entirely in the same pale brown ink from the Roman numeral heading to the monogram signature and marginal signature. It is therefore a good example of Wyatt's punctuation. When Wyatt signed this text in the margin, he also added his signature to the poem above it on the same leaf.

D H P U T: 1. that ar so] that be both *P*] wch are bothe *U*   2. sometyme ber] beare somtymes *P*] Beare flowers we se full fresh and faire of hue *T*   3.

poyson] and poyson *P*   offtyme] oft tymes *D U*] oftayne *H* ofte *P*] is also *T*
4. *om. U*] and to his helthe dothe make the mã renue *D*] And vnto man his helth doth oft renue *T*   and] w^{ch} *H*   5. fyre that all thing cõsumith so clene *D*] the fier eke that all consumeth cleene *P*] The fier that all thinges eke consumeth cleane *T*   6. hele /& hurt] hurt and heale *T*   and] then *T* thes bene] this be *D H U*] that this be *P T*   7. somtyme] *om. H*   may be] to be *H*   8. with] to *H*

78

My mothers madye when they did sowe & spȳn
   they sang sometyme a song of the feld mowse
   that forbicause her lyvelood was but thyn
Would nede goo seke her townyssh systers howse   4
   she thought her self endured to much pain
   the stormy blaste her cave so sore did sowse
That when the forowse swymmed wth the rain
   she must lye cold & whete in sorry plight   8
   and wours then that / bare meet ther did remain
To comfort her when she her howse had dight
   sometyme a barly corn sometyme a bene
   for which she laboured hard boeth daye & nyght   12
In harvest tyme whilest she myght goo & glyne
   and wher stoore was stroyed with the flodd
   then well awaye for she vndone was clene
Then was she fayne to take in stede of fode   16
   slepe if she myght her hounger to begile
   my syster ꝗ she / hath a lyving good
And hens from me she dwelleth not a myle
   in cold & storme she lieth warme & dry   20
   in bed of downe the dyrt doeth not defile

Her tender fote / she laboureth not as I
   richely she fedeth and at the richemans cost
   and for her meet she nyde not crave nor cry   24
By se by land of the delicate the moost
   her Cater seke & spareth for no pell
   she fedeth on boyled bacon meet & roost
And hath therof neither charge nor travaill   28
   and when she list / the licoꝛ of the grape
   doeth glad her hert till that her belly swell
And at this Ioꝛney she maketh but a Iape
   so fourth she goeth trusting of all this welth   32
   with her syster / her part so for to shape
That if she myght kepe her self in helth
   to lyve a Lady while her liff doeth last
   and to the dore now is she com by stelth   36
And with her foote anon she scrapeth full fast
   thothre for fere durst not well scarse appere
   of every noyse so was the wretche agast
At ⟨the⟩ last she asked softly who was there   40
   and in her langage as well as she cow⟨l⟩d
   pepe ꝙ the othre syster I ame here
Peace ꝙ the town⟨e⟩y⟨sshe⟩ mowse why spekest
              thou so lowde
   and by the hand she toke her fayer & well   44
                     by
   welcom ꝙ she my sister my the Roode
She fested her that Ioy it was to tell
   the faer they had they drancke the wyne so clere
   and as to poupose now & then it fell   48
She chered her with how syster what chiere
   amydde this Ioye befell a sorry chaunce
   that well awaye the straunger bought full dere
The fare she had for as she loke a⟨r⟩ scaunce   52
   vnder a stole she spied two stemyng Ise
   in a rownde hed with sherp erys / in fraunce
Was never mowse ⟨fe⟩ so ferd for tho
   had not I sene suche a beest before   56
   yet had nature taught her after her gyse
To knowe her ffoo and dred him evermore
   the towney mowse fled she knowe whether to goo

thothre had no shift but wonders sore   60
fferd of her liff / at home she wyshed her tho
   and to the dore alas as she did skipp
   thevyn it would lo and eke her chaunce was so
At the threshold her sely fote did tripp   64
   and ere she myght ⟨it⟩ recover ⁀it again
   the trayto^g Catt had caught her by the hipp
And made her there against her will remain
   that had forgotten her poure suretie & rest   68
   for semyng welth wherin she thought to rayne
Alas my poyngz, how men do seke the best
   and fynde the wourst by erro^g as they stray
   and no marvaill when sight is so opprest   72
And blynde the gyde anon owte of the way
   goeth gyde and all in seking quyete liff
   o wretched mynde there is no gold that may
Graunt that ye seke no warr no peace no stryff   76
   no no all tho thy hed were howpt with gold
   s$^?$geaunt with mace hawbert sword nor knyff
Cannot repulse the care that folowe should
   eche kynd of lyff hath with hym his disease   80
   lyve in delight evyn as thy lust would
And thou shalt fynde when lust doeth moost the please
   it irketh straite and by it self doth fade
   a small thing it is that may thy mynde apese   84
Non of ye all there is that is so madde
   to seke grapes vpon brambles or breers
   nor none I trow that hath his wit so badd
To set his hay for Conys over Ryvers   88
   ne ye se not a dragg net for an hare
   and yet the thing that moost is yo^g desire
Ye do mysseke with more travaill & care
   make playn thyn hert that it be not knotted   92
   with hope or dred and se thy will be bare
ffrom all affecte whome vice hath ever spotted
   thy self content with that is the assigned
   and vse it well that is to the allotted   96
Then seke no more owte of thy self to fynde
   the thing that thou haist sought so long before

for thou shalt fele it sitting in thy mynde
Madde if ye list to continue your sore   100
   let present passe and gape on tyme to cõm
   and diepe yo^9 self in travaill more & more
Hens fourth my poyngz, this shalbe all & some
   these wretched fooles shall have
         nought els of me   104
   but to the great god & to his high dome
None othre pain pray I for theim to be
   but when the rage doeth led then from the right
   that lowking backward vertue they may se   108
Evyn as she is so goodly fayre & bright
   and whilst they claspe their luste in armes a crosee
   graunt theim goode lorde as thou maist of thy myght
   to frete inward for losing suche a losse /   112

E ff. 50v-52v, hand *A*. *A* ff. 100r-101v. *D* f. 87v (fragment, ll. 1-18 only and first word of l. 19). *T* 124.

Hughey (II, 187) ovserved that *E* and *T* frequently agree against *A*, but never *A* and *E* against *T*. The *A* texts of the satires are notably less accurate than the *A* texts of the shorter poems.

In two instances I disagree with Hughey. In the *D* text (l. 2) she read "fildy," which mistakes a downstroke on the final "d" for a "y." In *E* (l. 43) the scribe apparently wished to preserve the "y" in "townysshe," which may originally have been "townesshe," but it is difficult to be sure. In any case, the "e" is not placed above the line, as Hughey suggested. Compare line 59.

The *E* text contains a number of colons, thus: "corn: sometyme" (l. 11), "hert: till" (l. 30), "fled: she" (l. 59), "lo: and" (l. 63), "marvaill: when" (l. 72), "no: no: all" (l. 77), "is: that" (l. 84), and "lorde: as" (l. 111). All the colons appear to be integral to the scribal text. All corrections in the *E* text are also scribal.

A D T: 1. did] do *A T*   and] or *D*   2. They sing a songe made of the fieldishe mowse *A T*   4. seke] se *A T*   5. much] greevous *A T*] myche *D* 13. whilest] when *A*] whylst *D*] while *T*   14. wher] when her *A T* stroyed] stroyd *D* 17. myght] cowlde 18.] *om. D* 19. And] *om. rest of ll. 19-112 D* 22. laboureth] labours *A T* 23. fedeth] feedes *A T* 24. nyde] neede *A*   25. of the] of *A T*   27. fedeth] feedes *A T*   boyled bacon meet &] boylde meat, bake meat, and on *A*]   boyle meat, bake meat, and on *T*   28. therof neither] therfore no whitt of *A T* 31. she maketh] makes she *A T*   32. goeth] goes *T*   34. myght] might theare *A T* 37. scrapeth] scrapes *A T*   38. scarse] *om. A*   40. At ⟨the⟩] At *A T*
                           by
43. town⟨e⟩y⟨sshe⟩] Towne *A T*   45. my] by *A T*   46. it was] was *A* 48. poupose] purpose *A T*   50. amydd-e] Amyd *A T*   52. loke a⟨r⟩ scaunce] lookt a scaunce *A T*   53. stole] stoole *A*   spied] espyed *A*   55. ⟨fe⟩ so] so *A T*   tho] the vnwyse *A T*   56. I sene] ysene *A T*   60. thothre] The other *A T*   61. wyshed] wisht *A T*   63. thevyn] The heaven *A T*   65. ⟨it⟩

recover ^it^] recover it *A T*   68. forgotten] forgote *A T*   poure] powre, *A*]
power, *T*   69. semyng] seeking *A*   71. wourst] worsse *A*   73. blynde]
blyndes *A T*   76. ye] you *A T*   77. were howpt with] weare hoope of *A*
78. hawbert] with hawlberd *A T*   nor] or *A*   79. Cannot] That can *A*
81. delight] delightes *A*   82. doeth moost the] thee most doth *A*   84. it is]
is it *A T*   85. ye] you *A T*   86. grapes vpon] for grapes on *A T*   or] or
on *A T*   87. his] a *A*   89. ne ye se] Nor ye sett   an] a *A*   91. Ye]
You *A T*   mysseke] myslyke *A*   92. thyn] thye *A*   94. ffrom] ffor *A*
ever] never *A*   95. assigned] assynde *A T*   99. sitting] stickinge *A T*
100. Madde] Made *A*   102. yo⁵] thie *A*   105. high] *om. A T*   107. then]
them *A T*   108. vertue] *om. A*

79

:	To cause accord or to aggre	
	two contraries in oon degre	
	and in oon poynct as semeth me	
	to all mans wit it cannot be	4
	it is impossible	
	Of hete and cold when I complain	
	and say that hete doeth cause my pain	
	when cold doeth shake me every vain	8
	and boeth at ons I say again	
	it is impossible	
Tho.	That man that hath his hert away	
	if lyff lyveth there as men do say	12
	that he hertles should last on day	
	a lyve & not to torn to clay	
	it is impossible	
	Twixt lyff and deth say what who sayth	16
	there lyveth no lyff that draweth breth	
	they Ioyne so nere & eke ⟨in⟩ I feith	
	to seke for liff by wissh of deth	
	it is impossible	20
	Yet love that all thing doeth subdue	
	whose power ther may no liff eschew	
	hath wrought in me that I may rew	
	these miracles to be so true	24
	that are impossible	

E f. 53r, hand A. *D* f. 69r. The *D* text is subscribed "fs⸪." The last three
words of the third line, "as semyth me," were added by the hand of the terminal "⸪." That hand contrasts markedly with the running hand of the text
and of the "fs." Line 16 of the text was first copied where line 11 should be,
then deleted.

In *E* Wyatt's signature in pale brown ink contrasts with the scribal copy, including the large colon preceding the first words. In line 16 the scribe may have written "saeyth" rather than "sayth." The deletion in line 18 is also scribal.

D: 4. mans] menns   12. lyveth] lyve   do] dothe   13. he] *om.*
14. torn] tone   21. thing] thinge   24. these] this

80

Though this port and I thy s⁾ unt true
   and thou thy self doist cast thy bemes from hye
   from thy chieff howse / promising to renew
   boeth Ioye and eke delite behold yet how that I   4
   bannysshed from my blisse carefully do crye
   helpe now Citherea my lady dere
   my ferefull trust en vogant la galere
Alas the dowbt that dredfull absence geveth   8
   withoute thyn ayde assuraunce is there none
   the ferme faith that in the water fleteth
   succoꝛ thou therefor in the it is alone
   stay that with faith / that faithfully doeth mone   12
   and thou also gevest me boeth hope & fere
   remembr thou me en vogant la galerie
By Sees & hilles elonged from thy sight
   thy wonted grace reducing to my mynde   16
   in sted of slepe / thus I occupy the nyght
   a thowsand thoughte & many dowbte I fynde
   and still I trust thou canst not be vnkind
   or els dispere my comfort & my chiere   20
   would she fourthwith en vogant la galerie
Yct on my faith full litle doeth remain
   of any hope whereby I may my self vphold
   for syns that onely worde do me retain   24
   I may well thinck the affection is but cold
   but syns my will is nothing as I would
   but in thy hande it resteth hole & clere
   forget me not en vogant la galerie   28

E ff. 53v-54r, hand A. *B* f. 171r. The variant for line 6 in *B* indicates an attempt to regularize the line metrically. This variant is not noted in *M3*. The *E* text contains six colons inserted within the first eleven lines, perhaps in an effort to puzzle out the meter of the poem: "port : and" (l. 1), "blisse : carefully" (l. 5), "Citherea : my" (l. 6), "ayde : assuraunce" (l. 9), "faith : that" (l. 10), and "therefor : in" (l. 11). They do not appear to be scribal.

B: 1. this] this thy   thy] the   6. Citherea my lady] cythera my ∧woffull ^{lady}
7. en] in *so also in ll. 14, 21, 28*   13. gevest] gevys   14. galerie] galere *so also in ll. 21, 28*   15. elongyd] enlongyd   20. els] ellys   23. any] *om.*

81

Vnstable dreme according to the place
be stedfast ons or els at leist be true
by tasted swetenes / make me not to rew
the sudden losse of thy fals fayned grace   4
By goode respect in such a daungerous case
thou broughte not her into this tossing mew
but madest my sprite lyve my care to renew
my body in tempest her succo⁹ to enbrace   8
The body dede the spryt had his desire
paynles was thone thothre in delight
Why then Alas did it not kepe it right
retorning to lepe into the fire   12
And where it was at wysshe it could not remain
such mocke of dremes they torne to dedly pain

E f. 54r, hand A. *A* f. 67 (*bis*) v. *T* 42. The *E* text contains two colons, thus: "ons : or" (l. 2) and "thone : thothre" (l. 10). It is impossible to tell whether they are scribal.

A T: 2. ons] ones *T*   6. broughte] broughtest *A T*   this tossing mew] these tossing seas *T*   7. lyve] to liue *T*   to renew] tencrease *T*   8. succo⁹ to enbrace] delight timbrace *T*   10. thothre] th'other *A*] the other *T*
12. retorning] But thus return *T*   13. it could] , could *T*   14. they] do *T*

82

iiij

In dowtfull brest, / whilst moderly pitie, /
w ⟨fa⟩ furyous famyn / stondyth at debate :/
saythe thebrew moder / o child vnhappye
Tho.   retorne thi blowd / where thow hadst milk of late · 4
yeld me those lyms / y I made vnto the ·

and entre there where y̆ wert generate ·

for of on body agaynst all nature/

to a nothr ⟨I⟩ must I make sepulture ·   8

TV

E f. 54v, Wyatt's holograph. T 123. The E text is in two inks. The Roman numeral in the head margin, the text, the monogram "TV," commas, full stops, and the single colon at the end of line 2 are in black ink. The "Tho." signature and the virgules are in pale brown. The extra "I" (l. 8) was deleted in pale brown, as if Wyatt noticed it only when he went over the text sometime later.

T: 1. whilst] whiles   3. saythe thebrew moder] The mother sayth
6. wert] were   8. a nothr⟨I⟩] an other

83

Off cartage he that worthie warier

could ouᵓ come / but cowld not vse his chaunce

and I like wise off all my long indeuᵓ

Tho   the sherpe cõquest tho fortune did avaunce   4

cowld not it vse / the hold y̆ is gyvin ouᵓ

I vnpossest / so hangith in balaunce

off warr my pees / reward of all my payne

            thus
At Mountzon ⟨lo⟩ I restles rest in spayne ·   8

TV

E f. 54v, Wyatt's holograph. T 120. The contrast of the simple and integral punctuation in this text with the double punctuation in the one above it on the same leaf is striking. The addition of the virgules to poem 82 may have occurred to Wyatt as a superior form of punctuation when he had finished this text.

T: 4. avaunce] aduance   5. cowld not it] Ne could I   8. ⟨lo⟩] thus

84

Processe of tyme worketh suche wounder

that water which is of kynd so ⟨fast⟩ soft

doeth perse the marbell stone a sonder

by litle droppes faling from a loft   4

And yet an hert that sems so tender
   receveth no dropp of the stilling teres
   that alway still cause me to render
   the vain plaint that ⟨sondҽ⟩ sowndҽ not in her eres   8
So cruel alas is nowght alyve
   so fiers so frowerd so owte of fframe
   but some way some tyme may so contryve
Tho   by mens the w⟨h⟩ild to tempre & tame   12
And I that alwaies have sought & seke
   eche place eche tyme for som lucky daye
   this fiers Tigre lesse I fynde her meke
   and more denyd the lenger I pray   16
The lyon in his raging furoᵍ
   forberis that sueth mekenes for his
   and thou Alas in extreme doloᵍ
   the hert so low thou ⟨doest excede⟩ tredis
               vnder thy foote   20
⟨Eche⟩
⟨and⟩ Eche fiers thing lo how thou doest excede
   and hidҽ it vnder so humble a face
   and yet the humble to helpe at nede
   nought helpeth tyme humblenes nor place   24

                                 Eche
E f. 55r, hand A. *A* f. 97r. The designation "⟨and⟩" (l. 21) indicates that hand A first wrote the word "and" evenly with the last line of the foregoing stanza, then "Eche" on top of the same letters (not above them). Although the deleted or overwritten "and" may have been an anticipation of line 22, its presence would have made the line a regular iambic pentameter. The cancellation of "h" in "w⟨h⟩ild" (l. 12) stands out because it was done in the pen and ink of poem 83.

A: 12. the] of   20. tredis] treadist

85

After great stormes the cawme retornis
   and plesanter it is thereby
   fortune likewise that often tornis
   hath made me now the moost happy   4
Thevin that pited my distres
   my iust desire and my cry
   hath made my langour to cesse
   and me also the most happy   8

Whereto dispaired ye my frende
  my trust alway in hid ly
  that knoweth what my though intende
  whereby I lyve the most happy   12
Lo what can take hope from that hert
  that is assured stedfastly
  hope therefore ye that lyve in smert
  whereby I ame the most happy   16
And I that have felt of yoᵍ paine
  shall pray to god continuelly
  to make yoᵍ hope yoᵍ helth retayne
  and me also the most happy /   20

E f. 55v, hand *A*. *A* f. 97rv. The *A* text is a close copy of *E* except for the negative form in the variant for line 16. Notably, *A* agrees with *E* in line 10. There are two silent emendations in *M3*, one of which is here, "always" (l. 10) for "alway." And *M3* adds a word, thus: "And make me" (l. 20), where *E* has simply "And me."

A: 5. Thevin] The heaven   11. though] thoughte   16. happy] vnhappie

86

A spending Hand that alway powreth owte
  had nede to have a bringer in as fast
  and on the stone that still doeth tourne abowte
There groweth no mosse these proverbis yet do last   4
  reason hath set theim in so sure a place
  that lenght of yeres their force can never wast
When I remembre this and eke the case
                            th
  where in thou stonde / I thowght forthw
           to write   8
  Brian to the / who knows how great a grace
In writing is to cownsell man the right?
  to the therefore that trotte still vp and downe
  and never reste but runyng day & nyght   12
ffrom Reaulme to Reaulme from cite strete & towne
  why doest thou were thy body to the bones
  and myghtst at home slepe in thy bed of downe
And drynck goode ale so noppy for the noyns   16

fede thy self fat & hepe vp pownd by pownd
lykist thou not this? no why? for swyne so groyns
In⟨i⟩ stye and chaw the torde molded on the grownd
and dryvell on perille the hed still in the maunger   20
then of the harp the Asse to here the sownd
So sacke of durt be filled vp in the cloyster
that servis for lesse then do thes fatted swyne
tho I seme lene and dry woute moyster   24
Yet woll I serve my prynce my lord & thyn
and let theim lyve to fede the panche that list
so I may fede to lyve both me & myn
By god well sayde but what and if thou ⟨lis⟩ wist   28
how to bryng in as fast as thou doest spend
that would I lerne / and it shall not be myst
To tell the how Now hark what I intend
thou knowest well first who so can seke to plese   32
shall pourchase frende where trowght shall but
            offend
ffle therefore trueth it is boeth welth and ese
for tho that trouth of every man hath prayse
full nere that wynd goeth trouth in great
            ⟨d⟩misese   36
Vse vertu as it goeth now a daye⟨s⟩ so
in word alone to make thy langage swete
and of the dede yet do not as thou sayse
Elle be thou sure thou shalt be farr vnmyt   40
to get thy bred eche thing is now so skant
seke still thy proffet vpon thy bare fete
Lend in no wise for fere that thou do want
onles it be as to a dogge a chese   44
by which retorn be sure to wyn a kant
Of half at lest / it is not good to lese
lerne at kittson that in a long white cote
from vnder the stall woute lande or feise   48
Hath lept into the shopp / who knoweth by rote
this rule that I have told the here before
sumtyme also riche age begynneth to dote
Se thou when there thy gain may be the more   52
stay him by the arme where so he walke or goo

be nere alway and if he kog̃h to sore
When he hat̃h spit / tred owte and please him so
    a diligent knave that pike his maisters purse   56
    may please him so that he wouten mo
Executoᵍ is and what is he the wourse
    but if so chaunce you get noug̃ht of the man
    the wedow may for all thy charge deburse   60
A ryveld skyn a stynking breth what than?
    a tothles mow̃th / shall do thy lips no harme
    the gold is good / and tho she curse or ban
Yet where the list thou maist ly good & warme   64
    let the old mule byte vpon the bridill
    whilst there do ly a swetter in thyn arme
In this also se ⟨thou⟩ be not Idell
    thy nece thy cosyn thy sister or thy dog̃hter   68
    if she be faire / if handsam by her myddell
Yf thy better hat̃h her love besoght her
    avaunce his cause & he shall help thy nede
    it is but love turne it to a lawghter   72
But ware I say so gold the helpe & spede
    that in this case thow be not so vnwise
    ⟨and⟩ pandare was in suche a like dede
ffor he the ffoill of conscience was so nyse   76
    that he no gayn would have for all his payne
    be nexte thy self for frendshipp beres no prise
Laughst thou at me? why do I speke in vayne?
    no not at the / but at thy thrifty gest   80
    wouldest thou I should for any losse or gayne
Chaunge that for gold that I have tan for best
    next godly thinge to have an honest name?
    should I leve that? then take me for a best   84
Nay then farewell and if you care for shame
    content the then with honest pouertie
    with fre tong what the myslike to blame
And for thy trouth sumtyme aduersitie   88
    and therewall this thing I shall the gyve
    in this worould now litle prosperite
    and coyne to kepe as water in a syve

E ff. 56r-57v, hand A. *A* ff. 99r[*bis*]-100r. *T*126. I view the variants slightly differently from Hughey (II, 184). It is impossible to tell whether the crucial emendations made for political caution (ll. 22,47) were first made in *A* or *T*. Given this ambiguity, the editor of the miscellany may possibly have collated both *A* and *E* for his printer's copy. As in the case of the other satires, *A* in this case shows greater independence of *E* than it does in the shorter poems. But once established that the satire had to be edited for prudential reasons, other minor changes could have occurred to the transcriber. In line 44, for example, the proverb could just as well concern a calf as a dog. Thus, the person or persons responsible for the *A* text could have had a good copy of *E* or even *E* itself before them; but being aware that some editing had to be done, they extended the process of prudential revision.

There is evidence of scribal checking and correction in *E*. In line 33 the last two words were added later in a slightly smaller script. The deleted "thou" (l. 67) was first written upon the letters "you" before "you" was finally written above the deleted "thou." But the corrected first word of line 75 is in black ink and is probably by Wyatt himself.

A number of colons were inserted in the text, perhaps by the scribe himself: "mosse: these" (l. 4), "no: why?" (l. 18), "how: Now" (l. 31), "trueth: it" (l. 34), "alway: and" (l. 54), "nece: thy cosyn: thy" (l. 68), "love: turne" (l. 72), "self: for" (l. 78), and "no: not" (l. 80).

A T: 4. groweth] growes *A*   8. stond̄e] stand'st *A*] standst *T*   15. myghtst] mightest *A T*   16. noppy] nappie *A*   noyns] nones *A T*   19. the tord̄e] donge *A T*   20. perilł̄e] pearells *A*] pearles *T*   the hed] with head *A T* 21. then of] So on *A*] So of *T*   to] dothe *A T*   22. filled vp . . . cloyster] fild. The neat Courtyer *A T*   23. that] So *A T*   24. woute] withouten *A T* 25. woll] will *A T*   27. fede to lyve] lyve to feede *A T*   34. boeth] for *A* 35. hath̄] have *A*   37. a daye⟨s⟩ so] adayes *A T*   39. the] thie *A* 44. dogge] calf *A*   45. by which retorn] but yf thow can *A*   46. it] I *A* 47. kittson] the Ladde *A T*   48. woute] withouten *A T*   49. knoweth] knowes *A T*   51. also riche age] ryche age also *A*   begynneth] begynnes *A T*   54. koggh] coughe *A T*   55. When] what *A T*   59. you] thow *A T* 60. charge deburse] payne disbursse *A*   64. maist] mayest *T*   65. mule] moyle *A*   66. whilst] whylest *A*   do] dothe *A*   thyn] thye *A*   67. ⟨thou⟩] that thow *A*] thou *T*   68. thy sister] *om. A*   69. by] be *A T*   71. avaunce] Advaunce *A*   72. turne] turne thow *A*   75. ⟨and⟩] as *A T*   76. ffoill] foole *A T*   78. prise] pryce *A T*   79. Laughst] Laughest *A T*   81. wouldest] would'ste *A*   85. you] thow *A T*   89. thing] guifte *A*   90. worould] worlde *A T*

87

All hevy mynde
   do seke to ese their charge
   and that that moost theim bynde
   to let at large   4
Then why should I
   hold payne win my hert

             and may my tune apply
             to ese my smart   8
         My faithfull lute
             alone shall here me plaine
             for els all othr*e* sute
             is clene in vaine   12
Tho   ffor where I sue
             redresse of all my grieff
             lo they do most eschew
             my hert*e* relieff   16
         Alas my dere
             have I des⁾ued so
             that no help may appere
             of all my wo   20
         Whome speke I to
             vnkynd & deff of ere
             Alas lo I go
             and wot not where   24
         Where is my thoght
             where wanders my desire
             where may the thing be soght
             that I require /   28
             light in the wynde
             doth fle all my delight
             where trouth & faithfull mynd
             are put to flyght   32
         Who shall me gyve
             fetherd wyng*e* for to fle
             the thing that doeth me greve
     that I may se   36
         Who would go seke
             the cause whereby to payne
             who could his foo beseke
             for ease of payne   40
         My chaunce doeth so
             my woofull case ᵱcure
             to offer to my ffoo
             my hert to cure   44
         What hope I then

to have any redresse
of whome or where or when
who can expresse   48
No/sins dispaire
hath set me in this case
in vain oft in the ayre
to say Alas   52
I seke nothing
but thus for to discharge
my hert of sore sighing
to plaine at large   56
                    t
And w my lut*e*
sumtyme to ease my pain
for els all othr*e* sute
is clene in vain   60

E f. 58rv, hand A. Line 36 got out of register when it was inserted later by hand A in a noticeably lighter ink. Line space had been left for it. The word "payne" (l. 38) is probably a scribal error for "playne." The phrase "in vain" (l. 51) may be linked by a continuous pen stroke. LInes 57-60 represent the first double column entry in *E*.

88

To seke eche where where man doeth lyve
the See the land the Rock the clyve
ffraunce Spayne and Ind & every where
is none a greater ⟨a⟩ gift to gyve   4
                                          and
lesse sett by oft and is so lyff ∧ dere
dare I well say / than that I gyve to yere
I cannot gyve browches nor Ring*e*
thes goldsmyth*e* work & goodly thing*e*   8
                  oryente
piery nor perle ⟨orent⟩ & clere
but for all that is no man bring*e*
leffer Iuell vnto his lady dere
Tho.   dare I well say then that I gyve to yere 12
Nor I seke not · to fetche it farr
worse is it not tho it be narr
and as it is it doeth appere
vncontrefaict mistrust to barr*e*   16
left hole & pure withouten pere

dare I well say the gift I gyve to yere
To the therefore the same retain
   the like of the to have again   20
ffraunce would I gyve if myn it were
   is none alyve in whome doeth rayne
   lesser disdaine frely therefore lo here
   dare I well gyve I say my hert to yer*e*   24

E f. 59r, hand A. Underneath the word "lyff" (l. 5) can be seen the first spelling "lieff," corrected by the scribe. A later hand made the following revision: "but for all that⟨is⟩ no man bring⟨e⟩^{can}" (l. 10). Probably the same hand inserted two colons, thus: "where: where" (l. 1) and "the land: the" (l. 2), but a large space had been left by the scribe as a divider of the first line.

89

O goodely Hand
   wherin doeth stand
   my hert distrast in payne
   faire hand Alas   4
   in litle spas
   my liff that doeth restrayne
O fyngers slight
   depted right   8
   so long so small so rownd
   goodely bygone
   and yet alone
   most cruell in my wound   12
Wth Lilis whight
   and Roses bright
   doth stryve thy colo^r faire
   nature did lend   16
   eche fyngers ende
   a perle for to repayre
Consent at last
   syns that thou hast   20
   my hert in thy demayne
   for s^r uice trew
   on me to rew
   and reche me love againe   24

And if not so
   then with more woo
   enforce thiself to strayne
   this simple hert   28
   that suffereth smart
   and rid it owte of payne

E f. 59r, hand A. *H* f. 28r. The text in H is headed "T. W." The manner of entry in H is double column, with this poem occupying one column, subscribed "finis." The "T. W." refers only to this column. The other column is headed *A balad of will* and subscribed "ffinis."

H: 4. faire] dere   6. that doeth] thou dost   10. bygone] begonne   15. stryve] strayne   26. then] Ther   29. suffereth] suffered

90

Lo What it is to love
   lerne ye that list to prove
   at me I say
   no ways that may   4
   the grownd is greiff remove
   my liff alwaie
   that doeth decaye
   Lo what it is to love   8
ffle alwaye from the snare
   lerne by me to be ware
   of suche a bayne
   which dowbles payne   12
   & endles woe & care
Tho.   that doeth retayne
   which to refrayne
   fle alwaye from the snare   16
To love & to be wise
   to rage wth good aduyse
   now thus now than
   now of now an   20
      vncerteyn as the dyse
   there is no man
   at ons that can
   to love & to be wise   24
Suche are the dyvers throws

suche that no man knows
that hath not profd
and ons have lofd   28
suche are the raging woos
soner reprofd
then well remofd
suche are the dyvers throws   32
love is a fervent fire
kendeld by hote desire
for a short pleasure
long displeasure   36
repentaunce is the hire
a poure tresoure
th
w oute mesure
love is a fervent fire   40

Lo what it is to love

E f. 60rv, hand A. *B* f. 117rv. The *E* text is smudged in lines 11-13. *M3*
recorded no variant for line 11 where I read "bayne" in *E*. Line 21 was filled
in later by Wyatt himself in black ink.

B: 1. it] hytt *so also in l. 8*   4. no ways that] that no wyse   5. grownd
is] growndyd   10. by] att   11. bayne] trayne   12. which dowbles] and
dubbyll   13. &] wyth   14. that doth retayne] wych to refrayne   15.
which to refrayne] and nott retayne   27. that hath not] but he haue   35.
for a short] a small   41. *om. B*

91

Leve thus to slaunder love
th
though evill w suche it prove
which often   vse
love to mysuse   4
and loving to reprove
such cannot chose
for their refuse
but thus to slaunder love   8
ffle not so much the snare
love sildom causeth care
but by deserfte

and crafty parte   12
som lese their owne welfare
be true of herte
and for no smarte
fle not so much the snare   16
To love and not to be wise
is but a mad devise
such love doeth last
as sure and fast   20
as chaunce on the dise
a bitter tast
coms at the last
to love & not to be wise   24
Suche be the plaisaunt daies
suche be the honest wayes
there is no man
that fully can   28
know it but he that sayes
lovinng to ban
were folly then
such be the plaisaunt daies   32
Love is a plaisaunt fire
kyndeled by true desire
and though the payne
cause men to playne   36
sped well is oft the hiere
then though som fayne
and lese the gayne
love is a plaisaunt fyre   40

E ff. 60v-61r, hand A. *B* ff. 117v-118r. Although poems 90-92 are themat-
ically linked, their manner of entry in *E* separates them more distinctly than
other entries in *E*. There is a larger space in *E* between poems 90 and 91, and
no heading for poem 91. In line 3 the scribe of *E* left space for an additional
word, which is not duplicated in *B*. In line 29 *M3* read the variant of *B* as
"them," which is a possibility.

B: *heading om.*] the answer   1. thus] thys *so also in l. 8*   2. evill] yll
it] hytt   4. mysuse] abvs   17. to be] be *so also in l. 24*   18. is but] hytt
were   21. chaunce on] chansys off   28. that fully] fully that   29. it] then
36. men] sum   38. som] ye   39. and . . . gayne] plesuer for payn

92

Who most doeth slander love
   the dede must alwaye prove
   trouth shall excuse
   that you accuse   4
   for slaunder & reprove
   not by refuse
   but by abuse
   you most do slaunder love   8
Ye graunt it is a snare
   and would vs not beware
   lest that yoᵍ trayne
   should be to playne   12
   ye colour all the care
   lo how you fayne
   pleasur*e* for payne
   and graunt it is a snare   16
To love and to be wise
   it were a straunge devise
   but from that tast
   ye vow the fast   20
   on zyns tho run yoᵍ dise
   ambs as may hast
   your payne to wast
   to love & to be wise   24
Of all such pleasaunt dayes
   of all suche pleasaunt playes
   ᵗwout deserft
   you have your part   28
   and all the worould so sayis
   save that poure hart
   that for more smert
   feleth yet suche pleasaunt dayes   32
Such fire & suche hete
   did never make ye swete
   for ᵗwoute payne
   you best obtayne   36
   to good spede & to great

who so doẽth playne
you best do fayne
suͨh fire & suche hete   40

Who now doẽth slaunder love /

E ff. 61v-62r, hand A. *B* f. 118rv. In line 29 of the *E* text, it is difficult
to tell whether the scribe wrote "says" or "sayis," but the latter would be
a better match for the rhyming words.

B: *heading om.*] the answer to thys   2. must] shall   4. you] ye *so also
in ll. 8, 14, 39*   9. Ye] yow *so also in ll. 13, 34*   it] hyt *so also in ll. 16, 18*
11. lest that] and lest   20. the] to   21. on zyns tho] an synne ye   32.
feleth yet suche] fele yett sum   33. &] nor   36. you best] ye dyd   38.
so] most   41. *om.*

93

I lede a liff/vnpleasant/nothing glad /
Crye/and complaynt offerre voydes Ioyfullnesse
      a   re
so chungethe   vnrest/that nought shall fade
Tho   payne and dyspyte hathe Altered plesantnes   4
ago/long/synnys / that she hathe truly/made /
dysdayne / ⟨for⟩ for trowght/sett lyght yn stedfastnes
I haue cause goode to syng this song
playne or reioyse / who felythe/wele/or wrong   8

E f. 62r, hand C. This is the first text in *E* copied by the second scribal hand
of the volume, hand C. There are two additions to the scribal text, both
probably by Wyatt himself. The final "s" on "voydes" (l. 2) was added later.
The letters "re" were placed above the third line before the word "vnrest."
Wyatt was probably contemplating the revision of "vnrest" to "rest."

94

And iff that ye may save or sley
and stryke more depe then wepon long
and iff an Iye by subtill play
may moue on more then any tong   4
how can ye say that I doo wrong
          t
thus to suspecte woute deserte
from the Iye is trayto꞊ of the herte
To frame·all well I ame cõtent   8
that itt were doõn vnwytyngly

butt yete I say who will assent
to doo butt well doo nothyng why
that men shulde deme the cõtrary   12
for itt is sayd by men expert
that the Iye is traytour of the hert
Butt yete Alas that loke all⟨nd⟩ sowle
that I doo clayme of right to haue   16
sholde nott me thynkethe go seke the skoole
to please all folk for who can crave
fryndlyer thyng then harte wittsaue
by looke to gyue in frendely parte   20
for the Iye is trayto⁹ of the harte

And my suspecte is woute blame
for as ye saye nott only I
butt other moo have demede the same   24
then is it nott of Ielowsy
butt subtill looke of rekeles Iye
dide raing to ferr to make me smarte
for the Iye is trayto⁹ of the harte   28

E f. 62v, hand C. The text in black ink contrasts with the six strokes in
brownish ink that cancel the whole. The cancellations are probably by Wyatt.
A corrected text of the same poem is copied by scribal hand D on f. 65r.

95

Yf in the world ther be more woo
then I haue yn my harte
Tho   wher so ytt is itt doithe cõm fro
and in my brest there doithe itt groo   4
from to encrease my smarte
Alas I ame recepte of euͨ y care
and of my liff eche sorrow claymes his parte
who list to lyue yn quyetnes   8
by me lett hym beware
ffor I by highe dysdayne
ame made withoute redresse
and vnkyndenes Alas hathe slayne   12
my poore trew hart all comfortles

E ff. 62v-63r, hand C. *D* f. 53v. The *D* text is subscribed "ffinis". Wyatt approved this text by signing it in *E*, probably at the same time he deleted the text above it on f. 62v.

D: 2. yn] now wi^tn   10. highe] grett   12. Alas] *om.*   13. my poore trew] a symple

96

Thanswere that ye made to me my dere
wha͞n I did sewe for my poore hartͤ redresse
hathe so apalld my countenaunce and my chere
that yn this case I ame all comfortelesse   4
sins I of blame no cawse ca͞n well expresse

I haue no wrong wher I can clayme no right
nowght tane me fro wher I nothing haue had
yete of my wo⁾ I ca͞n nott so be quyte   8
namely sins that another may be glad
w that / that y in sorowe makethe me sad

Another / why shall lyberty be bond
ffre hart may not be bond ⟨by⟩ but by desert   12

Nor none ca͞n clayme I say by form⁾ graunte
that knowithe nott of any graunt att all
And by deserte I dare well make avaunte
of faythfull will ther is no wher that shall   16
bere yo more trowthe / more redy att yo call

Now good then call agayne that frendly word
that seithe yo frende in saving of his payne
and say my dere that itt was sayde in borde   20
late or too sone lett that nott rule the gayne
wher w fre will trew des⁾ te retayne

E f. 63rv, hand C. *T* 83. Hand C made this entry on two occasions, as shown by the inking. Lines 13-22, perhaps also line 12, were added at a later time. As a result, three lines were lost from what was the third stanza, now represented only by lines 11 and 12. The stanzaic division between the second and third stanzas was also made less clear than between the first and second. *T*'s editor omitted lines 11-12 in order to preserve the stanzaic form of the whole. Thus, it is probable that he had no other manuscript source available. The form "wo⁾" (l. 8) is puzzling, since the mark added does not seem to be an apostrophe.

97

Most*e* wretchid hart most myserable
syns the c⟨or⟩te comforte is from the fled
syns all the trouthe is turned to fable
most wretchid harte why arte thow nott⟨d⟩ded   4

No no I lyve and must doo still
wherof I thank god and no mo
ffor I me selff have att my will
And he is wretchid that wens hym so   8

Butt yete thow hast bothe had and lost
the hope so long that hathe the fed
and all thy travayle and thy cost
most wretchid harte why arte thow nott ded   12

Som other hope must fede me new
yff I haue lost I say what tho
dyspayr shall nott throwghe ynsew
for he is wretchid that wenys hym so   16

The sonne the mone doth frowne on the
thow hast darkenes in daylighte stede
as good in grave as soo to be   u
moost wretched hert why art y not ded   20

Some plesaunt sterre may shewe me light
      e
but tho y heven wold worke me woo
who hath himself shal stande vp right
and he is wretched that wenis him soo   24

Hath he himself that is not sure?
his trust is like as he hath sped

against the streme thou maist not dure

most wretched herte why art y^u not ded   28

The last is worst, who feres not y^t

he hath himself where so he goo

and he y^t knoweth what is what

sayeth he is wretched that wens him soo   32

Seist y^u not how they whet their teth

which to touche ye somtime ded drede

they finde comforte for thy mischief

moost wretched hert why are y^u not dede   36

What tho that currs do fal by kinde

on him that hathe the overthro

al that can not opresse my minde

for he is wretched that wens him soo   40

Yet can it not be thenne denyd

it is as certain as thy crede

thy gret vnhap y^u canst not hid

vnhappy thenne why art y̆ not dede   44

Vnhappy / but no wretche therfore

for happe doth come again and goo

for whiche I kepe my self in store

sins vnhap cannot kil me soo   48

ffinis

E ff. 63v-64rv, hands C and D. The first sixteen lines are on the lower half of
f. 63v in hand C. The continuation is in a markedly different scribal hand,
hand D. However, both the refrain and the dialogue structure indicate either
a single poem or a closely knit unity of two or three shorter sections.

One should keep in mind the relative unreliability of hand C, who was
responsible for the text deleted by Wyatt on f. 62v and redone on f. 65r by
hand D (poem 99). Thus, the word "att" (l. 7). which *M3* read as "all" or
silently emended to that form, may have been a scribal error. Also, the form
"throwghe" (l. 15) may represent the adverbial form "thorough" for "thoroughly." However, *M3* may have been correct in assuming that the word
"it" was omitted as the object of a preposition.

98

You that in love finde lucke and habundance
 and live in lust and Ioyful Iolitie
 arrise for shame do away yor sluggardie
 arise I say do may some obs^aunce   4

Let me in bed lye dreming in mischaunce
 let me remembre the happs most vnhappy
Tho.   that me betide in may most comonly
 as oon whome love list litil to avaunce   8

Sephame saide true that my natiuitie
 mischaunced was w^t the ruler of the may
 he gest ⟨of⟩ I prove of that the veritie
In ⟨me⟩ may my ⟨self⟩ welth and eke my liff I say   12
 have stonde so oft in such pplexitie
 reioyse let me dreme of yor felicitie
                       TV

E f. 64v, hand D. *A* ff. 67 [*bis*] v-68r. *T*43. The *E* text copied and corrected
by hand D was signed twice by Wyatt himself on different occasions, as
shown by differences in the color of ink and pointing in the "TV" monogram
and "Tho."

    There are two direct links between the *E* and *A* texts. The manner of
linking the final "e" to "m" in "Sephame" (l. 9) could have been misread by
the scribe of *A* to suggest the form "Sephance." A similar phenomenon
occurs in the first corrected word or phrase in line 12 of *E*. Note also that
the deleted word "of" (l. 11) in *E* could account for the alternate phrasing
in the *A* variant. Although Hughey (II, 154-155) only suggested the inference,
this text definitely suggests that at least one copyist of *A* actually saw *E*.
However, none of the deletions in line 12 of *E* affected the text of *A* or *T*.
The omission of line 6 from *A* is explained by Hughey's observation that
both lines 5 and 6 begin with the same two words.

A T: 1. You] Ye *T*   habundance] swete abundance *T*   2. lust and] lust
of *T*   3. away] way *T*   5. in] of *T*   6. *om. A*   the happs most] my
missehappes *T*   8. avaunce] advaunce *A T*   9. Sephame] Sephance *A*]
Stephan *T*   10. mischaunced] Mischaunce *A*   11. of . . . that] of that I
prove *A*] (I proue) of that *T*   12. liff] wittes *T*   14. reioyse] Ioye *T*

99

And if an Ie may save or sleye
 and streke more diepe then wepon Longe
 and if an Iye by subtil play
 may move on more thenne any tonge   4

how canne ye say that I do wronge
thus to suspect w^out des^) te
for the Iye is traito^9 of the herte
To frame all wel I am content   8
that it were done vnwetingly
but yet I say who wol assent
to do but wel · do no thing whie
that men shuld deme the contrary   12
for it is said by men expert
that the Iye is traito^9 of the hert
But yet alas y^t loke all sowle
that I doo clayme of right to haue   16
shuld not methinke goo seke the scole
to plese all folke / for who canne crave
frendlier thing thenne hert witsaue
by loke to give in frendely pte   20
for the Iye is traito^9 of the hert
And my suspect is w^out blame
for as ye saye not only I
but other moo haue denyd the same   24
thenne is it not Ielowsye
but subtill loke of rekeles Iye
did rainge to farre to make me smart
ffor the Iye is traito^9 of the hert   28
But I your freende shal take it thus
sins you wol soo / as stroke of chaunce
and leve furder for to discus
wither the stroke did sticke or glaunce   32
but scuse who canne let him avaunce
dissembled loke but for my pte
my Iye must stil bitray my harte
And of this grief ye shalbe quitte   36
in helping trowth stedfast to goo
the time is longe that doth sitt
feble and weike and suffreth woo
cherish him wel continewe soo   40
let him not fro your hart astart
thenne feres not the Iye to shewe the hert
ffinis

E f. 65r, hand D. This entry is a corrected and completed text, of which twenty eight lines were copied by hand C on f. 62v. See poem 94.

100
Noli ⟨malignari⟩ emulari in maligna
Psalm. 37.

Altho thow se thowtragius clime aloft
Envie not thowe his blinde prosperitye
The welth of wretches tho it senith soft
Move not thy hert by theyre felicitye   4
They shalbe found like grasse turnd into hay
And as the herbe that wither sodenlye
Stablisshe thy trust in god / seke right allway
And on the yerth thowe shalte inhabite longe   8
ffede and encreace such hope from day to day
                 t
And if w god thow time thy hartie songe
He shal the giue what soo thy hart canlust
Cast vppon god thy will that right thy wrong   12
Gyve him the charge for he vpright and iust
Hath cure of the and of thy cares all
And he shall make thy trowgh to be discust
Vpright all the sone / and thy rightwisnes shall   16
(The cursids welth tho now do it deface)
Shine like the daylight that we the none call
Paciently abide the Lordes assured grace
                 t
Bere w even minde the trouble that he sende   20
            u
Dismay the not tho y se the purchace
Encresse of some, for such like lucke god sende
To wicked folke
Restrayne thy mind from wrath that ay offende   24
            u
Doway all ⟨a⟩ rage / and se y do estewe
By theire like dede suche dede for to comitt
ffor wikked folke theire overthrow shal rewe
Who pacientlie abid and do not flitt   28
They shall possede the world from heire to hayre
The wikked shall of all his welth be quitt
                   t
So sodainly and that wout repaire

That all his pompe and his staring aray   32
Shall from thyn Iye depte as blast ofayre
The sobre thenne the world shall weld I say
And live in welth and pes soo plentifull
Him to distroy the wikked shall assay   36

E f. 65v (fragment, ll. 1-36 only), hand D. *A* ff. 118r-119v. The thirty six
lines of the *E* text are entirely in hand D except for the words "theyre
felicitye" (l. 4), which were added by Wyatt in his own hand. The scribal
linking of final and initial letters in *E* is indicated by the words "canlust"
(l. 11) and "ofayre" (l. 33).

The variant "moone" (l. 18) in *A* was correctly included by Hughey in
the text (I, 206) but was not listed in the variants (II, 243). *M3* also
failed to list this variant. The complete text of *A* preserves the short line 23
of *E*, which is probably a deliberate metrical variation in the manner of
Virgil. As there is no reason to think that the scribe of *A* had any other
source but *E*, it is impossible to know whether two lines have been lost
between the present lines 69 and 70 of *A*. The missing seventy four or seventy
six lines would have fitted neatly on one leaf now missing from *E*.

A: Noli . . . maligna] Noli aemulari in maligna: 3. senith] seemythe
8. the yerth] the earthe   14. and] and eke   16. Vpright all] Vprighte as
rightwisnes] rightousnes   18. none] moone   20 sende] sendes   25. estewe]
eschew
                                                    u
28. abid] abydes   32. and his staring] and eke his straunge   37-110 *A only*
37.   And gnasshe his teethe eke with girninge yrefull
       The Lord shall scorne the threatninge of the wretche
       ffor he doth know the tyde is nighe at full
40.   when he shall syncke and no hand shall hym seeche
       Theye have vnsheathed eke their blouddye bronds
       And bent theire bowe to prove if they might reache
       To overthrowe the
44.   Bare of relief the harmlesse to devoure
       The sworde shall pearce the hart of suche that fonds
       Their bow shall breake in their moste endevoure
       A litle Livinge gotten rightfullie
48.   Passithe the ritchesse and eke the highe powre
       Of that that wretches have gatherd wickedlye
       Pearishe shall the wickede posterite
       And god shall stablishe the iuste assuredlye
52.   The iust mans dayes the Lorde doth know and see
       Their heritage shall Laste for evermore
       And of their hope beguylde they shall not be
       When dismolde dayes shall wrappe the tother sore
56.   They shall be full when other faynte for foode
       Thearwhyl'ste shall faile theise wicked men thearfore
       The gode ennemyes suche end shall be allowdd
       As hath Lambs greace wastinge in the fyre
60.   That is consumde into a smokye clowde
       Borow'th th'vniust without will or desyre
       To yelde agayne the iuste freelye dothe geve
       Wheare he seethe neede as marcye dothe requyre

64.   Who will'the hym well for right thearfore shall Leve
      Who bannyshe hym shall be rooted awaye
      His steppes shall god, directe still and relieve
      And please hym shall what lyf hym Lust assaye
68.   And thoughe he fall vnder foote lye shall not he
      Catchinge his hand for god shall streight hym staye
      Nor yet his seede foodelesse seene for to be
      The iuste to all men mercyfull hathe bene
72.   Busye to do well, thearfore his seede I saye

                          u
      Shall have habundaunce all waye fresshe and grene
      fflee yll do good that thow mayste last all waye
      ffor god dothe Love for evermore th'vpright
76.   Never his Chosen dothe he cast awaye
      ffor ever he them myndeth daye and night
      And wicked seede alwaye shall waste to nought
      The iust shall welde the worlde as their owne right
80.   And Longe thearon shall dwell as theye have wrought
      Withe wisdome shall the wyse mans mowthe hym able
      His tongue shall speake alwaye even as it ought
      With gode Learning he hathe his harte stable
84.   His foote thearfore from slydinge shall be sure
      The wicked watchethe the iust for to disable
      And for to se hym dothe his busye cure
      But god will not suffer hym for to quaile
88.   By tyrannye nor yet bye faulte vnpure
      To be condemn'd in iudgement without faile
      Awayte thearfore the commynge of the Lorde
      Live withe his Lawes in pacience to prevayle
92.   And he shall raise the of thyne owne accorde
      Above the earth in suretye to beholde
      The wickede deathe that thow maye it recorde
      I have well seene the wicked sheene lyke goolde
96.   Lustie and grene as Lawrell lasting aye
      But even anon and scantt his seate was colde
      When I have paste agayne the self same waye
      Wheare he did raigne he was not to be fownde
100. Vanyshte he was for all his fresshe arraye
      Let vprightnes be still thie stedfast grownde
      ffollowe the right suche one shall alwaye fynde
      Hym self in peace and plentie to habounde
104. All wicked folke reversyd shall vntwynde
      And wretchidnes shall be the wickede ende
      Healthe to the iuste from god shall be assignde
      He shall them strengthe whome troble shoulde offend
108. The Lord shall helpp I saye and them delyver
      ffrom curssed Hande and Healthe vnto them send
      for that in Hym they sett their trust for ever./
                  ffinis

                  101

From thes hye hilles as when a spryng dothe fall
              t   still
      it tryllythe downe w ⟨small⟩ and suttyll corse

off this & that ⟨& gad⟩ it gaders ⟨st^{ay}ill⟩ & shall

Tho.

tyll _∧^{it} have Iust off flowd th*e* streme and forse   4
th*e*n at th*e* fote it ragith*e* ou[?] all

so faryth*e* love when h*e* hath*e* tan a sorse
his rayne_∧^{is} rage ⟨then botyth*e* no deny⟩ ^{resistans vaylyth none}
th*e* first estew is ⟨only⟩ remedy alone ·   8

TV

E f. 66r, Wyatt's holograph. B f. 73r. T63. The B text is subscribed "W".
None of the deleted readings in the E text affected those of B or T. In E
there is a considerable space after the word "love" (l. 6) and a blot, but no
punctuation mark, which raises the possibility that Wyatt used spacing to
indicate a caesura or left spaces occasionally for some kind of punctuation
to be added later. The "TV" monogram signature beneath the text is very
faded, which suggests that it was added when the fragmentary lines of poem
102 were put on the leaf.

B T: 1. From . . . when] as from theys hyll*e* when that B   2. it] hyt B
w ⟨small⟩] by styll B] with still T   3. off . . . it] and of ech thyng hyt B
4. it] hyt B   Iust] full B   off flowd the] downflowed to T   7. his . . . rage]
Rage is his raine T   vaylyth] ys ther B   8. estew] extwe B] eschue T

102

prove wyth*e*r I do chainge my dere
or if y^t I do still remayne
like as I went [?] f [?]
and if ye fynde [?]   4

E f. 66r, Wyatt's holograph. This fragment of four lines is barely legible
beneath poem 101. Muir (M3) was able to read more of line 3 than I could:
"Lik as I went or ferre or nere."

103

If waker care if sodayne pale Coulo⁹
if many sighes w^t litle speche to playne
now ioy/now woo / if they my chere distayne
for hope of small*e* if muche to fere therfor   4
To hast to slake my passe lesse or more
by signe of love then do I love agayne

Tho.

if thow aske whome / sure sins I did refrayne
⟨her⟩ y ⟨ded⟩ set ⟨o⁹ country⟩ in _∧ a rore   8
^{brunet t} ^{my welth   suche}

Thunfayned chere of Phillis hath y̆ place
   ^t
  y brunet had she hath and ever shal
  she from my self now hath me in her grace
She hath in hand my witt my will and all   12
  my hert alone wel worthie she doth staye
  ^t
  wout whose helpe skant do I live a daye

E f. 66v, hand D. A f. 68r. T44. The revision of line 8 in E was done by
Wyatt himself. All the rest of the text is scribal.

T: 5. to slake] or slack   passe] pace to   6. by] Be

104

In Spayne

        ^t
So feble is the threde y dothe the burden stay
        ^t   hevy   ^t   ^t
  of my pore lyff ⟨y⟩ In ⟨sory⟩ plyght y fallythe ⟨w his sway⟩
                  some   some
That but it have ⟨frome⟩ elke where ⟨some⟩ aide or ∧ socours
  the runyng spyndell off my fate anon shall end his cours ·   4
                    ^t
⟨ffore⟩ sins thunhappy howre y did me to depart
                            staide
  from my swete wele one only hope hathe ⟨held⟩ my lyff apart ·
wych   ^t   such
⟨That⟩ doth ꝑswade ⟨w suche like⟩ ∧ worde vnto my
                sory
                ⟨wofull⟩ mynd ·
            e
  maytene thy sellff o wofull spryte some better luke to fynd   8
        u
ffor tho y be depryffd from thy desyerd syght
  who can the tell iff thi retorne be for thy most delyght?
              u^ʲ   maist
or who can tell/thy losse if y ⟨maist⟩ ons ∧ recover:
              e   e
  some plesant howre thy wo ∧ may ⟨w⟩rape and y defend
              & cover ·   12
        ^t
this is the trust y yet hath my lyff sustaynid
  and now alas I se' it faint and I by trust ame trainid ·
        flete   ei
the tyme doth ⟨passe⟩ and I ꝑceyve thowrs how y ⟨flye⟩ bend
        ^t
  so fast ⟨alas⟩ y I have skant the space to mᶜke
           my comyg end ·   16

westward the sonñe from owt thest skant doth shew his lyght
                  straite   t
   when in the west he hyds hym ⟨sellff⟩ w in the darke of nyght
         as fast
and cons ⟨agayne⟩ where he/began his path a wrye

   from est to west ⟨to est⟩ from west to thest so dothe
              Iorneı
        his ⟨viage⟩ ly   20
        t
the lyff so short so fraile y mortall men lyve here
                        t
   so gret a whaite so hevy charge the body y we bere
that when I thinke apon the distance and the space
     t
   y doth so ferr devid me from my dere desird face   24
                  t
I know not how tattayne the wynge y I require
           t
   to lyfft my whaite y it myght fle to folow my desyre
⟨t⟩us   t   t
y off y hope y doth my lyff some thing sustayne
   alas I fere and ptly fele full litill doth remayne   28
Eche place doth bryng me grieff/where I do not behold
            wich
             t
   those lyvely Iyes ⟨y⟩ off my thowghte were wont the
           kays to hold

                              t
those thowghte were plesaunt swete / whilst I enioyd y grace
                       wher
                          t
   my plesure past/my pꞌsent payne /⟨y⟩ I myght well embrace · 32
But for be cawse my want shold more my wo ecresse
   In wache in slepe both day and nyght my will doth
           neuꞌcesse
that thing to wishe wheroff / sins I did lese the syght
             t   faytfull
   I neuꞌ saw the thing y myght my ∧ hert delyght   36

thvnsesy lyff I lede doth teche me for to mete
                     t   em
   the flowde the sees/the land and hille y doth y entremete
                    t
twene me and those shiniḡ lyghte y wontyd to clere
   my darke pange off clowdy thowghte as bryght as phebus
           spere   40
It techithe me also ⟨to know⟩ what was my plesant state

                         t
   the more to fele by suche record how y my welth doth bate ·
if such record alas / provoke thenflamid ⟨my⟩ mynd

   wiche   t   t
⟨that⟩ sprang y day y I did leve the best of me byhynd 44
if love forgett hym sellff by lenght of absence let
  who doth me guyd o wofull wreche vnto this baytid net
where doth encresse my care? muche better were for me
     all thing forgott still
  as dome as stone ⟨to thinke on nowght and⟩ absent for
        to be ·   48
alas the Clere Crystall the bryght transparat glas
    bewray   neth
  doth not ⟨declare⟩ the colour hyd wich vnder it has
as doth thaccomberd sprite ⟨a⟩ thowghtfull throws discover
           t
  off fiers delyght / off fervent love/y in o⁹ herte we cover · 52
       t
owt by thes Iyes it shewth y euᶜ more delyght
        & that
  In plaint & teres to seke redresse/⟨to seke⟩ bothe day & nyght ·
        most
Thes new kynde off plesurs wherein ⟨all⟩ men reioyse /
  to me thei do redowble still off stormye syghe the voyce 56
ffor I ame one off them/whom plaint dothe well cotent
  it sitte me well / myn absent welth / me seems me to lamet
   t
and w my teris for to' assay to charge myn Iyes tweyne
  lyke as
   t
  ⟨sins y⟩ myn hert ⟨or eu⟩⟩ above the brink is frawtid
              full of pa[60
And forby cawse therto / off those fayre Iyes to trete
  do me provoke / I shall retorne/my plaint thus to repete/
        t   t
ffor there is nothing elle /y towche me so w in
  ei
  where y rule all / and I alone nowght but the cace or skyn · 64
wherfore I do retorne / to them as well or spryng
  from whom decende my mortall wo/above all othr thing ·
So shall myn Iyes in payne / accopagnie min hert
  t   t
  y were the guyde y did it lede of love to fele the smert · 68
The cryspid gold y doth sormount Apollos pryd
              t
  the lyvely strenes off plesaunt sterres y vnder it doth glyd
where in the bemes off love doth still encresse theire hete
  wiche yet so farre towch me so nere in cold to make
        me swet   72
The wise and plesaunt talk / so rare or elle alone
  t   t suche
  y did me gyve the courtese gyfft y ⟨erst⟩ had neu⟩ none

be
⟨ar⟩ ferre from me alas / and eu⟩ y other thing
            t   en   t
    I myght forbere w better will / y that y did me bryng   76
t
            lingerd
w plesant word & chere redresse off ⟨all my⟩ payne
           in
          t   to
    and wontyd offt ⟨w⟩ kendlid will ⟨in⟩ ɇtu me to trayne ·
thus ame I dryven to here / and herken affter news
    my confort skant my large desire / in dowtfull trust renew[80
      t   mone
And yet w more delyght to ⟨playne⟩ my wofull cace
                       fermely
                    t
    I must coplaine those handɇ those armes y ∧ do embrace
Me from my sellff / and rule / the sterne of my pore lyff
                               e
    the swete disdaynes / the plesant wrathes / & eke y
                     lovely stryff   84
t   well
y wontid ⟨offt⟩ to tune / in tempre Iust and mete
        t
    the rage y offt did make me erre / by furour vndiscrete
         t
All this is hid me fro / w sharp and craggyd hillɇ

    at other ⟨evill⟩ will   long abode   my diepe
    ⟨my faintyng hope⟩ / my ⟨brytill lyff⟩ / ⟨willing⟩
                   dispaire fulfillɇ ·   88
But if my hope somtyme / ryse vp by some redresse
    it stumblithe straite / for feble faint / my fere hathe
             such excess
        sort
suche is the ⟨fere⟩ off hope / the lesse for more desyre

    wherby I fere   t
    and yet I trust to se y I requyre
The restyng place of love / where ɇtu lyves and grose   92
                   also al
    where I desire my wery lyff/may sometyme take repose
      u   t
My song y shalt ataine / to fynd y plesant place
                    may
    where she doth lyve / by whome I lyve /⟨ρ⟩chaunce
                               the have
                               ⟨she shew⟩
                               this gce
when she hath red and seeñe the dred wherein I
                         ere   sterve e
    by twene her brestɇ she shall the put y   shall she y res⟩ve

           t
  tell her y   she shall me shortly se
Then ⟨say⟩ I come ⟨for here I may not tary⟩
    t   this
yff y for whay*te* th*e* body fayle ⟨my⟩ sowle shall to her fle   100

TV

E ff. 67r-68v, Wyatt's holograph. *A* ff. 97v-98v. *D* ff. 49r-50v. *T*104.
The *D* text is subscribed simply "ffins." The *E* text represents an extensive
specimen of Wyatt's holograph verse, combining both precision and error.
Fortunately, the errors are obvious: the spelling "cons" (l. 19) for "coms,"
the missing ∼ in "accopagnie" (l. 67).

Among the signs of precision suggesting metrical exactitude are the
apostrophes in lines 11 and 59 and the accent mark on "seene" (l. 97).
Another apostrophe occurs in line 13. Noteworthy also is the single semicolon
at the end of line 11, whose function seems more grammatical than
metrical. Internal punctuation is limited to the virgule. There may be a ·
after "frome" (l. 3).

Under "v" in the word "thvnsesy" (l. 37), an "o" is still visible. Because
of the clipping of margins and the intrusion of the binding, some final
letters are lost or hard to find. Part of an "s" on "renew" (l. 80) may still
be there. Other losses are indicated by [.

Despite Hughey's high degree of accuracy (II, 175-177), there were a few
errors among the variants, noted as follows: 24. variant "fro" in *A*   31.
no apostrophe in *E* or *D*   42. no *D* variant because *D* reads "fele"   50.
additional *E* and *D* variants   51. disagreement on the deleted letter or sign
59. *D* agrees with *A* and *E* by reading "m̃y"   62. additional *T* variant
66. additional *D* variant   80. additional *D* variant, perhaps by scribal error
   u
"remes"   90. final word in *E* is "excess," visible by spreading the binding
96. no *D* variant "the have" since that also appears in *E*. The issue of whether *A* was dependent on *T* is clarified by line 36, which demonstrates the
complete departure of *T*. If the person who supplied the copy for *A* had no
access to *E*−direct or indirect−he could not have supplied that line correctly
in *A*. Thus, while *A* is an edited text, it derives directly or indirectly from *E*.

Although *D* seems to be an unedited attempt to transcribe its copy within
the limits of human error, there may have been some change in habit for the
lines now on f. 68v in *E*. The variants for lines 81, 83, and 86 look rather
like editing in *D*, while the earlier variants of *D* seem to be scribal omissions
and pen slips made from sound copy of the revised version.

One of the most interesting group of variants is the last in line 74, where
A and *T* adopt the deleted reading "erst" while *D* is consistent in supplying
the revision "suche." This suggests that the editors of the *A* and *T* copy had
access to *E*. The fact that *T* preserves the word "spere" (l. 40), where *A*
revises to "spheare," indicates independent checking and editing on the part
of *T*. Since *D* nowhere gives a deleted or earlier reading of *E*, it is likely
that the copyist was following a fair copy of the revised text. The heading
of the *E* text, "In Spayne," was added later by Wyatt in the italic script he
used on f. 70r.

A D T: 3. have] hathe *A*   5. ⟨ffore⟩sins] ffor sens *A*] syñs *D*] For since *T*
 t
y] *om. D*   6. one] and *A*   7. sory] sored *A T*   8. spryte] wight *A T*
9. depryffd] depriued *T*   desyerd] desyred *A*] desired *T*   10. most] more

A T: 11. ons $\wedge$ maist
ons $\wedge$] mayste ones *A*] mayst once *T*]   ons must *D*   12. ⟨w⟩rape]
wrapp *A*]   wrappe *T*] rape *D*   13. this is the] Thus in this *T*   ẏ yet] as yet /
that *A*]   as yet it *T*   14. and] but *A T*   and I] & *D*   15. ꝑceyve] se how *T*
                                                                                   ei
thowrs] the howres *A*]   the howers *T*] the houres *D*   how y] do *T*   17.
thest] the easte *A*]   the East *T*   skant doth shew] dothe scantlye shew *A*]
scant shewes *T*   18. when] Butt *A*   19. cons] cõmes *A D T*   he] *om. D*
20. thest] to easte *A*]   to East *T*   22. body] bodies *A T*   24. from] fro *A*
desird] desyred *A*] desired *D T*   26. my whaite]·me vp *T*   it] I *A T*   fle]
flye *A*]   flie *T*   27. hope] hope as yet *A*   some thing] *om. A*   28. fele]
fle *D*   29. me] my *A*   30. lyvely] Lovelye *A*   31. whilst] whylest *A*
enioyd] enioyed *A T*   32. wher] when *A T*   well] *om. D*   33. But] And *T*
be cawse] by cause *D*   34. in slepe] and sleepe *A T*   35. sins] *om. D*
                  faytfull   full
36. The] that *A* $\wedge$] fayth$\wedge$*D*] faithfull *A*   I . . . delyght] Was neuer
thing that mought in ought my woful hart delight *T*   37. thvnsesy] thunesy
D] Th'uneasye *A*   38. land and hill] Landes the Hilles *A*] land the hylles *T*
39. shinig̃] shene *T*   to] for to *A T*   40. darke] darked *A T*   spere] spheare
A   44. sprang] sprong *T*   ẏ day] the daye *A*   46. doth] did *A*   48.
forgott] forgeat *A*   49. the bryght transparat̃] that bright transplendan̂t *A*]
                                                                         u
                                                                        neth
the bright transplendant *T*   50. colour] coulours *A T*   vnder it] vnder not
yt *D*   51. thaccomberd] thaccovmred *D*] thaccombred *A T*   ⟨a⟩] now *A*]
om. D] the *T*   53. shewth] shewethe *A*] shyweth *D*] sheweth *T*   54.
& teres] of teares *A*   & that] and eke *A T*   55. new kynde] new kynde *A*]
                     most
kindes *T*   wherin ⟨all⟩] most wherein *T*   men] men so *T*   56. thei] the *D*
                                                                          me
sygh̃e] sight̲e *D*   57. them] those *A*   58. me to] ˙for to *A T*] $\wedge$ to *D*   59.
for to' assay] to geve assaye *A*] for to assay *D*] tassay *T*   60. lyke] Loke *D*
myn] my *A T*   pa[*cut off*]] payne *A D T*   61. forby cawse] for because *A*]
A] for bycause *D*] forbecause *T*   62. shall] wyll *T*   63. towch̃e] toucheth
A T] toucheht *D*   65. do] shall *T*   66. above] abovte *D*   67. myn Iyes]
my Iyes *D*   min] my *A T*   68. were] wher *D*   guyd̃e] gooid̲e *D*   the
smert] smart *D*   70. strenes] streames *A T*   71. doth still] dothe so *A*]
doe styll *T*   72. me so] so *D*   74. did·me gyve] gave to me *A T* courtese]
                                 suche
Curteist *A*] courtesse *D*] curteis *T*   ⟨erst⟩] earste *A*] suc̃he *D*] erst *T*   76.
   t   t
that y] it that *A*] y I *D*] this that *T*   77. lingerd] linger *D*] lingred *A T*

78. and] whiche *A*   79. dryven] forst *T*   80. confort] compforte *A T*
                                       u   mone·
renew[*cut off*]] renewes *A T*] remes *D*   81. ⟨playne⟩] morn *D*   83. sterne]
         e   e
streme *D*   84. eke y lovely] y eke louyth *D*   86. rage] Charge *D*   87.
craggyd] Craggie *A*] ragged *T*   88. other] others *A T*   89. But] And *T*
                                            such   whereby
somtyme] some tymes *D*   90. such excess] $\wedge$ express *D*   92. and . . .
requyre] And yet I trust ere that I dye to see that I requyre *T*   93. lyves]
                                      also al
lyve *D*] dwelles *T*   wery] wearyd *A*   / may sometyme] somtyme may *A*]
                                      the have
also may somtym *D*] somtime may *T*   96. ⟨she shew⟩] to have *A T*] the
have *D*   97. dred] grief *T*   sterve] serve *A T*   98. by twene] betwene *A T*
      e   e   t
she ẏ] se ẏ *D*   99. ẏ] *om. D*   100. yff ẏ] and yf *A T*   this] the *A T*   fle]
flye *A D*

105

in Spayn

Tagus fare well y̌ westward w̌ thy strems
   torns vp the grayns off gold alredy tryd
w̌ spurr and sayle for I go seke the tems
   gaynward the soñne y̌ shewthe her welthi pryd   4
               wyche
and to the town ⟨y⟩ brutus sowght by drems
   like bendyd mone doth lend her lusty syd ·
              alone
My kyng my Contry ∧ for whome ⟨only alone⟩
      I ⟨s⟩lyve
   of myghty love the winge for this me gyve   8

         TV

E f. 69r, Wyatt's holograph. *T* 121. Surprisingly, there is no internal punctuation in any of these eight lines. Probably Wyatt's first thought for the end
rhyme of line 7 was the word "serve." The heading, partly cut off in the head
margin, is in Wyatt's italic script of f. 70r.
                                  wyche
T: 3. w̌...I] For I with spurre and saile   4. shewthe] sheweth   5.⟨y̌⟩] that
6. doth lend] that leanes   7. ∧...⟨s⟩lyve] I seke for whom I liue   8. love
the winge] Ioue the windes

106

Off purpos Love / chase first for to be blynd
      he w̌ sight of that
   for ⟨yff he myght ha⟨d⟩ve sene⟩ that I behold
vanquisht had bene   against all godly kynd
   ⟨yoͬ hand⟩ his bow yoͬ hand and trusse shold
          have vnfold   4
and he w̌ me to sͬve had bene assind ·
       he blind   and
   but for ⟨by ∧ cawse ∧ he⟩ rekelesse wold him hold
and still by chaunse his dedly stroke bestow
   w̌ suche as see I sͬve and suffer wow ·   8

         TV

E f. 69r, Wyatt's holograph. *T* 110. There is only one sign of internal punctuation in these eight lines. But there is also an unusual space after the word "bene" (l. 3), which may have been intended to indicate a break or to serve for later punctuation. The reading "ha⟨d⟩ve" (l. 2) within the deletion indicates a "v" written upon the earlier letter "d." The *T* text is an exact printing of Wyatt's revised wording, but with spelling variations such as "chose" for "chase" (l. 1) and "wo" for "wow" (l. 8). Considering the amount of editing *T* gives to poem 105 from this same leaf, the fidelity is surprising.

107

what kynd ?
What rage is this? what furour of ⟨excesse⟩ ?
    what plage
        ⟨Infect⟩   wery thus
    what powre // ∧ ⟨what poyson⟩ doth ∧ my mynd ⟨opresse⟩ ?
        m y   is assind
    with in ⟨the⟩ bons to rancle ⟨doth not cesse⟩

            t
        what
        ⟨the⟩ poyson⟨d⟩ plesant⟨nesse⟩ swet*e*   4

        ͠iyes   t
Lo se my ⟨chekes⟩ swell w contynuall terys
                    sleples
    the body still ⟨sleples⟩ away ∧ it weris
    my fode m⟨y⟩othing / my faintyng strenght reperis
                            ⟨redresse⟩
            nor doth*e* my ly͠ms ⟨ssustaine⟩ sustayne ·

    In diepe
    ⟨In to⟩ wid wound
⟨The strok doth streche⟩ th*e* dedly strok*e* doth torne
        to   t   ͡
    ⟨In⟩ curid skarre y neu shalle ⟨to⟩ retorne /
    Go to / tryvmph*e* / reioyse thy goodly torne
                    thi frend thow dost opresse ·   12

        u
Opresse y dost / and hast off hym no ⟨ruthe⟩ cure
        ⟨deth⟩ plaint
    nor yett my ⟨wowe⟩ ∧ no pitie can procure
                        t
    fiers tygre fell / hard rok w owt recure
    ons   u | rebell
    ⟨so⟩ may y love | cruell ⟨vnkynd⟩ to love?
        u   ‾‾‾‾‾‾‾‾‾‾‾‾‾‾‾‾‾‾‾‾
⟨Myghst y so love⟩ / neu͡ belovffd agayne
        u
    so love y still & not thi/love
            u
    ⟨myghst y so love & neu͡ more⟩ ob⟨a⟩ttayne ·

$$\overset{t}{w}\ spite\ of\ lust$$
so   e t
⟨myght⟩ wrathfull love ⟨so threte y w⟩ disdayne
cruelltyhert
may thret thy ⟨cruell hert⟩⟨to⟩⟨reprove⟩ ·

TV

E f. 69v, Wyatt's holograph. *T* 111. Nott (II, iii-iv) attempted to decipher the many deletions in this poem. From the difference in inking and the slightly slanted, crowded position of the present first stanza, it is clear that the first four lines were a later addition, the original beginning with line 5.

The deletion "Infect" (l. 2) may also be "& hete." Neither Nott nor *M3* offered a reading of that deletion. The reading "m⟨y⟩othing" (l. 7) indicates that the letter "o" was written upon the earler "y" and that the "m" was not clearly revised to "n." At the end of line 10 are two punctuation marks imposed one upon the other: · and /. The reading "cruelltyhert" (l. 20) shows that Wyatt failed to delete the letters "ty" when he made the final revision. The first two words of this last line are in a lighter ink, making possible the following versions: "thy cruell hert to prove," "thy cruellty to reprove," "may thret thy cruellty," or "may thret thy cruell hert."

T: 5. swell] flow   10. curid] cureles

108

ffrom thowght to thowght/from hill to hill Love dothe me lede
clene cõtrary from restfull lyff / thes cõmon pathe I trede ·

E f. 70r, Wyatt's holograph.

109

me
Vulcane bẏgat ∧ Mẏnerua me taught
yere
Nature mẏ mother craft norischt me yere[

Thre bodẏes ar mẏ fode mẏ strengh is in naught
Angre, wrath, wast, and noyse, are mẏ children
dere   4
Gesse frend what ẏ ame and how ẏ ame wrought
Monstre of see or of lande or of els where
Know me and use me and ẏ maẏ the defende
And if ẏ be thine enmẏe ẏ maẏ thẏ life ende   8

E f. 70r, Wyatt's italic holograph. *H* f. 29v. *T* 115. An italic script identical with this one occurs in the headings of poems 104 and 105. There are several reasons for regarding this italic script as Wyatt's own. First, his familiar book hand occurs in the two verses of poem 108 on the same folio. Second, the letter "y" in poem 109 is usually dotted, conforming with Wyatt's habit. Third and perhaps most important, the following scripts appear in the first line of poem 61 on f. 40v of *E*:

the furyous gonne   [Wyatt's ordinary script]
⟨bombard⟩ [italic script]
⟨Like as the cañon⟩ [scribal hand A]

In addition, the style of the word "bombard" there is very like that of the text of poem 109.

Wyatt was probably induced to use an italic script on particular occasions simply because of the nature of his material. Poem 109, for example, is based on a Latin epigram. When he had the second thought of changing "bombard" to "the furyous gonne," a similar chain of association probably called forth the italic script.

The *H* text is headed "A Ridell   Tho. *W*." Beneath the English text is a copy of the Latin source in italic script, headed "*Idem latine ex Pandulpho*." The Latin text was modernized in *M3* (p. 346) and contained three errors. The second line is in fact: "Edocuit genitrix ars fuit atꝗ dies" and the first two words of the third line are "Vis mea."

H T: 2. norischt] nurisseche *H*   yere [*cut off*]] yere by *H T*   3. strengh] strength *H T*   in] *om. H*   4. Angre] slawghter *H*   5. ẏ] I *H T throughout* and] or *H*   6. see or of lande or of] land see or *H*   7. Know] have *H* 8. enmẏe] enimye *H*

110

Love to gyve law vnto his subiect*e* hert*ę*

    stode in th*e* Iyes off barsabe th*e* bryght

    and in a look*e* anõne hymsellff convert*ę*

    cruelly plesant byfore kyng david syght   4

    first dasd his Iyes / and forder forth he stert*ę*

       t   venemd

    w ⟨poyson⟩ breth as sofftly as he myght

    towcht his sensis / and ouᵌ rannis his bonis

       t   creping

    w ⟨sparplyd⟩ fyre   sparplid for th*e* nonis ·   8

              t

And when he saw y kendlid was th*e* flame

          moyst

    the ⟨warme⟩ poyson in his hert h*e* launcy⟨dth*e*⟩d

       t   t

    so y th*e* sowle did tremble w th*e* same

                     he

    And In this brawle as ⟨it⟩ stode and trauncyd   12

    yelding vnto the figure and th*e* frame

       t

    y those fayre Iyes had in his pᶜsens glauncid

            that   had

    the*e* forme ⟨wheroff⟩ love pᶜ ntyd in his brest

he honorth it as thing off thing*e* best ·   16

                the wisdome ⟨ou⟩ all⟩ and fore cast
So that forgot ⟨and owt off mynd clene cast⟩
        to   t
(wych*e* wo ⟨the⟩ Remes when y th*e*s kyng*e* doth*e* lakk*e*)
for gettyng eke godd*e* maiestie as fast
             t
        forthw
⟨and⟩ ye and his own / ⟨anone⟩ he doth*e* to mak*e*   20
  vrye to go   in to the feld
⟨vnder pᶜ tence off victorye / in hast
    I say   t
Vrye ⟨to go⟩ / y was his Idoll*e* mak*e*)
vnder p⟩ tence off certen victorye
for enmys sword*e* a redy pray to dye ·   24

                owt of dowt*e*
Wherby he may enIoy her ⟨all alone⟩
                              myndyth
      more than god / or ⟨ell*e* he⟩   he⟨lovth⟩
whom ⟨he doth Love more than⟩ hym sellff ⟨or god⟩
     after
and ⟨when⟩ he had browght this thing abowt*e*
       that ⟨his⟩ lust
& off ⟨this delyght⟩ posest hym sellff he fyndyth*e*   28
  t
y hath & doth*e* reu⟩ se and clene torn⟨d⟩ owt
      from
kyng*e* ⟨and⟩ kyndomes & cytes vndermyndyth
he blyndy⟨th⟩d think*e* this trayne so blynd & closse
       t
to blynd all thing y nowght may it disclosse   32
                trecherye
But Nathan hath*e* spyd owt this ⟨gret*e*⟩
  t
w rufull chere & sett*e* afore his face
the gret offence outrage & Iniurye
  t
y he hath done to god as in this Case   36
by murder for to clok*e* Adulterye
        from   threte alas
he shewth hym ek*e* ⟨how⟩ hevyn th*e* ⟨sore menace⟩
so sternly sore this prophet*e* this Nathan
  t   agid
y all a masid this ∧ woofull man   40

    t   t   t
lyke hym y met*e* w horrour & w fere
the ⟨colour⟩ hete doth*e* strayt*e* forsake the lȳ̄s cold
the colour eke drowpith down from his ch*e*re

        his   er

so doth he fele ⟨the⟩ fy⟨re⟩ maynifold /   44

his hete his lust / and plesur all in fere

consume and wast / and strayt his crown of gold

               pall

his ⟨pall his⟩ purpirll his sceptre he lett͜e fall t

and ‿to the grownd he throwth hym sellff w all   48

The pompous pryd of state and dygnite

    t

  fortw rabat͜e repentant humblenes

    ⟨vile⟩

⟨athyn cloth⟩ thynner vyle clothe then clothyth pou⟩ ty

doth skantly hyde and clad his nakednes   52

    faire

his ∧ hore ⟨his⟩ berd of reverent gravite

  t   knowyng   wyknednes

w ruffeld here · ⟨repentyng⟩ his ⟨excesse⟩

          he

more lyke ⟨he⟩ was ∧ the sellff same repentance

then statly prynce off wordly governance ·   56

His harpe he ⟨hathe⟩ take⟨n⟩th in ⟨his⟩ hand to be his guyde

    t   his   his sowle to save

wherw he offerthe ⟨the⟩ plaint͜e ⟨and the Cryis⟩

  t

y from his hert distill͜e on eu⟩ y syde

  t

w drawyng hym in to a dark Cave   60

  t   hym

w in the grownd wherin he myght ∧ hyde

        as

fleing the lyght ∧ in pryson or ⟨in⟩ grave

Inwyche as sone as david enterd had

        did make

the dark horrour ⟨mad⟩ his fawte a drad   64

    t   or

But he w owt prolonging ⟨of⟩ delay

    rof that

  ⟨the thing⟩ that myght his lord his god apese

fallth on his knees · & w his harp I say

         t

a fore his brest / frawtyd w disese   68

off stormy sygh͜e / his chere colourd lyk clay

          sekyng to cōter pese

dressyd vpryght / ⟨he tunis his god to plese⟩

      t

his song w sygh͜e and towching of the stryng͜e

  t

w tendre hert Lo thus to god he syng͜e ·   72

E ff. 86r-87r, Wyatt's holograph. *A* f. 108rv. *R* ff. 2v-5v. *Q* sigs. Aiiir-Avir. On f. 85v in *E* is a copy of Surrey's *The great Macedon*, probably entered by John Harington the Elder, who drew his own initials "IH" on the inner margin and an interlaced "HS" for Surrey in the head margin.

In the *E* text an unusual space occurs after "fyre" (l. 8) but no punctuation. Wyatt first ended line 10 with "launcythe," then wrote a "d" over "the," and finally added a clearer "d" in the margin. I read "⟨it⟩" (l. 12) where Hughey read "⟨at⟩." The closed parenthesis at the end of line 22 has no mate. The abbreviation in "p⟩tence" (l. 23) is probably a pen slip rather than an alternate spelling. Cf. line 21. Beneath "for enmys" (l. 24) is a deleted

reading, perhaps "& by y̆." The revised spelling "fyer" (l. 44) indicates a precise care for the number of syllables in the line. After the first word in line 48 is a smudge but no readable deletion. It is possible that the word "tendre" (l. 72) is actually "tendrer."

Two of the variants show a distinction for *R*. The second variant for line 57, where *R* preserves the deleted "his" of *E*, is the only case among all the variants where a deleted reading of *E* is recovered elsewhere. *R* alone preserves Wyatt's careful spelling of "fyer" (l. 44) with "fier." Even the scribal error "emnis" (l. 24) may have resulted from attempting to catch Wyatt's spelling "enmys." Thus, the variants show that *R* could have been edited directly from *E*.

There is no similar evidence for the *A* text. The *Q* text is the most eccentric, and it could have been edited from *R*. In line 69, where *R* mistakenly repeats half of a line from *E*, the editor of *Q* noticed the repetition but could not supply the original phrase, so he made one up. At that point *A* has the *E* reading, so the *A* copyist was editing either from *E* directly or from good copy, with which he was not too careful.

A R Q: *title om.*] The prologue to the first psalm of Dauid *R*] The Prologe of the Auctor *Q*   1. subiecte] subiecte *A Q*   3. hymsellff] hym selfes *Q*   4. david] Davides *A R Q*   5. dasd] David *A*   6. ⟨poyson⟩] venemd *A*] venumed *R*] venemed *Q*   7. towcht . . . ou⟩ rannis] Towcht . . . over ranne *A*] Toucht . . . ouer runs *R*] Touche . . . senewes, . . . ouer runnes *Q*   8. sparplid] spark'led *A*] sparcled *R*] sparkeled *Q*   9. kendlid] kindeled *Q*   10. ⟨warme⟩] noysome *Q*   he] *om. A*   11. the sowle] his Sowle *A*   12. this] his *R Q*   16. honorth] honoreth *A R Q*   thing] a thinge *A Q*   17. forgot] he forgotte *Q*   18. the s kynge dothe] this kinges do *A R*] the kynge dothe *Q*   22. Idollѐ] Ieweles *Q*   24. enmys] en'myes *A*] emnis *R*] enemyes *Q*   dye] be *Q*   30. kyndomes] kingdomes *A Q*   31. this] his *A*   32. thing] thynges *Q*   nowght] nothing *Q*   33. this] his *R*   34. rufull] ruthfull *A*   setѐ] set *A*   38. shewth] shewith *A*] sheweth *R*]   shewethe *Q*   hym] *om. R Q*   40. this ∧woofull man] was, thys woful aged man *Q*   41. metѐ] mete *A*] meateth *Q*   42. lyms] lymyttes *Q*   43. drowpith] droppeth *R Q*   44. fy⟨re⟩] fyre *A Q*] fier *R*   45. hete] helth *R*   and] his *Q*   fere] fyre *A*   47. pall] pauler *Q*   letѐ] letteth *Q*   48. throwth] throweth *R Q*   49. The pompous] Then pompious *Q*   of state and] & statelie *R*   50. rabatѐ] rebates *A*] rebate *R Q*   51. thynner] Th'inner *A*   clothyth] clothyd *Q*   53. of] w *R*   54. here] hears *A*   wyknednes] wickednes *A*] wikednes *R*]   wyckednes *Q*   55. sellff] *om. Q*   repentance] repentante *A*   56. wordly] worldlye *A*] worldly *R*] worldelye *Q*   57. take⟨n⟩th] takes *A*] taketh *R*]

takethe *Q* ⟨his⟩ hand] his hand *R*   58. offerthe] offerith *A*] offerth *R*]
offreth *Q*   59. distill e] dystylleth *Q*   60. hym] hym selfe *Q*   dark] darke
depe *A*   61. wherin] whenne *R*] wher *Q*   62. fleing] fflyeing *A*] flyinge *Q*
63. enterd] entrid *A*] entred *R Q*   64. a drad] adrad *A*   65. he] *om. Q*
         rof that
66. ⟨the thing⟩] Of that *A R Q*   that] whyche *Q*   67. fallth] falleth *A Q*
68. frawtyd] yfraughted *A*   69. his . . . coloured . . . clay] his . . . colurid . . .
claye *A*]   and touching of the stringes *R*]   depe draughtes of hys decaye *Q*
70. dressyd] dressing *R*   71. song] songes *Q*

111

Domine ne in furore · Psal : 6 ·

                    in
O Lord sins ⟨off⟩ my mowght thy myghty name
    sufferth it sellff / my Lord to name and call
                       hope taken
    here hath my hert ⟨cawght cõfort⟩ by the same
that the repentance wyche I have and shall   4
                          marcy as the
    may at thi hand seke ⟨eu⟩ the same⟩ thing
                    wrechid
    only confort of ⟨vs⟩ synners all
                t
Wher by I dare w humble by monyg
                     this
    by thy goodnes off the ∧ thing require /   8
    chastyse me not for my des⟩ ving
Acordyng to thy Iust conceyvid Ire ·
                t
    O Lord I dred / and y I did not dred
    I me repent / and eu⟩ more desyre   12
                  open
the the to dred / I ⟨knolege⟩ here & spred
                       u
    my fawte to the / but y for thi goodnes
    mesure it not in ⟨lengh⟩ largenes nor in bred
u
pnish it not as askyth the grettnes   16
                  o
    off thi furour prov⟨eth⟩kt by my offence
    Tempre o lord the harme of my excesse
    t   ⁓   t   for recompense
w mendyg will y I ⟨p⟨ pare agayne⟩
    prepare agayne / & rather pite me   20
                       t
    for I ame weke / & clene w owt defence
                is the I have
⟨And have⟩ more nede of ⟨the for⟩ remede

for off th*e* hole th*e* leche takyth no cure

　the shepe y strayth*e* the sheperd sek⟨th⟩*e* to se　　24
　　　　　　　　　　　　　　　　ᵗ

I lord ame strayd / I sek*e* wᵗ owt recure
　　　fele　　　　　ᵗ
　⟨for⟩ al my lȳms y have rebelld / for fere
　　　in　　　　　onles u
　shake ⟨for⟩ dispayre ⟨if⟩ y me ⟨not⟩ assure

　　　ᵗ
　wᵗ secrett ⟨gy⟩ trapps to troble my penance
　　　sum　　　　　　　　to my weping
　⟨the and⟩ do⟨th⟩ pᶜ sent ⟨vnto myn⟩ yes lo　　84

The ch*e*re the manere bealte & countn͡ace
　off her whose lok*e* alas did mak*e* me blynd
　sum oth*e*r off*e*r to my rem͡ebrans

those plesant word*e* / now bitter to my mynd　　88
　and sum shew me th*e* powre of my armoᵍ
　tryumph*e* and c͡oquest / and to my h*e*d assind

dowble Diademe / sum shew the favoᵍ
　　　　　　　　　　　　ryches
　of peple frayle / palais / pompe / & ⟨glory⟩ /　92
　to th*e*s Marmayd*e* and th*e*yre bayt*e* off erroᵍ
　　　　ᵗ

I stopp myn eris wᵗ help of thy goodnes
　and for I fele it comith*e* alone of th*e*
　　ᵗ
　y to my hert th*e*s foes have non access　　96

8　I dare th*e*m bid avoyd wrech*e*s and fle
　the lord hath*e* hard th*e* voyce off my complant
　yoᵍ engins take no more effect in me
　　　　herd I say &
9　th*e* lord hath*e* ⟨pitid for to⟩ sen me faynt　　100
　vnder yoᵍ hand · and pitith*e* my distres
　he shall do mak*e* my sensis by c͡ostraint

Obbey the rule y reson shall expres
　　　　　ᵗ
　　　　the　　　　　ᵍ　　　baite
　wher/⟨bye⟩ deceyt*e* of yow glosing ⟨venim⟩　104
　made th*e*m
　⟨ther had⟩ vsurpt a powre in all exces
　　　　　　ᵗ so
10　Shamid be thei all y ∧ly in ⟨a⟩ whaite
　to compas me / by missing of th*e*ire pray

shame and rebuke redound to suche decayte   108

sodayne cōfusion ⟨a⟩s stroke w owt delay

shall so defface theire craffty ⟨entreprise⟩

y they to hurt my helthe no more assay

sins I olord remayne in thi protection   112

⟨finis⟩ TV

E ff. 87r-88v, Wyatt's holograph, *om.* ll. 28-81. *A* ff. 109r-110r, *om.* 1.59.

R ff. 6r-10r. *Q* sigs. [Avi^r] – Bii^r. Between the present ff. 87 and 88 in *E* is a blank modern unnumbered leaf indicating the loss of a folio containing lines 21-81. For the missing lines, *A* is the best source, although line 59 must be taken from *R*. *A* is a good copy of *E* except at the end of the poem, from line 103. Lines 103 and 104 contain what looks like the only serious editing of *E* in *A*. The scribe of *A* probably took Wyatt's "decayte" (l. 108) for "decaye" because the final "te" might seem to be a large open "e" whereas the poet's final "e" is just a hook on the "t."

At this point an error suggests that the scribe of *A* had the *E* copy before him, for the next poem begins in *A* without a break to indicate the beginning of a new unit. This scribal error was made most likely because Wyatt had deleted his own "finis" in *E*. Wyatt must have thought of extending his version of Psalm 6 for another verse or two before deciding to begin the next prologue.

Another significant aspect of the *E* text is the appearance in the margins of arabic numbers, 8 opposite line 97, 9 opposite line 100, and 10 opposite line 106. These numbers were one of the clues that led H. A. Mason to discover Wyatt's use of a paraphrase of the psalms by Ioannes Campensis. Since Wyatt also makes occasional use of a paraphrase by Zwingli, one can assume that the poet's text was an edition which printed both prose explications. The full title is *Enchiridion Psalmorum. Eorundem ex ueritate Hebraica uersionem, ac Ioannis Campensis e regione paraphrasim, sic ut uersui respondeat, complectens* (Lyons, 1531). See H. A. Mason, "Wyatt and the Psalms—1," *TLS*, 27 Feb. 1953; Mason, *Humanism and Poetry* (London: Routledge and Kegan Paul, 1959), pp. 206-207.

At the end of line 8 in *E* occurs the puzzling combination of a full stop and a virgule occupying the same place.

Although Hughey's variants were helpful (II, 217-219), a number of additions and corrections were necessary. For example, what Hughey took as an "i" written upon the deleted "a" in line 108 is in fact an apostrophe.

A R Q: *Domine . . . furore*] Dne ne infurore tuo arguas me../*A title*] Domine ne in furore tuo *R title*] Domine ne in furore *Q title*   1. in] *om. Q*   mowght] mowthe *A*] mouth *R*] mouthe *Q*   2. sufferth] Suffereth *Q*   and] & to *Q*   3. hert] harpe *Q*   taken] he taken *Q*   6. only] Of onely *Q*   of] to *Q*   8. thy] the *R Q*   13. the the] thee for *R*] Thee *Q*   15. not] *om. A*   17. furour] furie *R*   my] myne *R Q*   18. my] mine *R*   24. straythe] straieth *A*] strays *R*] strayeth *Q*   25. I seke] and seke *Q*

28-81. *om. E A*
28.   mye flesshe is troubled my hart doth feare the speare
       That dread of death, of death that ever lastes
       Threateth of right and draweth neare and neare

Moche more my sowle is trowbled by the blastes
32.   Of theise assawltes that come as thick as hayle
Of worldlye vanytie that temptacõn castes
Agaynst the weyke bulwarke of the flesshe frayle
Wheare in the sowle in great perplexitie
36.   ffeelethe the sensis with them that assayle
Conspyre, corrupte by vse and vanytie
whearby the wretche dothe to the shadowe resorte
Of hope in the, in this extreamytie
40.   but thow o lord, how longe after this sorte
fforbearest thow to see my myserye
Suffer me yet in hope of some comforte
ffeare and not feele that thow forgettest me
44.   Returne o lorde, O lorde I the beseche
Vnto thie olde wonted benignitie
Reduce revyve my sowle be thow the leche
And reconcyle, the great hatred and stryfe
48.   That it hath tane agaynste the flesshe the wretche
That stirred hathe thie wrathe bye filthie life
Se how mye sowle doth freat it to the bones
Inwarde remorce so sharp'the it like a knife
52.   That but thow helpp the caitife that bemones
His great offence / it turnes anon to dust
Heare hath thie mercye matter for the nones
ffor if thie rightuous hand that is so iuste
56.   Suffer no Synne or stryke with dampnacõn
Thie infinyte marcye want nedes it must
Subiecte matter for his operacion
        for that in deth there is no memorie
60.   Amonge the Dampnyd nor yet no mencion
Of thie great name grownd of all glorye
Then if I dye, and goe wheare as I feare
To thinck thearon, how shall thie great mercye
64.   Sownde in my mowth vnto the worldes eare
ffor theare is none that can thee lawde and love
ffor that thow nilt no love among them theare
Suffer my Cryes thie marcye for to move
68.   that wonted is a hundred yeares offence
                    u
In momente of repentance to remove
How ofte have I calde vpp with diligence
This slowthfull flesshe longe afore the daye
72.   ffor to confesse his faulte and negligence
that to the done for ought that I coold say
Hath still returnd to shrowde it self from colde
whearbye it suffers nowe for suche delaye
76.   by mightye playntes in stede of pleasures olde
I wasshe my bed with teares contynuall
To dull my sight that it be never bolde
To stirr mye hart agayne to suche afall
80.   Thus drye I vpp among my foes in woe
That with my fall do rise and grow with all

30. Threateth] Tretith *R*   33. worldlye] worlds *R*   vanytie] vanities *Q*
34. weyke] *om. Q*   37. vse] pleasure *Q*   38. shadowe] shade *Q*   44. o lorde

. . . beseche] (o lorde) I beseche thee o lorde *Q* 45. thie] thine *R* 48. tane]
had *Q* 51. sharp'the] sharpth *R*] sharpeth *Q* 53. great] *om. R* turnes]
turneth *Q* 55. rightuous] rightwise *R* 59. *R*] *om. A*] For that in deathe,
there is no memorye *Q* 66. nilt] wilt *Q* 67. thie marcye for] thee mercye
Q 68. a] an *R* 69. In] In a *Q* 73. done] denne *Q* 74. it self] hym
selfe *Q* 75. suffers] sufferth *R*] suffreth *Q* nowe] none *Q* 76. mightye]
nightly *R* 79. stirr] stere *Q*

82. bysett] besettes *A* 84. to] to me *Q* yes lo] eyes Lo *A* eyes *R Q*
85. the manere] manere *R* bealte &] bewtie and *A*] beaultie & *R*] bewtye,
or *Q* 88. those] These *Q* 89. my] myne *R* 91. the] *om. Q* 93. thes] the
R Q 94. myn] my *A* 95. comithe] comes *A* 96. hert] harpe *Q* thes]
those *A* 97. I] *om. Q* 100. sen] seme *R* 101. pitithe] pittieth *A*] pitieth *R*]
pytyeth *Q* 103. the rule] therefore *A* 104. wher] Where that *Q* glosinge]
glawncynge *A* 105. vsurpt] vsurpp *A*] usurpe *R Q* 106.∧ly] so do lye *Q*
(so above ∧)
108. decayte] decaye *A*

112

fevour
Who so hathe sene the sikk in his ⟨dolour⟩
    t   the hete
   affter ⟨the⟩ treux taken w ⟨thete⟩ or cold
   and that the fitt is past off his faruour
             t let him I say behold
   draw faynting syghe / ⟨w sobbyng double fold⟩   4
   ⟨let hym⟩ sorowfull david affter his langour
 t t   ʼ   t   down
y w the terys y from his iyes ∧ rold
   pausid his plaint / and layd a down his harp
   faythfull record of all his sorows sharp ·   8

It semid now that of his fawt "the horrour
   did make a ferd no more his hope of grace
   the threte whereoff in horrible errour
   did hold his hert as in dispaire a space   12
                his
till he had willd to seke for ∧ socour
          beknowyng
   hym selff accusing / ⟨and knoleging⟩ his cace
   thinking so best his lord for to apese
   esed not yet held he felith his disese   16

   eesd

⟨Now⟩ semythe horrible no more the darke Cave

<pre>
                t   for   tremble
y erst did make his fault to ⟨be a drad⟩
a place devout or refuge for to save
the socourles / it rather doth resemble   20
                     him   t
for who had sene so ∧ knele w in the grave
the chieffe pastor of thebrews assemble
wold Iuge it made by terys of penitence
a sacrid place worthi off reu⁾ ence   24

      t
 W vapord iyes he lokyth here & there
and when he hathe a while hym sellff bethowght
                          t
gadryng his sprit͜ey where dismayd for fere
his harp agayne ⟨v⟩ In to his hand he rowght   28
tuny͡g accord by Iugem͡et of his ere
his hert͜e botum for a sigh he sowght
              t
and there w all apon the holow tre
              ⟨syghing⟩
  t strainid   agayne
w ⟨lowd⟩ voyce ⟨lo⟩ thus ⟨oft⟩ cryth he   32
                TV
</pre>

E ff. 88v–89r, Wyatt's holograph. A f. 110rv. R ff. 10v–11v. Q sigs. [Biii^r-

Biv^r]. In A the first stanza of this poem was added onto the conclusion of poem 111 by the scribe and marked "ffinis" beneath line 8. There is another "ffinis" for the next three octaves, which occur on f. 110v in A.

The text of E includes some noteworthy signs of Wyatt's careful attention. In line 11, for example, the rhyme word was first written with only the rhyme ending and space for the body of the word:

horrible] our]

Wyatt then added "err" in the same ink in slightly larger letters; still later he underlined the "err" in black ink. That black ink is notable elsewhere. The surprising revision beneath the first word of line 16 is in black ink. The variants show that only R precisely keeps Wyatt's revision. The word "where" (l. 27) was underlined in E in black ink, and the three striking marks upon "fawt" (l. 9) were also apparently done later in the same color of ink.

At two points there is evidence that Q was edited directly from E. In line 17 only Q preserves the deleted "Now" of E and could therefore have found that word only in E. In line 28, the Q reading "vnto" could have been suggested by Wyatt's own deleted "v." Wyatt himself must have considered using "vnto" rather than "In to."

Hughey's variants (II, 220) were incorrect for line 28 in A, which reads "raught" rather than "caught." Thus, A agrees with E and the other two texts in this instance. Hughey also failed to note that the inserted "him" (l. 21) in E was later deleted. It is possible that this "him" is the one word on the leaf not written by Wyatt. M3 (p. 105) repeated Hughey's error concerning the reading of A in line 28.

A R Q: 2. ⟨thete⟩] ^{the hete} heat *A R*   or] or w th *A*   3. faruour] furour *A*] feuour *Q*
6. the] his *Q*   iyes] eyen *Q*   7. a down] down *Q*   11. errour] terrour *Q*
13. willd] wyll *Q*   14. ⟨and knoleging⟩] ^{beknowyng} by knowing *A*   15. for to] to *Q*
16. esed] Easyd *A*] Eesd *R*] And *Q*   held] healed *Q*   felithe] tilleth *A*]
eesd
feleth *R*] fealethe *Q*   17. ⟨Now⟩semythe] Semethe *A*] Semeth *R*] Nowe
semeth *Q*   horrible] feareful *Q*   19. or] of *Q*   20. doth] dyd *Q*   21. had]

hathe *A*   so . . . grave] so knele within a grave *A*] so knele w^tin the graue *R*]
so kneeling with in the graue *Q*   22. pastor] pasture *Q*   thebrews]
Th'ebrues *A*] the hebrewes *Q*   25. lokyth] loked *Q*   26. a while hym sellff]
himself a while *R*   bethowght] besought *A*   27. gadryng] Gatheringe *A Q*
sprite] spirite *R Q*   where] weare *A*] were *R Q*   28. ⟨v⟩In to] vnto *Q*
32. cryth] Cryethe *A*] crieth *R*] cryed *Q*

113

Psal : 32 beati quoꝝ remisse sūt ū

1   Oh happy ar they ⟨ that ⟩ y̆ have forgiffnes gotte
     off theire offence / (not by theire penitence
     as by meryt wyche recõpensyth not
     altho y·yet pardone hath non offence   4
       w owte the same /) but by the goodnes
     off hym y̆ hathe ꝑfect intelligens
       Off hert contrite / ⟨y̆⟩ ^{and} coverth the grettnes
       w in a marcifull discharge
     off syn ⟨vnder the mantell off mercy⟩ ·   8
     ^{and}   the willfullnes
     ⟨oh⟩ happy ar they y̆ have ⟨forgiffe⟩
     Off lust restraynd / afore it went at large
     provokyd by the dred of godde furour
     wherby thei have not on theyre bake the charge   12
     of w   to suffer the dolour
     ⟨off⟩ others fawte ⟨examplid theire errour⟩
                    was   excecute
     for y̆ theire fawte ⟨did⟩ neu ⟨it extend⟩
     in opyn syght/example of errour
                    he
2   And happi is ∧ to whom god doth impute
     no more his faute by knoleging his syn
     but clensid now the lord doth hym repute

         fresh*e* /

as adder ∧ new / ⟨y⟩ stryppid from his skin

        owght

    nor In his sprit*e* is ⟨nothing⟩ vndiscoverd   20

    by cawse   t

3   ı ⟨I⟩ for ⟨that⟩ I hidd it still w in

     k

  thying by state in   to be deberd pᶜferd

⟨and for to shew my⟩ fawt*e* ⟨have bene aferd⟩

    ⟨and⟩ do

    ⟨do⟩ fynd⟨e⟩ by hyding of my fawt*e* my harme

    as h*e* that fells his h*e*lth*e* to be hinderd   24

by secret*e* wound concelid from th*e* charme

           t

    of lechis cure / y elk*e* had had redresse

    and

    ⟨dyd⟩ fele my bonis cõsume and wex vnfarme

       rage   t   ⟨did still⟩ roryng in excess*e*

by dayly ⟨plaint y I by force express*e*⟩   28

              ⟨did⟩ was

4   ⟨and for⟩ thy hevy hand on me ⟨hath⟩ so encrest

    both*e* day and nyght / and h*e*ld my h*e*rt in presse

  t priking

w ⟨restles⟩ thowght*e* by reving me my rest

    t

    y ⟨I am⟩ wyth*e*rd is my lustynes à way   32

         t

    a⟨s⟩ somer hett*e* y hath*e* th*e* grene oprest

5   wherfore I did an oth*e*r way assay

               t

    and sowght forthw to opin in thi syght

    my fawt / my fere / my filthines I say   36

          from

And not to hide ⟨to⟩ th*e* my gret vnryght

    I shall ꝗ I agaynst my sellff ⟨bemon⟩ cõfesse

    vnto th*e* lord all my synfull plyght

   ù   t

And y forthw didst wash*e* th*e* wikk*e*dnes   40

    off myn offence · of trowght ryght thus it is

6   wh*e*rfor th*e*y that have tastid thi goodnes

At me shall take example as of this

             ⟨to⟩ for

    and pray and sek*e* in tyme ⟨for⟩ tym⟨s⟩e of grace 44

        stormes

    then shall th*e* ⟨waves⟩ and fludd*e* of harme him mis

and hym to rech*e* shall neuᵗ have th*e* sp⟨l⟩ace

7   Thow art my refuge and only save gard

             t

    from th*e* trobles y compasse me th*e* place   48

         t

Such*e* Ioy as he y skapis his enmis ward

^t
w losid bonde hathe in his libertie
suche Ioy / my Ioy thow hast to me p^r pard

⟨8⟩   ^t
y as the seman in his Ieopretie   52

               the
by soden lyght perceyvid hathe ∧port
so by thy gret marcifull propertie

8   ^t
w in thi loke thus rede I my confort

               ond
I shall the teche and gyve vnderstyng   56
and poynt to the what way ÿ shalt resort

for thi adresse to kepe the from wandryng
myn yIe shall take the charge to be thy guyde ·

9   ⟨be⟩ I aske therto / of the alone this thing   60
           ^t
be not like horse or mule y man dothe ryde
^t
y not alone dothe not his master know
          u
but for the good y dost hym must be tyde

        ^t
and brydeld ⟨y⟩ lest his guyd he bite or throw ·   64
10   Oh dyu⁾ se ar the chastysinge off syn
                  ^t
in mete / in drynk / in breth y man dothe blow
                   ^t
In slepe/in wache / In fretyng styll w in
^t
y neu⁾ soffer rest vnto the mynd   68
   ^t   ^t
filld w offence / ⟨but⟩ y new & new begyn
^t   hart
w thowsand feris the ⟨mynd⟩ to strayne & bynd
             ^t
but for all this he y in god dothe trust
^t
w m^r cy shall hym sellff defendid fynd ·   72
       I say   ^t
11   Ioy & reioyse ∧ ye y be⟨ne⟩ Iust
        t   makth & holdyth
in hym y ⟨dothe cotynew⟩ yow so still
                  alwey set
in hym ⟨I say set all⟩ yo^ꝯ glory ⟨&⟩ yow must
       ^t
all ye y be off vpryght hert & will ·   76
           TV

E ff. 89r-90v, Wyatt's holograph. *A* ff. 110v-111v. *R* ff. 12r-15r. *Q* sigs. [Biv^v-Bvii^v]. The heading of this psalm in *E* is in two hands. The abbrevia-

tion of "psalm" and the number match the entire heading of Psalm 6 on
f. 87v. However, the Latin incipit "*beati* . . ." is in a pale brown ink and larger
italic script, very like that Wyatt employed on f. 70r.

Hughey (II, 221) offered the variant "Leathis" (l. 26) for *A*, which is a
misreading of "Leachis." *M3* did not correct this error, although elsewhere
M3 corrected a few errors in Hughey's variants from *Q*.

The peculiar form "emnis" recurs in *R* at line 49. Yet once again *Q* is the
most eccentric text. The variants for lines 53 and 55 suggest that *Q* could
have been edited from *R*. Of the more difficult lines to read in *E*, line 73
stands out. The scribe of *R* got it exactly right and the scribe of *Q* edited it
slightly. In this instance the scribe of *A* confused the line.

A R Q: 4. non] not *R Q*   7. coverth] couereth *R*] couert *Q*   10. restraynd]
restrayned *A*] restraygned *Q*   13. oth*e*rs fawt*e*] other faultes *Q*   18. but]
And *Q*   19. new] and new *A*   20. sprit*e*] spirite *R*   vndiscoverd]
undiscouered *R*   21. I] In *R*   hidd] had *A*   22. p᷑ferd] preferred *Q*
24. fells] feles *A*] feleth *R*] fyndeth *Q*   to be] *om. Q*   hinderd] hindred *R*]
hyndered *Q*   29. thy] The *Q*   31. by reving] bireuing *R*   32. wytherd]
wethered *Q*   33. a s] As *A R Q*   hath*e*] haue *R Q*   41. trowght] trouthe
A] trouth *R*] truthe *Q*   45. him mis] *om. Q*   49. Ioy] Ioyes *Q*   skapis]
scapeth *Q*   enmis] emnis *R*] enemyes *Q*   50. bond᷑e] bandes *Q*   his] *om. Q*
51. Ioy my] is my *Q*   53. lyght] sight *R Q*   port] light *R Q*   55. loke]
booke *R Q*   rede] reade *A Q*   58. adresse] redresse *A*   wandryng]
wanderynge *Q*   59. myn] My *R Q*   yIe] eyes *A*   60. alone] onelye *Q*
61. mule] moyle *A*   man doth*e*] men do *Q*   62. doth*e* not] doth *R Q*
63. the . . . tyde] thee good, thou muste hym betide *Q*   64. brydeld]
bryd'led *A*] brideled *Q*   guyd] maister *R*   65. ar th*e*] there are *Q*   66. in
drynk] and drynke *Q*   67. in wach*e*] and watche *Q*   69. filld] Feld *R*]
                                                                         I say
Felde *Q*   70. bynd] blynde *A Q*   73. Ioy] Ioyce *Q*   ye . . . Iust] saye ye
that be just *A*] I saye : you that be iuste *Q*   74. makth] makethe *A*]
maketh *Q*   75. alwey] alwayes *Q*   75. all ye] All *A*] All you *Q*   off] of
an *A*

114

     song   did stint   voyce
This endid / ⟨did, o᷑⟩ david ⟨hold⟩ his ⟨pees⟩
                    about h*e*   t
    and In that while ⟨did seke⟩ w his iye
    did sek*e*   t   t
    the darke Cave / w wich*e* / w owten noyce
    his sylence semid / ⟨his⟩ to argew & replye   4
                      t
              pees · this pees y
    apon this ⟨marcy wheron he⟩ did reioyce
          sowle   t   ᶜ   t
    the ⟨hert for⟩ w mᶜcy / y mercy so did Crye
                     plentifull
    and fownd mᶜcy at mercy full hand
                    t
    neuᶜ denid but wh*e*re it was w stand   8

〈And〉 as the s⁾vant y in his masters face

fyndȳg pardon〈s〉 of his passid offence

cõsyderȳg his grete goodnes and his grace

glad teris distills / as gladsome recõpense   12

ryght so david / 〈and〉 semid in that place

a〈nd〉 ymage 〈made〉 off singuler reu⁾ ence

Carffd in the rokke w Iyes and hande 〈lyfft vp〉

〈semȳg〉∧ by crafft to 〈syghe〉 to sobbe to

〈svpp〉 sygh ·   16

This while a beme 〈down from〉

that sonne ∧ 〈disc〉 sende

that sonne the wyche was neu⁾ clowd hide

percyth the cave / and on the harpe discende

〈and w the luster on〉 the corde 〈it〉 glyd〈e〉e   20

and suche luyster apon the harpe extende

as lyght off lampe apon the gold clene tryde

the torne wheroff In to his Iyes did sterte

surprisd w Ioye / by penance off the herte ·   24

He then Inflamd w farr more hote 〈desire〉

of god / then 〈off his Idolle〉 Bersabe

his lifft fote did on the yerthe erecte

and Iust therby remaynthe the tother kne   28

to his lifft syde his wayght he dothe directe

〈assured〉 hope of helthe and harpe agayne takth he

his hand his tune / his mynd sowght his lay

wyche to the Lord w sobre voyce did say   32

                        T V

E ff. 90v-91r, Wyatt's holograph. *A* ff. 111v-112r. *R* ff. 15r-16r. *Q* sigs.
[Bvii ᵛ]-Ci ʳ. The most important variant is that for line 7. The scribe of *R* assumed that Wyatt meant to cancel the workd "mercy full," while the scribes
of *A* and *Q* kept it. The editor of *Q* therefore had access to either *A* or *E* in
addition to *R*.

A R Q: *om. title*] The prologue *R*] The Auctor *Q*   1. stint] skant *R*

2. abowt he] he aboute *Q*   3. darke] *om. A*   w^t owten] wythoute *Q*

4. semid] seem'de *A*   5. this ⟨marcy⟩] hys harpe *Q*   6. Crye] cal *R Q*
7. mercy full] plentifull mercyes *A Q*] at plentifulles *R*   8. where] whi *R*

9. y̆] *om. Q*   10. pardon⟨s⟩] the pardon *A*   13. ⟨and⟩ semid] did seme as *R*]
semed *Q*   that] thee *Q*   14. a⟨nd⟩] *om. A R*   15. the] *om. A*   hand⟨e⟩]
hande *Q*   16. as] is *Q*   17. This] The *A*   ⟨disc⟩send⟨e⟩] sendeth *Q*   18. was]
theare was *A*   clowd] sonne *R Q*   19. the harpe] his harppe *A*   discend⟨e⟩]
descende the *Q*   20. cord⟨e⟩] world *Q*   21. luyster] glister *A*   22. tryde]
tryed *A Q*   23. sterte] stette *Q*   24. surprisd] Supprysed *Q*   25. then
Inflamd] more enflamed *Q*   affecte] effecte *Q*   27. lifft] list *R*   the
yerthe] the earthe *A*] therthe *R*] thee earthe *Q*   28. and] *om. Q*
remaynthe] remayneth *A Q*   the tother] the other *Q*   29. his] thee *Q*

30. sure] For *Q*   and] hys *Q*   takth] takethe *A Q*   31. sowght] ∧sought *A*
32. voyce] looke *A*

115

Psal : 38 dñe \ ne in furore tuo arguas me

1   O Lord as I the have both*e* prayd & pray
                    no
      (altho ⟨be⟩ in th*e* be ⟨no such⟩ alteration⟨s⟩)
             like as
    but that we men /⟨as we⟩ o⁹ sellff*e* we say)
    ⟨And⟩ mesurȳg thy Iustice by ⟨thi⟩ o⁹ Mutation⟨s⟩)   4
    Chastice me not o lord in thi furour
    nor me correct in wrathfull castigation⟨s⟩
2   ffor that thi arrows / off⟨?⟩fere / off terrour
               f⟨y⟩ amine   fyre
    of sword / of sek*e*nes / off ⟨derthe⟩ & ⟨of deth⟩   8
    stikk*e* diepe   lo
    ⟨ar stykyd⟩ in me / I ⟨now⟩ from myn errour
    Ame plongid vp / as horse owt of th*e* myr*e*
      t
    w stroke off spurr / such is thi hand on me
      t   terrour
3   y̆ in my flesh*e* for ⟨fere⟩ of thy yre   12
    Is not on poynt of ⟨helthe⟩ ferme stabilit*e*
    nor in ⟨?⟩ my bonis there is no stedfastnes
             drede
    such*e* Is my ⟨fere⟩ of mutabilit*e*
              frailefull
    ffor that I know my ⟨sinfull⟩ wykednes ·   16
      for why   hed ar ⟨w⟩bovnd
4   ⟨by cause⟩ my sinns ⟨ar clome⟩ above my ⟨hed⟩ ⟨crowne⟩

                  ^t
like hevi wheght y doth*e* my force oppresse

                     to
Vnder th*e* wych*e* I stopp & bowe ⟨a⟩ gr⟨d⟩own⟨e⟩d ·

⟨by force wh*e*roff the evill Curid skarris⟩

          whilow plant
as ⟨doth a bow⟩ haled by vyolence   20

      ^t   and   not well
5   ⟨y⟩ ∧off my fleshe eche ⟨evyll⟩ curyd wound

     ^t   is
⟨Is⟩ y festred ∧by foly and neclegens

                  vnder t   skyn
by secret lust hath*e* ranklyd ⟨styll w⟩ ⟨sin⟩ ⟨in⟩

not duly Curyd by my penitens   24

6   Perceyving thus the tyranny off sin

     ^{t t}
y w his wheit*e* hath humblid & deprest

          gruging   ^t
my pryd / by ⟨gnawyng⟩ off th*e* worme w in

 ^t   ^t
y neu⟩ dyth / lyve w owten rest   28

                   ^t
7   So ar myn entrayles infect w farvent sore

          ^t   welthe
fedyng th*e* harme y hath*e* my ⟨helth⟩ oprest

that in my flesh*e* is lefft no helth*e* th*e*r fore ·

8   so wondrus gret hath*e* bene my vexation   32

     ^t   it hath forst   to crye
y ⟨forcyd hath*e*⟩ my hart ⟨for⟩ / & ⟨to⟩ rore

9   O lord thow knowst*e* the in ward cōtemplation

                u
off my desire / y knowst my syghe & plaint*e*

thow knowst th*e* teres of my lamētation   36

Can not express*e* my hert*e* in ward restraint*e*

                          quaile
10   my ⟨force⟩ hart pantythe / my force I fele it ⟨faile⟩/

my syght / myn Iyes / my loke dekays and faynt

11   And when myn enmys did me most assayle   40

       frende most sure   most
my ⟨n owne ꝟtus⟩where in I sett ⟨my⟩ trust

my own ꝟtus
⟨as frend*e* most sure⟩ / sonest th*e*n did ffaile

     &
⟨Did⟩ stond apart · reson and witt vniust

     ⟨naturall⟩   fardest
as kyn vnkynd ⟨&⟩ were gone ⟨farr off⟩ at nede   44

12   So had th*e*i place th*e*ire venim owt to thrust

that sowght my deth*e* by nowghty word and dede

          reproche
their tong*e* ⟨deceyt*e*⟩ th*e*ire witt*e* did fraude aplye

1⟨8⟩3   and I like deffh and dome forthe my way yede   48

1⟨9⟩4   Lyk one that heris not / nor hathe to replye
                        t

⟨15⟩
                    knowyng y from thi hand
    one word agayne / ⟨ffor that to the O Lord⟩
                and
      thes thingeprocede⟨but⟩ o lord shalt
    ⟨I me dyrect⟩ / thow ⟨shalt my hope⟩ supplye ·
    my   in
    ⟨the⟩ trust ⟨off⟩the / where in I stikk and stand   52

16   yet have I had gret cawse ⟨to⟩ ⟨off⟩ dred and fere
                            to
    u
    t y woldst gyve my foos
    y ⟨myn Enmys shold have⟩ the ou hand
                  suche plesant
  ffor in my ffall they shewd ⟨reioysing⟩ chere

1⟨6⟩7   and therw all I alway in the lashe   56
           t

    abyd the stroke · and w me euy where
                  t

  I bere my fawte / y gretly doth a bashe
                t

18   my dowlfull chere / ffor I ⟨confess⟩ my fawt cofesse
                all
    and my desert dothe ∧ my coffort dashe ·   60

1⟨8⟩9   In the mene while myn Enmys saffe / encresse
          provokars
    and my ⟨Evill willers⟩ herby do augemet
    t   hurt
    that w owt cawse to ⟨harme⟩ me do not cesse
                    be bent

⟨19⟩20   In Evill for good agaynst me they ⟨shall assent⟩   64
    and hinder shall my good p'suyte off grace
          god   t   seist

2⟨0⟩1   lo now my ⟨lord⟩ ⟨my⟩ y ⟨knowst⟩ my hole Intent
    lord
  My ⟨god⟩ / I ame thow knowst well in what case
                    farr
  fforsak me not / ⟨nor⟩ be not ∧ from me ⟨farr⟩ gone 68

⟨22⟩   hast to my help hast lord and hast a pace
  O lord the lord off all my helth alone ·

              finnis

E ff. 91r-92r, Wyatt's holograph. *A* ff. 112r-113r. *R* ff. 16v-19r. *Q* sigs. Ci^r -
[Ciii^v]. The title of the *E* text is in the hand of Sir John Harington. The
"finnis" was added by Wyatt, probably at a later time when he looked over
his text. Two indecipherable deletions in *E* are indicated as follows: "off⟨?⟩"
(l. 7) and "in⟨?⟩" (l. 14). In the case of line 7, "off" was written over a longer
word. A later unknown hand added the word "acquaintance" (l. 42) over the
deletion "most sure." Hughey stated correctly that this word is surely not in
the hand of Nott and is certainly not in Wyatt's. The only variant that indi-

cates direct use of a deleted word in *E* is for line 41, where the scribe of *A*
chose to keep the deleted "my."

A R Q: *dnẽ . . . me*] Dñẽ ne infurore tuo arguas me· / *A*] Domine ne in
furore tuo arguas me *R*] Domine ne in furore tuo. *Q*   1. th*e* have] haue
ỹ *Q*   prayd] prayed *Q*   2. ⟨no such)⟩] none *R*   7. thi] thine *R*   8. off] a *R*
10. plongid] plucked *Q*   as] like *R*   myr*e*] mier *R*   12. thy yre] thine ier *R*
13. on] one *A Q*   18. wheght] weightes *Q*   19. stopp] shrinck *A*] stoupe
R Q   to] to the *Q*   19+ ⟨. . .⟩] *om. A R Q*   20. vyolence] violente[?] *A*
22. festred] festerd *A*] festered *Q*   23. ranklyd] rancled *R*] ranked *Q*
26. his] *om. Q*   27. worme] wounde *R*   28. dyth] dyeth *A Q*   29. myn]
mye *A*   30. the] my *R Q*   hath*e*] *om. Q*   33. ⟨forcyd hath*e*)⟩] forced
Q   34. knowst*e* th*e* in ward] know'ste the inward *A*] knowest in ward *R*]
knowest, thinwarde *Q*   35. knowst] know'ste *A*] knowest *R Q*
36. knowst] know'ste *A*] knowest *R Q*   39. myn] my *A Q*   40. myn
enmys] mye enmyes *A*] myne emnis *R*] myne enemyes *Q*   41. ⟨my⟩] my *A*
42. did] did me *A*   43. stond] stode *Q*   44. were] *om. A*   47. witt*e*]
wit *Q*   50. one] Not one *Q*   thi] thyne *Q*   51. o] *om. A R Q*   lord] *om.*
R   supplye] replye *Q*   52. th*e*] that *Q*   where in] where *R*   54. woldst]
wouldeste *Q*   55. shewd] shew *A*] shewed *R Q*   56. and] That *Q*   alway]
alwais *R*   58. ỹ] and *A*   61. Enmys saff*e*] en'myes safe *A*] emnis sauf *R*]
enemies styll *Q*   62. ⟨Evill willers)⟩] provokes *A*] prouokers *R Q*   do] do
moche *A*   65. p⟨suyte] presente *Q*   67. knowst well] knoest wel *R*]
knowest *Q*

116

Like as the pilgryme that ⟨hath*e*⟩ a long way
fayntyng for het*e* / provokyd by some ⟨shaad⟩ wind
in some freshe ⟨wynd⟩ rests ⟨yth⟩ at ∧ myd*e* ∧ day
so dothe off David the weryd voyce and mynd   4
take breth*e* off sygh*e* when he had song this lay
vnder suche shaad as sorow hath*e* assynd
a⟨s⟩nd as th*e* tone ⟨t⟩ ⟨sekys still⟩ his viag*e* end
so dothe the tother to m⟩ cy still p⟨ tend ·   8
⟨His fyngers strike apon the sonour cord*e*⟩
w owt heryng or Iugemet off th*e* sownd
down from his Iyes a storme off terys discend*e*
w owt feling that trykill on the grownd   12
as he y bled*e* in baigne / ryght so intend*e*
⟨his sensis sparplid⟩ sensis to y y th*e*i ar bownd

but syght and wepe he can non other thing
and loke ⟨on⟩ vp still vnto the hevins kyng ·   16

            t
        w owt
But who had bene ⟨forth at⟩ the Cavis mowthe
        terys   syghte t
and herd the ⟨syghte⟩ and ⟨terys⟩ y he
            did
      ⟨powrd owt⟩ strayne
he wold have sworne / there had owt off the sowthe
a lewk warme wynd/browght forth a smoky rayne · 20
     t
but y so close the Cave was and vnkowthe
    t
y none but god was record off his payne ·
elte had the wynd blowne in ⟨to⟩ all Israelte erys
the woffull plaint and off theire kyng the terys ·   24

                      vpp
Off wyche some part / when he ⟨had⟩ suppyd hade
like as he whom his owne thowght affrays
he torns his looke · hym semithe that the shade
off his offence / agayne his force assays   28
by violence dispaire on hym to lade
   stertyng
⟨he sterte⟩ like hym when sodeyne fere dismays
  t
⟨w⟩ his voyce he strains and from his
         hert owt brynge
   t
this song y I not wyther he crys or singe·   32
      TV

E f. 92v, Wyatt's holograph. A f. 113rv. R ff. 19v-20v. Q sigs. [Civ^r-Cvi^r].
One reading of E is open to disagreement. I read "when" (l. 30) where the
scribes read "whom." M3 also read "whom."

   The variants to this poem indicate a remarkable independence. Q is again
the most heavily edited text, so much so that it is impossible to argue any necessary dependence on A or R. Only the scribe of R read line 9 accurately,
and it is generally true that R has the most faithful text of this poem. Hughey
(II, 229) was wrong in giving the reading "so that" (l. 14) for A. At that
point A agrees perfectly with E. Hughey was also in error in giving the reading "slepe" (l. 15) for R. The correct reading is "wepe."

                       the   off
A R Q: 3. lith] lyeth A Q] lieth R   at∧myde] at mydds of A R] at middes
of the Q   4. weryd] wery Q   7. the tone] the one A   8. the tother] the
other A Q   9. sonour] Sower A] foure Q   extende] pretendes Q   11.
from] of Q   storme] streame A Q   13. baigne] vayne Q   intende]

thaltryd
entendes *A*   14. ⟨his⟩   ] Thalterid *A*] Thaltred *R Q*   15. syght] sighe
A R Q   16. th*e* h*e*vins] theuins *R*] the heauen *Q*   17. who] who so *A*
had] hath *Q*   Cavis] caue *Q*   18. h*e*] hym *Q*   21. so . . . was] the Cave
close ⟨[?]⟩ was & eke *A*   vnkowth*e*] vnkoweth *Q*   23. blowne] blowen *Q*
Israell-e] Isr'ells *A*] Israels[?] *R*] Israell *Q*   24. Of theyr kynge, the wofull
                                                        vpp
playnte and teares *Q*   25. some] sonne *Q*   ⟨had.⟩suppyd] vp sapped *Q*
26. affrays] affayres *Q*   27. semith*e*] semed *Q*   29. violence] vyolente *Q*
30. when] whome *A R Q*   fere dismays] dispayre dismayde *Q*   31. his
voyce] his hert *R Q*   his h*e*rt] the same *R*   32. not] note *A Q*   wyther]
wheather *A*] whither *R*] wether *Q*   crys] cryeth *Q*

117

Miserere mei d̃ne ·

Psal : 51 ·

1   Rew on me lord for thy goodnes and grace
            t
         y off thy nature art so bountefull
                      t   in
         ffor that goodnes y ⟨all⟩ the world doth*e* brace
      repug̃at natures In quiet*e* wonderfull ·   4

                                 t
            and for thi m⁾ cys nomber w owt end
            In hevin and yerth*e* ℘ceyvid so plentefull
      that ou⁾ all th*e*y do th*e*m sellff℮ extend
            ffor those marcys much*e* more th℮̃ man can sỹn   8
                      t
            do way my sỹnns y so thy grace offend ·
         agayne   t
2   Offttyms wash*e* me but wash*e* me well w in
            and from my synn y thus makth me affrayd
               u
            make y me clene as ay thy wont hath*e* byn   12
      ffor vnto th*e* no nombre can be layd
            for to p⸍ scrybe remissions off off*e*nce
            In hert℮ retornd / as thow thy sellff hast sayd ·
3   And I/beknow ⟨f⟩ my ffawt my neclegens   16
                               is fixid fast
            & in my syght my synn ⟨shall still remayne⟩
            theroff to have more ℘fett penitenc*e*
4   To the alone to th*e* have I trespast

                                     u
            ffor none can mesure my fawt*e* but y alone   20
            for in thy syght I have not bene agast
      for to offend/Iuging thi syght as none

      ^t
so y my fawt were hid from syght of man
   thy maiestye so from my mynd was gone   24
This know I and repent / pardon thow than
        shalt   kepe still
wherby thow ∧⟨hold farme and fast⟩ thi word ⟨still k⟩
        stable ·
       pure   ^t
thy Iustice ⟨stable⟩ and clene / by cawse y whan
      then   t
I pardond ame / ⟨and⟩ forthw Iustly able   28
     I ame
   Iust ⟨to be⟩ Iugd / by Iustice off thy grace

5   ffor I my sellff / lo thing most vnstable
    fformd in offence / conceyvid in like case
              from my natyvite
    ame nowght but synn ⟨by corruppt nature⟩   32
           u
⟨6.⟩   ⟨yet lo y loves so the herte trowgh in Inward place⟩
    be not this sayd for my excuse alase
   But off thy help to shew necessite
        u
6   ffor lo y loves the trowgh off inward hert
    wiche yet dothe lyve in my fydelite
   tho I have fallen by fraylte ou⟩ thwart
               no the
    ffor willffull malice ⟨hathe not⟩ led me ⟨a⟩ way ·
    so muche as hathe the fleshe drawn me apart
   Wherfore o lord as thow hast done alway   40
    teche me the hydden wisdome off thy lore
    sins that my ⟨tr⟩ faythe dothe not yet dekay
7   and as the Iuyz to hele the liepre sore
     t
    w hysope clense / clen⟨e⟩se me / & I ame clene   44
    ⟨do⟩ thow shalt me washe / & more then snow therfore
   I shall be wight · how fowle my fawt hathe bene
8   thow off my helthe shalt gladsome tydȳge bryng
    when ⟨he⟩ from above remission shall be sene   48
   descend on yerthe / then shall for Ioye vp spryng
             t
    the bonis y were afore cõsumd to dust
9   Looke not o lord apon myn / offendyng
           t
   But do a way my dede y ar VnIust   52
     a   the
10   make clene hert in myd ⟨e⟩ de off my brest
      spryte
   t   voydyd   fylthye
   w vpryght ⟨spryte / purgid⟩ from ⟨all vile⟩ lust

11   ffrom thyn Iys cure / cast me not in vnrest

      nor take from me thy spry*te* of holynesse   56

       rendre to

12   ⟨retourne⟩ me/Ioye off thy help and rest

   my will   t

     ⟨and me⟩ conferme w spry*te* off stedfastnesse ·

 3   and by this shall th*es* goodly thingⳋ ensue

      sinners I shall in to thy ways adresse   60

   th*ey* shall retorne to th*e* and thy grace sue

14   My tong shall prayse thy Iustification

15   my mowgh shall spred thy gloryus praysis true

      But off thi sellff o god this ⟨repenta⟩ operation   64

      it must proced / by purging me from blood

          t

      among th*e* Iust y I may have relation

   And off thy lawdⳋ for to let owt th*e* flood

      thow must o lord my lypps furst vnlose   68

         u

16   ffor if y hadst estemid plesant good

            t

   the ovttward dedⳋ y owtward m̄e disclose

      I wold have offerd vnto th*e* sacryfice

         u

      but y delyghtⳋ not in no such*e* glose   72

   off owtward dede / as men dreme & devyse

            t   the lord lykyth*e*

17   The sacryfice / y ⟨plesith*e* god⟩ most /

      is spry*te* co͞trite / low hert In humble wyse

   thow dost accept o god for plesant host   76

18   make Syon lord acordyng to thy will

      in ward syon / the syon of th*e* ghost

   off hertⳋ ⟨I⟩ Hierusalem streg͞h the wallⳋ still

         u

19   then shalt y take for good th*es* vttward dedⳋ·   80

      As sacryfice thy plesure to fullfyll

   Off th*e* alone thus all oⳋ good procedⳋ·

               TV

E ff. 93r-94r, Wyatt's holograph. *A* ff. 113v-114v. *R* ff. 21r-24r. *Q* sigs.
[Cv^v-Cviii^v]. The headings in *E* were entered at two different times by two
different hands. The psalm number is in the hand of Sir John Harington;
the Latin incipit is in another hand, not Wyatt's.
   There may be an accent mark over the "u" in "repugnā͡t" (l. 4) in *E*. The
division "myn/offendyng" (l. 51) does not seem to be metrical. Rather, it was
added simply to separate the words.

Two of the variants indicate direct knowledge of *E*. That for line 10 shows that the editor of *Q* knew that Wyatt had not deleted the word "agayne." The scribe of *A* recovered the deleted word "all (l. 54) and inserted it. Equally interesting is the fact that the scribe of *R* followed Wyatt's peculiar spelling of "on yerthe" (l. 49).

In this poem *Q* follows the title of *A*, but if *Q* was edited from *A*, its editor must also have had access to *E*. *R* could have been copied directly from *E*. But the errors of *R* and *Q* in line 37 would require that two scribes independently misread one of Wyatt's final hooked "t's" as a final "e."

A R Q: *Miserere mei dñe ·*] Miserere mei Deus : -*A Q*] Miserere mei dñe *R*
1. lord] good lorde *R*   3. the world] thy worde *Q*   6. and yerthe*] and earthe *A*] & erth *R*] and earth *Q*   8. those marcys] hys mercye *Q*   9. way] a way *Q*
           agayne
syñns] synne *Q*   so] *om. Q*   10. Offttyms] Ofte tymes *A*] Oft times *R*] Ofte tymes agayne *Q*   11. synn] synnes *Q*   makth] makes *A R Q*   12. ay] euer *Q*   13. no nombre] nowe, none *Q*   14. remissions] remyssyon *Q*   15. herte] harte *Q*   16. my] and my *Q*   17. &] *om. Q* synn] synnes *Q*   18. theroff] Thearfore *A*   19. alone] aboue *Q*
20. mesure] cure *Q*   24. mynd] sight *Q*   28. pardond] pardoned *A Q* Iustly able] iusticiable *Q*   29. Iugd] iudged *A R Q*   31. fformd] fform'de *A*] Fourmed *R*] Formed *Q*   32+. ⟨. . .⟩] *om. A R Q*   33. this] these *Q*   my] myne *A R Q*   alase] alace *A*] alas *R*] ah alas *Q*
34. necessite] necessitie in warde *Q*   35. loves] lov'ste *A*]   louest *R Q* trowgh] truthe *A Q*] trauth *R*   inward] the *Q*   36. my] mooste *Q*
37. fraylte] fraile *R*] frayle *Q*   ou'thwart] ouerthawrte *Q*   38. led] leade *Q*
      no
me ⟨   ⟩] me not *A R Q*   39. drawn] drawen *A Q*] draune *R*   42. yet] as yet *A R*   43. Iuyz] Iuyce *A*] iuyze *R*] Iewes *Q*   liepre] leaper *A*]lipre *R*] lypper *Q*   44. hysope] ysope *A R*] Isoppe *Q*   47. shalt] shall *Q*   49. on yerthe] on earthe *A*] on yerth *R*] on earth *Q*   then shall] thou shalt *Q*
50. afore] before *Q*   cõsumd] consum'de *A*] consumed *R Q*   52. VnIust] vniuite *Q*   myd⟨e⟩de] middell *Q*   54. spryte] spirite *R*   voydyd] voyde *A*
     fylthye   all
from ⟨all ⟩   ] from ∧ filthie *A*   55. thyn] thye *A*   56. thy] thee *Q* spryte] spyryte *Q*   57. rest] heste *Q*   58. spryte] the spirite *Q*
59. goodly] godlye *A Q*   60. ways] waie *R*   61. they] Theise *A*
63. mowgh] mowthe *A*] mouth *R Q*   praysis] prayse *Q*   68. furst] at furst *A*   69. hadst] hadd'st *A*] haddeste *Q*   72. delyghte] delyghtest *A*] delightest *R*] delytest *Q*   75. spryte] spirite *Q*   78. ghost] hoste *Q*
79. stregh] strengthe *A Q*] strength *R*   the] thy *Q*   80. thes] the *Q*
81. As] Of a *Q*   82. *om. Q*

<h2 style="text-align:center">118</h2>

     off   t   here
⟨The⟩ diepe secrete y david ⟨here⟩ did sing
                                        off
     off mercy off faythe off frailte ⟨and⟩ grace
     off godde goodnes and off Iustyfying
         t ⟨whi⟩ grettnes dyd so   selff
     ⟨did w⟩ the ⟨wonder⟩ ∧astonne hym ∧ a space   4
     as who myght say · who hatthe exprest this thing?
     I synner I / what have I sayd alas?

y godde goodnes wold w ^my ⟨me⟩ song entrete
let me agayne cosidre and repete ·   8

And so he dothe / but not exprest by word
but in his hert he tornith and paysithe
eche word y erst / his lypps myght forth aford ·
he poynte / he pawsithe / he wonders /
he praysythe   12
the marcy y hyde off Iustice the swoord
the Iustice y so his promesse complysythe
for his worde sake / to worthilesse desert
⟨so⟩ gratis ⟨dothe⟩ his graces to men ^depert   16

Here hathe he cofort when he dothe mesure
⟨thes⟩ mesureles marcys ⟨&⟩ mesureles fawte
to prodigall siners Infinite tresure
tresure termeles y neuᶜ shall defawte   20
ye when that sinn shall fayle & may not dure
Mercy shall reygne / gaine whome shall no assaute
off hell pᶜvaile / by whome lo at this day
off hevin gatte Remission is the kay ·   24

And when ⟨o⟩ david hathe ⟨cosiderd this⟩ and tryd
and seith hym sellff not vtterly deprivid
from lyght of grace / y sinn ⟨had mad hym mis⟩
dyd hyde
he fynde hys hope ⟨so⟩ muche ther w revivid   28
he dare Importun ⟨th⟩⟨he⟩ the lord on euʳ y syde
for he knowth well to mercy is ascrybid
respectles labour Importune crye and call
and thus begynth his song ther w all   32

TV

E f. 94v, Wyatt's holograph. *A* ff. 114v-115r. *R* ff. 24v-25v. *Q* sigs. Di^r-
Dii^r. Two deletions in *E* are conjectural. The canceled "whi" (l. 4) may be

"whe." The canceled "ẙ" (l. 16) may be simply another "h." The only notable feature of the variants is that wherever *E* is difficult to read, *Q* edits widely. The scribes of *R* and *A* did a good job of following Wyatt's revisions and deletions. But there is some carelessness in following Wyatt's syllabification in lines 26, 30, and 32.

A R Q: om. title] The Auctor *Q*   1.⟨here⟩] ther *Q*   3. goodnes] goodnes eke *A*   4. Thy goodnesse dyd so, astony hym apace *Q*   5. exprest] expressed *Q*   6. alas] ah alas *Q*   9. not exprest] expressed *Q*   11. erst] om. *Q*   forth aford] foorde abrode *Q*   12. poynte] poīteth *Q*   wonders] wōdreth *Q*   13. hyde] hydethe *Q*   14. complysythe] accomplysheth *Q*   16. graces] grace *Q*   18. marcys] mercye *Q*   fawte] fautes *Q*   19. Infinite] Infinytye *Q*   tresure] mercie *R*   20. termeles] celestyall *Q*   21. dure] endure *Q*   22. gaine] gaynste *A*]   agayne *Q*   no] not *A Q*]   none *R*   25. hathe] had *Q*   ⟨cōsiderd⟩] ponderid *A*] pondered *Q*   tryd] tried *A*] tryed *Q*   26. vtterly] outterly *Q*   deprivid] depryvde *A*   27. from] For *Q*   fynde] fyndeth *Q*   revivid] revyv'de *A*   29. dare Importun⟨th⟩⟨he⟩] importeth on *Q*   30. knowth] know'the *A*] knoweth *R*] knowethe *Q*   to] that to *Q*   ascrybid] ascryb'de *A*] ascribd *R*] ascribed *Q*   32. begynth] beginnithe *A*] beginneth *R*] begynneth *Q*

119

Dne exaudi orationem meam
Psal : 102 ·

1   Lord here my prayre / and let my crye passe
        vnto the lord wowt ⟨en stopp or lett⟩
2   do not from me torne thy mercyfull fase
    Vnto my sellff leving my government   4
        In tyme off troble and adu⁾ sitye
        Inclyne to me thyn ere and thyn Intent
    And when ⟨so⟩ I call ⟨ffor⟩ help ⟨vnto the⟩
        redely graunt theffect off my desyre ·   8
        thes bold demaunde do plese thy maiestye
    And ek my Case suche hast dothe well require ·
3   ffor like as smoke my days bene past awaye
        my bonis dryd / vp as forneis w the fyre   12
4   My hert my mynd is wytherd vp like haye
        by cawse I have forgot to take my ⟨foode⟩ brede
        my ⟨foode⟩ off lyff / the word off trowthe I saye ·
⟨5⟩   And ffor my plaintfull ⟨my⟩ syghe and my drede   16
        my bonis my strenght my very force off myde

cleved to the fleshe / and from thi spryte were flede

⟨In diepe⟩ dispaireite thy mᶜ cy for to fynd ·
<small>as</small>

⟨6⟩5   so made I me the solaine pelycane   20

and lyke the owle that fleithe by propre kynd

Lyght of the day and hathe her sellff betane

to ly⟨ve⟩ff alone owt off all companye
<small>ruyne</small>

⟨7⟩6   w waker care / y w this wo bygane   24
<small>t   t t</small>

like the sparow ⟨I ame⟩ I solytarye ·
<small>was</small>

y sitte alone vnder the howsis e ⟨v⟩ ffes
<small>t</small>

⟨8⟩7   this while my foes c͠ospird continually

And did ⟨assaute⟩ the harme off my dises   28
<small>ρvoke</small>

⟨9⟩8   wherfor like ashes my bred did me savour

⟨In trowgh I fownd no tast y⟩ myght me ples ·
<small>of thi Iust word the tast   t   not</small>

W⟨w⟩herfore my drynk I temperd w lycour
<small>t</small>

⟨Off ⟩off weping teris y ⟨haile downe⟩ from myn
<small>t</small>
y les · do rayne

⟨10⟩9   by cawse · I know the wrathe off thy furour

provokt by ryght had off my pride disdayne

for y didst lyfft me vp to throw me downe
<small>u</small>

to teche me how to know my sellff agayne ·   36

10   Wherby I knew y helples / I shold drowne
<small>t</small>

my days like shadow declyne / and I do drye

11   and the for euᵒ eternite doth crowne

World w owt end ⟨shall⟩ last thy memorye ·   40
<small>t   dothe</small>

12   ffor this ⟨misery⟩ y yokythe ⟨euᵒ y⟩ mane kynd
<small>frailte   t   all</small>

y shallt a wake / and rue this misery
<small>u</small>

Rue on Syon / Syon y as I ⟨a⟩ ffynd
<small>t</small>

⟨ffor⟩ the people y lyve vnder thy law ·   44
<small>is   t</small>

for now is tyme the tyme at hand assynd

13   The tyme so long y dothe thy svante draw
<small>t</small>

in gret desyre to se that plesant day

day off redem͠ig syon ffrom ⟨the⟩ Aw   48
<small>sins</small>

ffor th*e*y have ruth*e* to se in such*e* dekay

    in

⟨off⟩ dust and stines this wrechid syon ⟨ly⟩ lowr

    then

14   ⟨And so⟩ the gentill*e* shall dred thy name alway

All erthly king*e* ⟨shall honour⟩ thy glory shall honour   52

    ⟨u⟩ i grace   thus

15   then / when y ⟨hast⟩ this syon ⟨thus savid⟩ redemith*e*

    u

when thus y hast dcclarid thy myght powre

    lord   wishis so

16 The ⟨lord hath*e*⟩ his sᵛaunt*e* ⟨crys⟩ estemi⟨d⟩the

that h*e* hym tornth*e* vnto the poores request   56

    o⁹ discent   to be wrytten

17   to ⟨all mankynd⟩ thys ∧⟨publysht me⟩ semith*e*

Off all cõfort*e* as ⟨conffor⟩ cõsolation best

    t

⟨wherb⟩ and th*e*i y then shalbe regenerat*e*

shall praise th*e* lord th*e*rfore both*e* most & lest ·   60

18   ffor he hath*e* lokt from th*e* heyght off his astat*e*

    vs

th*e* lord from hevyn in yerth*e* hath*e* lokt on ⟨vs men⟩

    t

19   to here th*e* mone off th*e*m y ar algate

In fowle bondage / to lose and to discus   64

the sonns off deth*e* owt from theire dedly bond

20   to gyve th*e*rby occasion gracius

In this syon ⟨t⟩hys holy ⟨to⟩ name to stond

    in

and ∧ Hierusalem ⟨t⟩hys laud*e* lastyng ay ·   68

    e

21   when in one chirch*e* the peple off y lond

    bene gaderd   to

And remes ⟨shall ranged⟩ to sᵎ ve / to lawd / ⟨&⟩ pray /

    t aboue

the lord ⟨y is⟩ so Iust and mˢ cyfull ·

22   But to this samble runỹg in th*e* way   72

My strenght faylyth*e* to rech*e* it at th*e* full

he hath*e* abrigd my days th*e*y may not dure

    that

to se ⟨th*e*⟩ terme / that terme so wonderfull

23 Altho I have wᵗ herty will and Cure   76

prayd to th*e* lord / take me not lord away ∤

In mydd*e* off my yeres / tho thyn euᵎ sure

remayne eterne / whom tyme can not dekay ·

24   thow wrowghtst th*e* yerth*e* / thy hand*e* th*e*vyns

did make   80

25   thei shall peryshe / and y̅ shalt last alway

and althinge age shall were and ou’ take

    like clothe / and y̅ shalt them like aparell

    tourne

    ⟨torne⟩ / and translate / & thei in worth it take ·   84

26   But y thy sellff / the sellff remaynist well thi yeres

    y y wast erst / and shalt ⟨w owten⟩ extend

    then sins to this there may nothing rebell

the gretest cõfort y I can pretend   88

    is that the childerne off thy svante dere

    y in thy word ar gott / shall wowt end

byfore thy face be stabisht all in fere

TV

E ff. 95r-96r, Wyatt's holograph. *A* ff. 115r-116r. *R* ff. 26r-29v. *Q* sigs. Dii^r-[Dvi^r]. The headings in *E* are once again in two hands and two colors of ink. The psalm number is in black ink in the hand of Sir John Harington. The Latin incipit is in brown ink and may be by Wyatt himself. In the *E* text there may be a full stop after "by cawse" (l. 33). There may also be a double "s" under the double "f" in "⟨a⟩ffynd" (l. 43). At the end of line 77 is double punctuation, thus ⁄.

Only *A* shows concrete evidence of direct connection with *E*. The lightly canceled "I" of "In" (l. 19) in *E* was picked up by the scribe of *A*. The variants for lines 23 and 76 illustrate the use of punctuation to fill in for an eliminated word. The peculiar emendation in line 38 (not noted in Hughey, II, 234) suggests that the editor of *Q* had consulted the text of *R*.

A R Q: Dne . . . meam] Dñe exaudi orationem meam : - *A*] Domine exaudi orationem meam *R Q*   4. my sellff] meself *R*   6. Inclyne to] Enclyne vnto *Q*   thyn . . . thyn] thye . . thie *A*   7. my] myne *Q*   9. thes . . . plese] Boldelye too please *Q*   11. as smoke] a synke *Q*   bene] are *Q*   12. dryd] dry'de *A*] dried *R*] dryed *Q*   as] as a *Q*   13. wytherd] wythered *Q*   14. by cawse] Because *A R*] But *Q*   16. plaintfull] paynfull *Q*   and] and for *A*] & eke *R*   17. off] & *R*   18. cleved] Cleav'd *A*   thi spryte] the sprite *A*] y spirit *R*] y spirite *Q*   19. ⟨In⟩] I as *A*] As *R Q*   dispaireite] desp'rate *A*] desperate *R Q*   20. I me] I am *Q*   solaine] solemne *A*] soden *Q*   21. fleithe] flyeth *A Q*] flieth *R*   23. alone owt] oute *A*] , out *R*] , oute *Q*   26. e⟨v⟩ffes] eaves *A Q*   27. cõspird] conspyr'de *A*] conspired *R*] conspyred *Q*   29. me] *om. R*   30. myght me] might me not *A*   31. temperd] temp'rid *A*] tempered *Q*   32. myn] mye *A*   do] downe *A*] did *R Q*   33. by cawse] Because *A R Q*   34. provokt] Prouoked *Q*   35. didst] didest *A*] dyddest *Q*   36. my sellff] meself *R*   37. knew] knowe *R Q*   38. drye] crie *R Q*   39. crowne] drowne *Q*   44. thy] the *Q* sins

46. dothe] *om. Q*   s᾿vant̴e] seruaunt *R*   47. desyre] desier *R*   48.⟨the⟩]
his *R*   50. stines] stones *A Q*] stonis *R*   lowr] lore *Q*   53. this] thi *R*]
thy *Q*]   54. declarid] declarde *A*   myght] myghtie *Q*   55. wishis so]
wysshes and so *Q*   56. he] *om. Q*   turnthe] turn'the *A*] turneth *R*]
turnethe *Q*   poores] power *Q*   61. lokt] loked *Q*   the heyght] th'height *A*]
the high *Q*   62. in yerthe] in earthe *A*] on earth *Q*   lokt] loked *Q*
64. fowle] soche *Q*   and to] and or *Q*   65. bond] band *R*   66. gracius]
glorious *Q*   67. ⟨t⟩hys] his *A*] this *R*] thys *Q*   70. gaderd] gathered *Q*

    t aboue
71. ⟨y is⟩   ] that is aboue *Q*   72. to] *om. R*   this] these *Q*   samble]
Sample *A*] semble *R*] feble *Q*   74. abrigd] abredged *Q*   may not dure] are
not sure *Q*   76. herty] hart, *Q*   77. prayd] Pray'de *A*] Prayed *Q*   take . . .
lord] Lord take me not *A*] take me not *Q*   78. mydd̴e] the middes *Q*   my]
om. A   80. wroughtst] wrought'ste *A*] wroughteste *Q*   the yerthe] the
earthe *A Q*] the erth *R*   thevyns] the heavens *A Q*] theuins *R*   81. alway]
ay *R*   82. age] aye *Q*   85. the sellff] thy selfe *Q*   well] hole *Q*   86. wast]
was *Q*   shalt] shal *R Q*   yeres] yere *R Q*   89. childerne] Children *A*]
chyldren *Q*   90. thy word] the world *Q*   91. stabisht] stablishte *A*]
stablisht *R*] stablyshed *Q*

120

When david had ρceyvid in his brest
                t
   the sprit*e* off god retournd y was exild
   by cause   he hath   alone
   ⟨ffor ⟨y⟩ he knew / ⟨off hym were not⟩ exprest
                  t
               y   spryt*e*
   thes grete thing̴e ⟨by⟩ greter ⟨thing*e*⟩ compild   4
   as shalme or pype let̴e owt th*e* sownd inprest
   by musik̴e art forgid to fore and fyld
   I say when david had ρceyvid this
   the sprit*e* of confort in hym revivid is ·   8

   ffor th*e*rapon he makyth*e* argument
   off reconsiling vnto th*e* lord̴e grace
   altho sometyme to prophecy have lent
   both brut best̴e & wikkyd hert̴e a place   12
   but ⟨he⟩ oᶜ david Iugith in his intent
   hym sellff by penance clene owt off this cace
   wherby he hath*e* remission off offence
   and gynnyth*e* to Alow his payne and penit*e*nce · 16

         t
   But when ⟨y⟩ he weyth*e* ⟨the⟩ the fawt & recõpes̃e
   he damth*e* his dede / and fyndyth playne

a twene th*e*m to no whitt equivalence

     all owtward dede in

wherby he take ⟨all recōpense as⟩ vayne   20

to bere th*e* name off ryghtfull penitence

  wich*e*

⟨that⟩ is alone the h*e*rt retornd agayne

       t

and sore contryt y doth*e* his fawt bymone

      the sygne or

and⟨[?]⟩owtward dede ⟨is⟩ fruyt ⟨th*e*roff⟩ alone ·   24

  t

W this h*e* doth*e* deff*e*nd th*e* slye assault

off vayne alowance off his voyde desert

     glory

and all the ⟨meryt⟩ off his forgyven fault

to good alone he doth it hole convertt   28

his owne merytt he fyndyth in deffault

        d

and whilst he   poder⟨the⟩ thes thinge in his h*e*rt

  knee

his ⟨arme⟩ his arme his hand sustenid his chyn

when he ⟨th⟩ his song agayne thus did begyn   32

        TV

E f. 96v, Wyatt's holograph. *A* f. 116rv. *R* ff. 30r-31r. *Q* sigs. [Dvi[r]-Dvii[v]].
One striking feature of the *E* text is that a large open "e" has been added in
black ink to the word "compild" (l. 4). It seems unlikely that this single addition was by Wyatt. There is an indecipherable deletion after "and" (l. 24).

    The second variant in line 19 suggests a dependence of *Q* upon *R*. The
interpretation of Wyatt's "good" (l. 28) by the three other texts as "God"
illustrates a psychological subtlety that the scribes or editors could not
understand.

A R Q: om. title] The prologue *R*] The Auctor *Q*   2. sprite] spyryte *Q*
retournd] retourne *Q*   exild] exyled *Q*   3. by cause] Because *A R Q*

            spryte

4. thes] Theise same *A*   ⟨thinge⟩compild] spyryte compyled *Q*   5. as]
Is *Q*   inprest] imprest *A R*] impreste *Q*   6. musike] musyke *Q*   fyld]
fylde *A*] fild *R*] fyled *Q*   7. this] that, I wys *Q*   8. sprite] spirite *Q*
11. have] hathe *Q*   13. intent] entent *A*] entente *Q*   14. this] his *R*
16. gynnythe] begynneth *Q*   18. damthe] dampnethe *A*] dampth *R*]
dampneth *Q*   his] this his *A*   19. to] two *A R Q*   whitt] what *R Q*
20. takes] takethe *Q*   dede] dedes *Q*   22. retornd] returned *Q*

           t

23. contryt y] contryte hart, that *Q*   bymone] bemone *A Q*] bimone *R*
24. sygne] synne *Q*   26. voyde] worde *A*] owne *Q*   28. good] god *A R*]

                    d

God *Q*   30. whilst] whyl'ste *A*] whyles *Q*   ponder⟨the⟩] pondreth *A*]
ponderd *R*] pondered *Q*   31. sustenid] sustaynde *A*] sustaind *R*]
susteyned *Q*

121

De profundis clamavi
Psal : ⟨129⟩ 130

                 &   a

1   ffrom depth*e* off sin ∧ from diepe dispaire

        from depth off deth*e* from depth*e* off herʰe sorow

                    off   diepe

        from this diepe Cave ⟨wh*e*re⟩ darknes ⟨doth*e*l repayre

      ⟨To⟩ the ⟨o lord⟩ have I cald o lord to be my borow   4

        thow in my voyce o lord peceyve and here

2   my hert my hope my plaint my ouʳ throw ·

      My will to ryse / and let by graunt apere

        that to my voyce thin eres do well entend ·   8

                that   is   not

        no place so farr ⟨but⟩   to the ∧ is ∧nere

                 t u

      No depth so diepe y y ne maist extend

           ere

        thin ⟨sellff⟩ th*e*rto / Here then my wofull plaint

          lord   u

3   ffor ∧ if y do obsʲve what men offend   12

      & putt⟨Ec⟩ Th⟨e⟩y natyff mᶜcy ⟨to put⟩ in restraint /

        if Iust exaction demaund recōpense

        who may endure o lord? who shall not faynt

      A⟨a⟩t such*e* acompt? dred / and not reuʳ ence   16

                  u

        shold so raine large · But y sekᵉ rath*e*r love ·

          in thi hand

            t

4   ffor ⟨mᶜcy is w the⟩ / is mᶜcys resedence

              u

      By hope wheoff y dost oᵍ herʰe move ·

5   I in the lord have ⟨euʳ⟩ set my ⟨trust⟩ cōfydence   20

        my sowle such*e* trust doth*e* euʳ more aprove

                eterne

      Thi holly word off ⟨excellence⟩ excellence

          ⟨pro⟩   mercys   t   alway Iust

        thi ⟨Iust⟩ promesse y is ⟨infallible⟩ ·

        have bene my stay my piller & pᶜ tence   24

6   My sowle in god hath*e* more desyrus trust

        en   man ⟨t⟩   ng

        y hath*e* the wach*e* ⟨y⟩ loky⟨th⟩ for th*e* day

         by th*e*

        ⟨for⟩ his releff*e* to quench*e* of ⟨the⟩ slepe th*e* thrust

         vnto

7   Let ⟨al⟩ Israell trust ⟨in⟩ th*e* lord ⟨I say⟩ alway   28

　　　　　　ffor grace and favour arn his propertie
　　　　　　　　　us　　　　shall com　　　t
8　　　　　plente⟨fful⟩ / rannzome ⟨is⟩ w hym I say :
　　　　　　　　　　　redeme
　　　　　And ⟨he⟩ shall ⟨rannzome⟩ all o℥ iniquitie
　　　　　　　　　　　　TV

E f. 97r, Wyatt's holograph. A ff. 116v-117r. R ff. 31v-32v. Q sigs. [Dvii^v-
Dviii^v]. The heading in E is divided between two hands. The psalm and the
two numbers, one deleted, are in the black ink and hand of Sir John Harington. However, the pen and brown ink of the Latin incipit match the text of
the poem and indicate that Wyatt wrote it. Several variants indicate the
scribes' efforts to deal with Wyatt's deletions, ll. 11, 13, and 27. The variant
for line 11 suggests that the editor of Q tried to make sense out of the
deleted word included by the scribe of R.

A R Q: De . . . clamavi] De profundis clamaui / A] Deprofundis clamaui R]
Deprofundis clamaui ad te domine. Q　1. a] om. Q　diepe] dirk R
　　　　　　　　　　　　　　　　　　　　　　　　it　not
3. repayre] dispayre A　8. entend] intende A] attende Q　9. ∧ is ∧] is
　　　　　　ere
not A R Q　11. thin ⟨sellff⟩] Thyne eare A] Thine eare self R] Thyne eare
sette Q　12. do obs⟩ve] observe A R　offend] doo offende Q　13. & putt
. . . natyff] And putt natyve A] And put thi natif R] And putte the natyue Q
14. recōpense] a recompencc A　16. dred / and not] dede, and no Q
17. raine] runne at Q　sek̲e] seekest A] sekest Q　18. m⟨cys] mercye A
　　　　　　　　　　　　　　　　　　　　　　　man
19. move] eke move A　21. trust] trueth Q　26. wache] watchmen Q
　　　by the
27. ⟨for⟩ his] By this his A] By ȳ R] By thy Q　28. ⟨in⟩] to Q　29. arn]
are A Q

　　　　　　　　　　　　122

　　　　　　　　　t
　　　This word redeme y in his mowght did sownd
　　　　did　　　　　　　　　　　　　　　vn
　　　⟨hathe⟩put david ⟨in to a diepe as⟩ it semyth ∧to me
　　　　as in a traunce to starre apon the grownd
　　　　　　　　t
　　　　and w his thowght the ⟨hye⟩ heyght of hevin to see　4
　　　　　　　　　　　　　　t　　　con
　　　　where he beholde̲ the word y shold ⟨res⟩ fownd
　　　　the sword off dethe / By humble ere to be
　　　　In mortall mayd / in mortall habitt made
　　　　Eternall lyff in mortall vaile to shade　　　　　　8

　　　　　　　　　　　full rype　　　　shold
　　　He seithe that word / when ⟨pl[?] e⟩ tyme ⟨was⟩ come
　　　　　do way
　　　　⟨shake off⟩ that vayle / by fervent affectione
　　　　　　t
　　　torne off w dethe / for dethe shold have her dome ·

and leppeth lyghter from such*e* coruptione   12

the glint of lyght ŷ^t in th Ayre doth lome

〈siĉe〉 redemid deth*e* hath*e* h*e*r distructione

that mortall vaile hath*e* immortalit*e*

david assurance off his iniquit*e*   16

Wherby he frames this reson in his hert

                             his sonne

that goodnes wych*e* doth*e* not forberre 〈the deth*e*〉

        from deth*e* for me

〈of his dere sonne〉 and can therby côvert

       my

〈o^ȝ〉 deth*e* to lyff / my synn to salvation   20

     can

both*e* 〈c may〉 & woll a small⁾ grace depert

to hym ŷ^t suyth*e* by humble supplication

             grace

& sins I have 〈then〉 his larger 〈bonte〉 assayd

to aske this thing whi ame I then affrayd?   24

                        t

He grauntyth*e* most to th*e*m ŷ 〈aske hym〉 most

          do crave

                t

         suyt*e* ŵ owt respect

and he delyght‒*e* in 〈forceable request〉

               t

alas my sônne po^ȝsuys me 〈ŵ his ost〉 to the grave

sufferd by god my sinne for to correct   28

but of my sinne sins I my ƨdonne have

my sonnis po^ȝsuyt shall shortly be reiect

             t

then woll I crave ŵ suryd côfidence

and thus begynns th*e* suyt off his p^ftence ·   32

               TV

E f. 97v, Wyatt's holograph. *A* f. 117rv. *R* ff. 33r-34r. *Q* sigs. Ei^r-[Eii^r]
The variants for lines 13 and 18 were the result of a possible misreading of
the author's script in *E*. The deleted word in line 9 of *E* which is very hard to
make out may be "plenteuse." The phrase "th Ayre" (l. 13) includes neither
a final hooked "e" nor an apostrophe.

A R Q: *om. title*] The prologue *R*] The Auctor *Q*   1. mowght] mowthe *A*]
mouth *R*] mouthe *Q*   6. sword] worde *Q* humble ere] humilite here *Q*
8. Eternall lyff] Eternallye *Q*   10. way] awaye *Q*   13. glint] glutt *A*]
glute *Q* th Ayre] in ayre *A*] in the ayre *R Q*   14. redemid] redemeth *Q*
16. david] Too Dauid *Q*   18. sonne] sôme *R*   23. have 〈then〉 his] haue

thys *Q*   28. sufferd] Suffered *Q*   sinne] synnes *Q*   29. sinne] synnes *Q*
my] may *Q*   30. poᵍsuyt] suyte *Q*   31. suryd] sure *Q*   32. begynns]
begynnethe *A*] begynne *Q*] beginnes *R*

123

Dne exaudi orationem meam CXliij

1   Here my prayer o lord / here my request
                answere   to
          complyshe my bone / ⟨supply ẙ⟩ my desire
          not by desert / but for thyn own byhest
                   u
          In ⟨trc⟩ whose ferme trowgh y promest myn empyre   4
                  after
          to stond stable / And ⟨for⟩ thy ⟨n own⟩ Iusty⟨c⟩se
          pforme o lord the thing that I require
                law
            off⟨Iustise⟩aftre⟨suche⟩the forme &
2   But not ⟨acordyng to Iust ryght In the⟩ guyse
                  t   thrall
          to entre Iugement w thy ∧ bond slave   8
               ⟨my⟩ his
          to plede ⟨thy⟩ ryght / for in suche maner wyse
          By fore thy syght no man his ryght shall save ·
          ffor off my sellff / lo this my ryght wisenes
                  prykyng spurrs /
          By skourge & whipp / and ⟨suffrans that⟩ I have ·   12
          e   rysen
      skant⟨ly rysn⟩ vp / suche is my bestlynes /
3   ffor that my enmy hath pursuyd my lyff
          and in the dust hathe foyl⟨y⟩d my lustynes
                   rage
               to fle his ⟨furyus stry⟩ so ryff
      ffor that in heins / ⟨as man in dr mortall stryff ⟩   16
          me forst   as ded
          he hathe ⟨constraind me for⟩ to hyd my hed
               t   in
4   and for by cawse w ∧my sellff at stryffe
                 t
          My hert and spryte w all my force were f⟨e⟩led
                   to
5   I had recourse ⟨vnto the⟩ tyms that have ben past   20
                   dede
          and did remembre thy ⟨worke⟩/ in all my dred
      and did peruse thi worke ẙ euᵗ last
          wherby I knew above those wondres all
                 were
6   thy mᵒcys ⟨ar⟩ · Then lyfft I vp in hast   24

did
My hand&e to the / my sowle to the ⟨doth⟩ call
  like bareyne soyle for moystre off thy grace ·
7 Hast to my help o lord / afore I fall
  ffor sure I fele my spryte dothe faynt a pace   28
              that I be layd
    torne not thi face from me / ⟨to make me seme⟩
                  t
    in compt off them / y hedlyng down do pase
8 In to the pitt · shew me by tyms thyn Ayde
    ffor on thy grace I holly do ⟨I⟩ depend ·   32
        and in thi hand
    ⟨do me to know⟩ sins all my helthe is stayde
                u
  Do me to know / what way y wolt I bend
    ffor vnto the I have reysd vp my mynd ·
                    t
9 ⟨do⟩ Rydd me o lord / from that y do entend   36
      to   me
  My foos ⟨on⟩ me · ffor I have ⟨bene⟩ assind
            t
    allway ⟨vnto⟩ w in thi secrette protection
10 Teche m⟨y⟩e ⟨w⟩ thy will ẙ I by the may fynd
  the way to worke the same in affection   40
        u   vpryght
    ffor y my god / thy blyssyd ∧spryte
        ⟨shall guyde⟩
    in lond off trowght shalbe my d⟨e⟩yrection
              lord
11 Thow for thy name ∧ shalt revive my spryte /
      t   t
    w in the ryght y I receyve by the   44
    wherby my lyff off danger shalbe quyte
12 ⟨There whilst thow shalt off thi benignite⟩
    ⟨confound my foos / & them destroy that seke⟩
    ⟨to hurt my lyff / by theyre iniquite⟩
        thus
    ⟨sins I thi s⟩vant humbly the beseke⟩
              TV
  Thow hast fordon theire grete Iniquite
                u
    that vext my sowle / y shalt also c͠ofownd
    my foos olord for thy benignite   48
  ffor thyn ame I thy s⟩vant ay most bownd

E f. 98rv, Wyatt's holograph. *A* ff. 117v-118r. *R* ff. 34v-36r. *Q* sigs. [Eii^r -
Eiv^r]. The entire heading in *E*, including the Roman numeral, matches the

text in ink and is by Wyatt. The variant for line 16 shows the dependence of
Q's editor on *A* for the emendation while the scribe of *R* made his own solution. Yet in line 2 both *R* and *Q* adopt a deleted reading, where *A* follows the
revision. In line 41 both *R* and *Q* misplace an inserted word. These variants
indicate that *A* and *R* stem independently from *E* and that the editor of *Q*
consulted both *A* and *R*. Again, in line 43, where *R* omits an inserted word,
the editor of *Q* filled in with a comma.

A R Q: Dne . . . meam] Dne exaudi orationem meam · / *A*] Domine exaudi

orationem meam · / *R Q*]   2. ⟨supply $\overset{u}{y}$⟩] awnsweare to *A*] supplie $\overset{u}{y}$ *R Q*
3. by] for my *Q*   4. trowgh] trouthe *A*] trouth *R Q*   6. the] that *Q*
7. not] *om. Q*   8. thy] thee *Q*   10. my sellff] meself *R*   ryght wisenes]

rightuousnes *A*] rightwisnes *R*] righteousnesse *Q*   12. $\overset{spurrs /}{⟩}$ I have] sourrs

have *A*   13. skant⟨ly $\overset{e}{rysn}$⟩vp] Scante $\overset{rysen}{rysyng}$ vppe *A*] Skant risen up *R Q*
14. my enmy] myne enmye *A*] myne emny *R*] myne enemyes *Q*   15. foyl⟨y⟩d]
foyled *A*] foiled *R*] foyled *Q*   16. ffor . . . heins] fforreyne Realmes *A Q*] for
in hernes *R*   fle] flye *A*] flee *Q*   ryff] rife *A*] rief *R*] ryfe *Q*   17. forst] first *A*
18. by cawse] because *A R*] bycause *Q*   my sellff] meself *R*   19. and spry*te*] &
spirite *R*] , spirite *Q*   20. to] two *R*   have] *om. Q*   23. knew] knowe *Q*
those] these *Q*   wondres] wonders *A R Q*   26. bareyne] bare *Q*   moystre]
moysture *A*] moisture *R*] moyster *Q*   27. spry*te*] spirite *R*] spiryte *Q*
29. layd] layede *Q*   30. hedlyng] headlonge *A*   33. hand] handes *Q*
stayde] stayed *Q*   34. wolt] wilt *A R*] wylte *Q*   35. reysd] raysed *Q*

36. that $\overset{t}{y}$] those that *A*] them that *Q*   37. ⟨$\overset{to}{on}$⟩ me] to ⟨m⟩bee *A*] to be *Q*
assind] assigned *Q*   39. Tech*e*] Theache *A*   40. affection] effection *R*
41. $\overset{vpryght}{\wedge}$ spry*te*] spirite upright *R Q*   42. lond] Lawde *A*] laude *R Q*   trowght]

trouthe *A*] trouth *R*] truthe *Q*   43. $\overset{lord}{\wedge}$] *om. R*] , *Q*   shalt] shal *Q*
spry*te*] spiryte *Q*   45+. ⟨. .   *om. A R Q*   ⟨. . .⟩] *om. A R Q*   ⟨. . .⟩]

om. A R Q   ⟨. . .⟩] *om. A R Q*   46. theire] the *Q*   47. $\overset{u}{y}$ shalt] *om. A*
49. ay] *om. Q*

124

Iopas Song ·

When Dido festid first / the wandr$\widetilde{yg}$ troian knyght

    whom Iunos wrath / $\overset{t}{w}$ stormes did force / in lybyke sand$e$

                      to lygh [

that myghty' Atlas did tech*e* / the souper lastyng long

    $\overset{t}{w}$ cryspid lokk$e$ / ⟨$\overset{on}{and}$⟩ golden harpe / Iopas sang

        in his song ·   4

That same $\wp$ he $\overset{t}{y}$ we / the world do call & name off hevin and yerth / w all cotent̃e/ it is the very frame ·

Or thus : off hevinly powrs / by more powre kept in one

⟨the dyu⁾ se⟩ kynd̃e/ in mydd̃e of whome / the yerthe

hathe place alo[8

firme / round / off ⟨lyvely⟩ thyng̃e/ the moder place & nourse

w owt the wyche in egall whaight / this hevin doth hold his

course

and it is calld by name / the first moving hevin

the ⟨stery skye⟩ / ⟨vnder the wiche there movith⟩ othr sevyn   12

Off hevinly powrs ⟨this skye⟩/ is plantid full & thikk

as shynĩg lyght̃e/ wych we call steres y ⟨therto⟩ cleve & stikk

W gret swifft sway ⟨this hevin⟩ / and w restles ⟨recours⟩

carythe it sellff / and all those ⟨sevin/ w⟩ in evin

cotinuall cours   16

And off this world so rownd / w in that rollyng case

there be ij ⟨signs⟩ / that neu⁾ move / but fermely kepe

there plac[

the tone we se alway / the tother stond̃e ⟨direct⟩

against the same / devididng Iust / the round by line direct   20

wiche by' ymagination / draune from ton to tother

⟨passethe⟩ the centre of the yerth ⟨for⟩ way there is no nother

and thes bene calld the poles / ⟨as Axell is this lyik⟩

Artyke the tone /⟨y⁾ we ⟨do⟩ se / Antartyke tother hight   24

The lyne y we devise / from ton to tother so

as Axell is / apon the wiche / ⟨thevin⟩ abowt doth go

Wyche off water nor yerth / of Ayre nor fyre ⟨hathe⟩ kynd

therfore the substance of ⟨the⟩ same were herd for man

to fynd ·   28

⟨ffor it is⟩ vncorrupt / ⟨vnmixt⟩ symple and pure ṽmixt

and so we say bene ∧ those sterrys y in ⟨the⟩ same bene fixt
      all   t   those
and eke those ⟨wandryng⟩ sevin / in cyrcles as thei stray
    erryng

so calld by cawse ⟨y⟩ / against y ⟨hevin⟩ thei have
       t   ⟨e⟩ ·first
             repugnãt way   32
and smaller by ways to / skant sensible to man

to busy worke for my pore harp / let sing them he y can ·
                                    t
the widest saff the first off all thes nyne⟨y⟩ above
                                     t
on hunderd yere dothe aske of space for on degre to move   36
Off wiche degres we make / In the first moving hevin
thre hunderd and thre skore in partę Iustly devidid evin ·
And yet there is an other by twene those hevins tow
            sli so slake   name it not
whose moving is so ⟨slow to prove⟩ / I⟨let it passe⟩ for now   40
                       next to
                  t ⟨vnder⟩ the ⟨firmamẽt⟩ sterry skye
The sevent hevyn or the shell⟨y movethe vnder that⟩
             t   t
all those degrees y gaderthe vp / w agid pas so slye
and doth ꝑforme the same / as elders compt hathe bene
                  complete
in nyne and twentye yeres / and days almost sixtene   44
Doth cary in his bowght the sterr off satarne old
         all   t
a thretner of ∧ all lyving thingę / w drowfft and ⟨eke⟩
                 t
              w his cold ·
                         t
The sixt whom this containes doth staulke w yonger pase
                                   viage
and in tweff yere doth sum what more / then tothers ⟨Iorney⟩
                wase ·   48
And this in it doth bere the sterre of Ioue benigne

                    frendly
twene saturn⟨e⟩s malice and vs men deffendy͠g
               ⟨and frendly⟩ signe
      berthe   t   in iij hunderd days
The fift ⟨hathe Cruell⟩ blody Mars y ⟨movithe all this war⟩
                   t
and twise elefn / w on full yere hath finisht all thoseways 52
               houres
⟨A⟩ the yere doth aske the fourt / and ∧ therto ⟨houres⟩ six
and in the same the day his yie the sonne there in he stix
      t   t
The third y goverd is / by that y governthe me ·

and love for love / and for no love / provoke as offt we se   56

                      did the

In like space dothe pforme / that course y̆ tother

     ⟨and⟩ so doth the next to the same / y̆ second is in order

But it doth bere the sterr y̆ calld is mercury

     y̆ mayni' a craffty secret stepp dothe tred as calcars try ·   60

                  vs those ways hath gone

that skye is last and first ⟨and⟩ next ⟨that path [?]⟩

     In sevin and twenty comon days and eke the third of one ·

And berythe w his sway the diuᵒ se mone abowt

     now bryght now browne / no bent now full / and now her

                            light is ow[64

               thire owne

Thus have thei of ⟨them sellffe⟩ ij movinge all those sevin

     one wherin they be carid still eche in his sevrall hevin

              ⟨as he⟩

an other of hym sellffe⟨his body⟩ where theire bodis ben layd

     in by ⟨y⟩ ways and in lesser rownde / as I afore have sayd ·   68

Saff of them all   the sonne doth stray lest from the straight

     the sterry sky hath but on cowrse / y̆ we have calld the eigh[

And all these movinge eight ar ment from west to thest

               alofft

     al tho thei seme to clymb ⟨thevin⟩ I say from est to west   72

But y̆ is but by force / of the first moving skye

     In twise twellff howres / from est to thest ẙ carythe them

                        bye & by[

but mᶜke we well also thes movinge of these sevin

     be not⟨ap⟩bout that axell tre of the first moving hevin   76

for thei have theire ij poles directly tone to tother

E ff. 100r-101r, Wyatt's holograph. *A* f. 99rv. *T* 127. On f. 100v in *E*, about an inch and a half below line 52, Wyatt wrote the following couplet in a rapid and vague hand:

     nor is it lyke ẙ men may think thes sters all

            streys ther pathe as thei do passe ẘ in that hevinly hall

The title of this poem is in a brown ink that matches the text. It is italic in style and by Wyatt himself. Line 7 contains one of Wyatt's few colons. Revisions in black ink in lines 12, 15, and 26 indicate that Wyatt returned to the text at a later time.

    Despite the influence of the *A* text on *T*, certain variants show that the editor of *T* had access to *E*. *T* reflects *E* in lines 49, 65, and 69, where *A* shows emendation.

A T: 1. wandrỹg] wanderyng *T*   2. lygh[ ] light *A T*   3. did teche]
taught *A T*   4. his] *om. T*   6. and yerth] and earthe *A*] and earth *T*
8. the yerthe] the earth *A T*   alo[ ] alone *A T*   9. moder] mother *A T*

11. first] first and *A T*   12. /] is placed *A T*   othr] other *A T*

16. carythe] Carieth *A T*   18. there be ij⟨] Two poyntes theare be *A T*
plac[ ] place *A T*   20. devididng] devyding *A*] deuidyng *T*   round]
grownd *A T*   21. by'] by *A T*   ton to tother] the one to thother *A T*

22. ⟨passethe⟩ the centre] Touche the ⟨S⟩ Centre *A*] Toucheth the centre *T*
the yerth] the earthe *A*] the earth *T*   ⟨for⟩way] for waye *A*] for way *T*

no nother] none other *A T*   23. ⟨   ] discryde *A*] discriyde *T*   24. the
tone] the one *A T*   tother] thother *A T*   25. ton to tother] thone to th'
other *A*] thone to thother *T*   26. ⟨thevin⟩] the heavens *A T*   27. nor yerth]
nor earth *A T*   30. bene fixt] be fixt *T*   31. cyrcles] circle *A T*   32. by
cawse] because *A T*   36. hunderd] hundred *A T*   38. hunderd] hundred *A T*
39. by twene] betwene *A T*   tow] two *A T*   41. sevent] Seventhe *A*]
seuenth *T*   42. gaderthe] gathrith *A*] gatherth *T*   45. bowght] boute *A*]
bowt *T*   46. drowfft] drought *A T*   48. tothers] thothers *A T*   viage]
vyoage *A*   49. in] is *A*   doth bere] that beares *A*   50. saturn⟨e⟩s]
Saturnes *A*] Saturns *T*   51. berthe] beares *A*] bears *T*   hunderd] hundred
A T   53. day his yie] daye his eye *A*] dayes eie *T*   he] her *T*
55. governthe] governes *A*] gouerns *T*   58. to] vnto *A T*   60. mayni']
many *A T*   61. first] fyxte *A*] fixt *T*   64. no bent] now bent *A T*   ow[ ]
oute *A*] out *T*   65. Thus . . . owne] Thus of their owne have they *A*
66. carid] caried *A T*   sevrall] severall *A*] seueral *T*   67. hym] them *A T*
bodis ben layd] bodies be layde *A*] bodyes be layed *T*   69. lest] still *A*
70. eigh[ ] eight *A T*   71. to thest] to east *A*] to the east *T*   74. est to
thest] east to east *A T*   carythe] carieth *A T*   76. ⟨ap⟩bout] about *A T*
77. tone to thother] to the tother. &c' *A*] tone to the tother. &c. *T*

General Index

Index of First Lines

This list is arranged according to normalized spelling. Poems for which the first line does not occur in the Egerton Manuscript are listed according to their first lines in either the Arundel or the Devonshire Manuscript. In such instances the number of the first line to occur in the Egerton Manuscript is noted in parentheses.